民航机务专业英语

English for Aircraft Maintenance Engineers

第4版

李永平 编著

清华大学出版社

北京

内 容 简 介

本书结合飞机维修的工作实际,涵盖了与飞机及其维修工程相关的技术内容,如民航飞机的一般知识、飞机的若干系统、飞机健康管理、飞机航材管理、飞机客户支持、飞机复合材料、飞机适航管理等,旨在使读者通过精读的方式掌握一定的飞机专业技术英文词汇,同时掌握初步的、较为全面的飞机维修工程及其管理方面的专业知识。

本书可作为普通高等院校、高职高专、中专等学校的飞机维修各相关专业"民航机务专业英语"或"专业英语"课程的教材或教学辅助材料使用,也可用于航空公司、飞机制造公司、飞机设计研究所等民航企事业单位飞机机务工程技术人员的培训和学习。

图书在版编目(CIP)数据

民航机务专业英语/李永平编著.—4 版.—北京:清华大学出版社,2022.5(2024.8重印)
ISBN 978-7-302-60470-9

Ⅰ. ①民… Ⅱ. ①李… Ⅲ. ①民用航空—英语—教材 Ⅳ. ①F56

中国版本图书馆 CIP 数据核字(2022)第 051425 号

责任编辑:许　龙
封面设计:常雪影
责任校对:赵丽敏
责任印制:曹婉颖

出版发行:清华大学出版社
　　　　网　　　址:https://www.tup.com.cn,https://www.wqxuetang.com
　　　　地　　　址:北京清华大学学研大厦 A 座　　　邮　　编:100084
　　　　社 总 机:010-83470000　　　　　　　　　邮　　购:010-62786544
　　　　投稿与读者服务:010-62776969,c-service@tup.tsinghua.edu.cn
　　　　质量反馈:010-62772015,zhiliang@tup.tsinghua.edu.cn
印 装 者:三河市少明印务有限公司
经　　销:全国新华书店
开　　本:185mm×260mm　　　　印　　张:15.5　　　　字　　数:373 千字
版　　次:2011 年 3 月第 1 版　　2022 年 5 月第 4 版　　　印　　次:2024 年 8 月第 5 次印刷
定　　价:49.80 元

产品编号:096242-03

前　　言

21世纪是中国民航高速发展的重要时期,为了满足中国民航运输业的需要,中国民航需要大量引进欧美等国家的飞机,如波音、空中客车飞机,尽管我国也在努力研发自主知识产权的飞机,但学好飞机维修领域的专业英语,在当前乃至未来很长一段时间都具有重要的意义。

当前,中国民航主要的飞机为波音、空中客车飞机,这些飞机的随机技术资料均为英文,飞机维修(简称"机务")人员必须掌握相应的专业技术词汇才能阅读并使用这些技术资料,如AMM(Aircraft Maintenance Manual,飞机维护手册)、IPC(Illustrated Part Catalogue,图解零部件目录)等,这对机务人员排除飞机故障和更好地维护、修理飞机具有重要的作用;同时,学好飞机维修专业英语对于有志考取各类执照(尤其国外的飞机维修执照,如FAA维修人员执照)和在外国航空公司或外航驻中国办事处工作的机务人员,有很好的助力作用。

本书在总结中国"民航机务专业英语"相关教材编写情况和经验的基础上,结合飞机维修的实际工作情况,精心挑选、编写了15篇课文,内容包括飞机的一般知识、数量最多的机型B737飞机家族、最先进的机型B787、飞机自动驾驶系统、飞机电气系统、飞机液压系统、辅助动力装置、新一代的空中交通系统和飞机复合材料,以及飞机维修工程管理类的知识,如飞机健康管理、飞机航材管理、客户支持、飞机载重与平衡、飞机适航等。本书期望尽可能地涵盖飞机维修及其管理的各个方面,使读者使用后,达到如下目的:掌握飞机专业技术英文词汇,能够阅读飞机各类英文技术手册和相关文献;更多地了解飞机维修的相关知识,能够认识到飞机维修不仅是严谨的技术工作,也是庞大的系统管理工程;对飞机维修工作提供帮助。

本书还有如下几个特色:

(1) 附录中列出了B737NG(New Generation)飞机航后维修工作单,中英文对照的编排供读者检验学习效果;

(2) 附录中列出了飞机维修较为常见的专业英文缩略语,另外,在每一课结尾有本课的词汇并在课文中按顺序加粗提示;

(3) 附录部分还提供了每一篇课文课后问题的参考答案,为读者自学提供帮助;

(4) 每一篇课文都提供了本课生词、长难句翻译、课后问题和延伸阅读,以利于读者自学,其中延伸阅读能进一步拓展读者的知识面。

本书第1版自2011年3月出版以来,由于特色鲜明,内容全面、丰富,易于学习和掌握,深受读者喜爱,多次重印,被全国各地多所普通高校、高职高专院校选作教材或参考书,同时本书也被国内各家航空公司、飞机制造公司等的培训部门选用,供飞机工程技术人员平时业务学习使用。

根据各地读者的热情反馈,为提高本书的质量,以便更好地服务读者,也为方便授课教师使用,2014 年 1 月出版了第 2 版教材。书中做了勘误,同时补充了新内容,如在每一课后面补充单项选择题、在每一课原文中插入相关图片等。2022 年,为紧跟数字化出版的趋势,全书增加了与课文内容相关的视频链接,读者可以获得更多直观的阅读体验,有助于拓展知识面。

  本书的编写工作得到上海工程技术大学航空运输学院/飞行学院郝勇教授的大力支持,魏鹏程老师编写了部分内容并提出了宝贵意见,上海航空公司机务部马银才高级工程师提供了部分资料,上海航空公司飞行部陶毅超飞行员对本书部分内容进行了校对,在此一并表示衷心感谢。

  本书可作为大、中专院校飞机维修各相关专业(如航空机电设备维修、航空器械维修、民航机电工程、飞行器动力工程、飞行器制造工程、机场工程与管理、民航电子电气工程)"民航机务专业英语"或"专业英语"课程的教材或教学辅助材料使用,也可供航空公司等民航企事业单位的飞机工程技术人员培训和学习使用。

  由于水平有限,错误和不妥之处在所难免,敬请读者提出宝贵意见,以便再版订正,从而能为广大读者更好地服务。

编著者

2022 年 1 月

Contents

Lesson 1

Airplanes and Main Manufacturers Introduction

Airplanes in a manufacturing factory

Airplanes come in many different shapes and sizes depending on the mission of the aircraft, but all modern airplanes have certain components in common. These are the **fuselage**, wing, **tail assembly** and control **surfaces**, landing gear, and **power plants**.

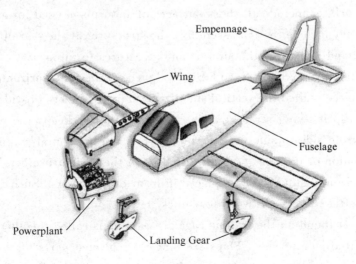

Aircraft components

For any airplane to fly, it must be able to lift the weight of the airplane, its fuel, the passengers, and the cargo. The wings generate most of the **lift** to hold the plane in the air. To generate lift, the airplane must be pushed through the air. The engines, which are usually located beneath the wings, provide the **thrust** to push the airplane forward through the air.

The fuselage is the body of the airplane that holds all the pieces of the aircraft together and many of the other large components are attached to it. The fuselage is generally **streamlined** as much as possible to reduce **drag**. Designs for fuselages vary widely. The fuselage houses the **cockpit** where the **pilot** and **flight crew** sit and it provides areas for passengers and cargo. It may also carry armaments of various sorts. Some aircraft carry fuel in the fuselage; others carry the fuel in the wings. In addition, an engine may be housed in the fuselage.

The wing provides the principal lifting force of an airplane. Lift is obtained from the **dynamic** action of the wing with respect to the air. The **cross-sectional** shape of the wing as viewed from the side is known as the **airfoil** section. The **planform** shape of the wing (the shape of the wing as viewed from above) and placement of the wing on the fuselage (including the **angle of incidence**), as well as the airfoil section shape, depend upon the airplane mission and the best compromise necessary in the overall airplane design.

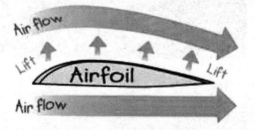

The generation of lift

The control surfaces include all those surfaces of an airplane used for **attitude**, lift, and **drag** control. They include the tail assembly, the structures at the rear of the airplane that serve to control and maneuver the aircraft and structures forming part of and attached to the wing. The tail usually has a fixed horizontal piece (called the **horizontal stabilizer**) and a fixed vertical piece (called the **vertical stabilizer**). The stabilizers provide stability for the aircraft—they keep it flying straight. The vertical stabilizer keeps the **nose** of the plane from swinging from side to side (called **yaw**), while the horizontal stabilizer prevents an up-and-down motion of the nose (called **pitch**). (On the **Wright brothers'** first successful aircraft, the horizontal stabilizer was placed in front of the wings. Such a configuration is called a canard after the French word for "duck").

The hinged part found on the **trailing edge** of the wing is called the **aileron**. It is used to roll the wings from side to side. **Flaps** are hinged or **pivoted** parts of the **leading** and/or trailing edges of the wing used to increase lift at reduced airspeeds, primarily at **landing**

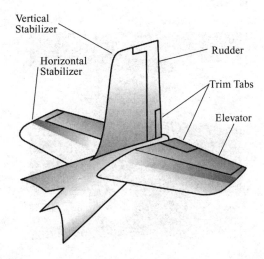

Tail assembly

and **takeoff. Spoilers** are devices used to disrupt the **airflow** over the wing so as to reduce the lift on an airplane wing quickly. By operating independently on each wing, they may provide an **alternate form** of roll control. **Slats** at the front part of the wing are used at takeoff and landing to produce additional lift.

At the rear of both the aileron surfaces and **elevators** and **rudders** are small moving sections called **trim tabs** that are attached by hinges. Their function is to (1) balance the airplane if it is too nose heavy, tail heavy, or wing heavy to fly in a stable cruise condition; (2) maintain the elevator, rudder, and ailerons at whatever setting the pilot wishes without the pilot maintaining pressure on the controls; and (3) help move the elevators, rudder, and ailerons and thus relieve the pilot of the effort necessary to move the surfaces.

The landing gear, or **undercarriage**, supports the airplane when it is resting on the ground or in water and during the takeoff and landing. The gear may be fixed or retractable. The wheels of most airplanes are attached to **shock-absorbing struts** that use oil or air to cushion the **blow** of landing. Special types of landing gear include skis for snow and floats for water. For carrier landings, **arrester hooks** are used.

Forward motion, or thrust, is generated by a thrust-producing device or power plant to sustain flight. The power plant consists of the engine (and propeller, if present) and the related **accessories.**

The main engine types are the reciprocating (or piston type), and the reaction, or jet, engine such as the **ram jet, pulse jet, turbojet, turboprop,** and **rocket** engine. The propeller converts the energy of a reciprocating engine's rotating **crankshaft** into a **thrust force.** Usually the engines are located in **cowled pods** hung beneath the wings, but some aircraft, like fighter aircraft, will have the engines buried in the fuselage.

Other configurations have sometime been used. For instance, the Wright brothers' 1903 Flyer had pusher propellers (propellers at the rear of the plane) and the elevators at the front of the aircraft. Many fighter aircraft also combine the horizontal stabilizer and el-

Landing grar

evator into a single **stabilator** surface. There are many possible aircraft configurations, but any configuration must provide for the four forces needed for flight.

The Boeing Company

Boeing Commercial Airplanes, a business unit of The Boeing Company, is committed to being the leader in commercial aviation by offering airplanes and services that deliver superior design, efficiency and value to customers around the world. There are more than 12,100 Boeing Commercial Jetliners in service, flying passengers and freight more efficiently than competing models in the market.

Boeing traces its history to aviation pioneer **William Boeing** who, in 1916, built the company's first airplane, a seaplane for two with a range of 320 **nautical miles** (515 km). Since then, Boeing has defined the modern jetliner and introduced the **twin-aisle** cabin, the glass cockpit and countless other innovations.

Today, Boeing Commercial Airplanes offers a family of technologically advanced airplanes, including one that can seat more than 500 and another that boasts the longest range in the world, at more than 9,300 nautical miles (14,966 km).

Meanwhile, Boeing Commercial Airplanes and its global network of suppliers are hard at work building the airplane of tomorrow, a **next-generation** jet that will set the standard for fuel-efficiency and passenger comfort.

Boeing Commercial Airplanes employs about 65,400 people under the leadership of President and CEO James (Jim) F. Albaugh. The business unit brought in revenues exceeding $28 billion in 2008.

With headquarters in Renton, Wash., Boeing Commercial Airplanes has operations in more than a dozen cities and countries. The business unit comprises five airplane programs, VIP-derivative airplanes, extensive fabrication and assembly facilities, and a glob-

Boeing Company's
founders

Boeing aircraft family

al customer support organization.

Air transport contributes 2 percent of human-produced CO_2 emissions and this could reach 3 percent by 2050, according to updated figures from the Intergovernmental Panel on Climate Change (IPCC). The industry is now working towards carbon-neutral growth—no increase in carbon emissions in spite of traffic growth—as a first step towards a future of carbon-free energy. Boeing takes this commitment very seriously. Today, more than 75 percent of our commercial airplane research and development efforts are focused on advancing environmentally progressive innovations. See below for more information.

Aircraft entering today's fleet are 70 percent more fuel efficient than early commercial jet airplanes, consuming about 3.5 liters per passenger per 100km. Technological innovation is a fundamental part of this industry.

Boeing is actively driving the development of sustainable **biofuels** for use by the aviation industry. Technology is advancing faster than expected. Many airlines could be flying on a percentage of biofuels within the next five to ten years.

Advanced technologies for generating and harnessing energy are reducing the need to produce electricity from non-renewable resources. Boeing is developing applications within key energy harvesting technologies, including **electrodynamic**, **thermoelectric**, **piezoelectric**, **hydrogen** fuel cells and solar cells.

Boeing continually pursues noise-reducing innovations, making each new airplane quieter than its **predecessor**. New technologies promise even greater improvements.

Today's airspace systems are inefficient. Though safe, the current model is serving increased demand with **outmoded** technologies—the result: system congestion and delays that waste fuel and increase emissions. Boeing is helping solve this complex problem by

5

collaborating with governments and industry partners.

Boeing is working to continually improve the environmental performance of our operations, our products and the aviation system overall. We have a plan and a set of commitments to which we hold ourselves accountable.

The Airbus Company

Airbus is one of the world's leading aircraft manufacturers, and it consistently captures approximately half or more of all orders for airliners with more than 100 seats.

Airbus' mission is to provide the aircraft best suited to the market's needs and to support these aircraft with the highest quality of service. The Airbus product line comprises 14 aircraft models, from the 100-seat single-aisle A318 jetliner to the 525-seat A380—which is the largest civil airliner in service.

Airbus made 483 deliveries in 2008, surpassing the previous year's total by 30. Its total number of aircraft provided to customers worldwide was above the 5,600 mark as of April 2009, with combined orders reaching more than 9,200 single-aisle and **widebody** Airbus jetliners.

Airbus also has expanded into the military transport aircraft sector. The A400M multi-role military **airlifter**—being produced under management of the Airbus Military company—will replace ageing fleets of C-130 Hercules and C-160 Transalls. In addition, aerial tankers for in-flight refueling and transport missions are available in aircraft variants derived from the A310 and A330.

The A318 brings all the benefits of Airbus commonality and comfort to the 100-seat market segment.

The A318 retains all of the A320 Family's advantages while providing highly efficient operations in the 100-seat airliner category.

With an overall length of 31.44 metres (103 ft. 2 in.), the A318 has the shortest fuselage of the A320 product line.

The A318 seats 107 passengers in a typical two-class cabin layout, with eight in first class and 99 in economy.

The A319 provides a new standard of service to markets where only the smallest jets have operated.

The A319 brings a new standard of comfort and performance to markets previously only served by the smallest jet aircraft.

The A319 operational flexibility provides range possibilities of 3,700 **nm.**/6,800 km., and longer for non-stop trans-Atlantic flights.

The A319 offers a variety of seating configurations, from an all business-class layout to an optional high-density version.

The founding member of the best-selling Airbus single-aisle Family, the A320 is the only all-new aircraft in its category.

Airbus innovation means better performance and reliability with reduced fuel burn and easier maintenance.

The A320's 3. 96-metre-wide (13 ft.) fuselage provides wider seats and more room for carry-on baggage in the cabin, and the ability to load containerized cargo in the **lower hold**.

The A320 set a new generation of comfort standards, accommodating 12 first class and 138 economy passengers in the widest cabin available for single-aisle jetliners.

With lower operating costs and more profitability available than with any other aircraft in its class, the A310 also offers wide body passenger comfort and exceptional cargo capacity.

The A310 offers maximum comfort, versatility and efficiency—making it the world's most profitable jetliner in the 200-seat size category.

The A310 uses the Airbus 222-inch widebody fuselage cross-section, providing the optimum balance between aerodynamic efficiency, passenger comfort and underfloor cargo capacity.

The A310 accommodates 220 passengers in a typical two-class layout with 20 first-class and 200 economy-class seats.

The shortest fuselage member of the A330 series provides airlines with excellent range and cargo capacity.

The A330-200 offers superior payload/range capability and greater cargo volume on medium-capacity routes to extended-range operations.

The shortest-fuselage version of Airbus' A330 series, the A330-200 has an overall length of 59 metres (193 ft. 7 in.), with a range of up to 6,750 nm. /12,500 km.

The A330-200 typically carries 253 passengers in a first/business/economy class layout, while the aircraft's two-class configuration seats 293 passengers.

The A340-200 enabled airlines to open long-range non-stop routes between cities that previously needed **intermediate stops.**

The A340-200 is the shortest-fuselage version of the A340 series, with an overall length of 59. 3 metres (194 ft. 10 in.).

The typical seating configuration for the A340-200 includes 216 passengers in a three-class cabin arrangement.

The A380 Navigator has enjoyed huge popularity and allowed many thousands of visitors worldwide to follow the design and industrial development of Airbus' 21st century **flagship** and share the excitement of the programme as it progressed.

Now that the A380 is in regular commercial service, the role of the A380 Navigator has come to an end. The dedicated site, which was created to follow the progress of the A380, is no longer being updated. We thank you for the enthusiastic interest you have shown for the A380 and encourage you to browse back through the milestones of this exceptional aircraft programme, review its development and continue to enjoy its many photos and videos.

The successful entry into service of the A380 is a tribute to the giant leap forward in technology and innovation embodied in the A380, which makes it the new industry's tech-

Airbus future
aircrafts

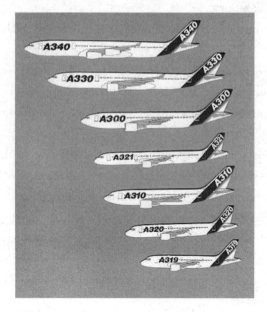

Airbus aircraft family

nology benchmark. This is highlighted by the more than 380 patent applications filed for A380 technologies.

Since its first flight in April 2005, the A380 has flown at air shows and carried out several worldwide tours, demonstrating its airport compatibility, its magnificent handling qualities and **eco-friendly** operation, and meeting with an enthusiastic welcome in every one of the 71 airports it visited.

The "Gentle Giant" as the media dubbed it, now belongs to the airlines and passengers who fly it. As more and more A380s are delivered and enter into service, its majestic and quiet flight will become a normal sight at airports all around the world.

The Bombardier Company

Bombardier is a global transportation company, present in more than 60 countries on five continents. It operates two industry-leading businesses:
- Aerospace
- Rail transportation

Our 66,900 employees design, manufacture, sell and support the widest range of world-class products in these two sectors. This includes commercial and business jets, as well as rail transportation equipment, systems and services.

With more than 32,500 employees and well-positioned in global markets, Bombardier Aerospace ranks as the world's third largest civil aircraft manufacturer. Our high-performance aircraft and services set the standard of excellence in several markets, including:
- Business aircraft

Bombardier business jet

- Commercial aircraft
- **Amphibious** aircraft
- Jet travel solutions
- Specialized aircraft solutions
- Aircraft services and training

The Embraer Company

Embraer was Brazil's largest exporter from 1999 to 2001 and the second largest in 2002, 2003 and 2004. It currently employs more than 16,853 people, 94.7% based in Brazil.

Embraer has become one of the largest aircraft manufacturers in the world by focusing on specific market segments with high growth potential in commercial, defense, and **executive aviation**. We develop and adapt successful aircraft platforms and judiciously introduce new technology whenever it creates value by lowering **acquisition price**, reducing direct operating costs, or delivering higher reliability, comfort, and safety.

"E"series aircraft

As a result, our aircraft provide excellent performance with day-in and day-out reliability, while being economical to acquire and cost-effective to operate and maintain. Equally important, we provide a superior product package, with comprehensive aircraft and after-sales support for parts, services, and technical assistance.

New Words & Phrases

fuselage　机身

tail assembly　尾翼组件

surface　舵面

power plant　动力装置(一般简称发动机或引擎)

lift　升力

thrust　推力

streamline　使……成流线型

drag　阻力

cockpit　驾驶舱

pilot　飞行员

flight crew　飞行机组人员(一般包括飞行员和空中乘务员)

dynamic　动态的

cross-sectional　横截面的

airfoil　翼面

planform　俯视图

angle of incidence　入射角;安装角

attitude　姿态

horizontal stabilizer　水平安定面

vertical stabilizer　垂直安定面

nose　机头

yaw　偏航

pitch　俯仰

Wright brother　莱特兄弟

trailing edge　后缘

aileron　副翼

flap　襟翼

pivoted　转动的;回转的;装在枢轴上的

leading　前面的;前端的

landing　着陆

takeoff　起飞

spoiler　扰流板

airflow　气流

alternate form　备用方式

slat　缝翼

elevator　升降舵

rudder　方向舵

trim tab　调整片

undercarriage　（飞机的）起落架；车盘；着陆装置

shock-absorbing strut　减振支柱

blow　撞击

arrester hook　制动钩

accessory　附件

ram jet　冲压喷气

pulse jet　脉冲喷气

turbojet　涡轮喷气

turboprop　涡轮螺旋桨

rocket　火箭

crankshaft　曲轴

thrust force　推力

cowled pod　整流罩罩体

stabilator　全动平尾

William Boeing　威廉·波音（波音公司创始人）

nautical mile　海里

twin-aisle　双通道

next-generation　下一代

biofuel　生物燃料（指曾经为活质的燃料，如煤）

electrodynamic　电力学的

thermoelectric　热电的

piezoelectric　压电的

hydrogen　氢

predecessor　前辈；前任；（被取代的）原有事物

outmoded　过时的

widebody　宽体的

airlifter　运输机

nm.＝nautical mile　海里

lower hold　腹舱（即一般客机的货舱）

intermediate stop　中转站

flagship　旗舰

eco-friendly　对生态环境友好的；不妨害生态环境的

amphibious　两栖的

Embraer　巴西航空工业公司

executive aviation　公务航空

acquisition price　购买价格

Choose the Best Answer

1. Which component generates most of the lift to hold the plane in the air?

A. Fuselage.　　B. Tail assembly.　　C. Wing.　　D. Power plant.

2. ＿＿ is a force provided by engines to push airplane forward through the air.

A. lift　　　B. gravity　　　C. thrust　　　D. drag

3. The place where the pilot and flight crew sit is called ＿＿.

A. cabin　　B. cockpit　　C. power plant　　D. hold

4. The ＿＿ provide stability for the aircraft.

A. wings　　B. fuselage　　C. landing gears　　D. stabilizers

5. ＿＿ are devices used to disrupt the airflow over the wing so as to reduce the lift on an airplane wing quickly.

A. Flaps　　B. Ailerons　　C. Slats　　D. Spoilers

6. The wheels of most airplanes are attached to ＿＿ that use oil or air to cushion the blow of landing.

A. undercarriage　　　　　　B. shock-absorbing struts

C. arrester hooks　　　　　　D. crankshaft

7. Jet engine and ＿＿ engine are two main engine types.

A. rocket　　B. turboprop　　C. reciprocating　　D. ram

8. ＿＿ is an aircraft manufacturer based in Brazil.

A. Boeing　　B. Airbus　　C. Bombardier　　D. Embraer

9. A ＿＿ is equal to 1852 meters.

A. mile　　B. nautical mile　　C. statute mile　　D. kilometer

10. The airliner is a ＿＿ aircraft if it has a twin-aisle cabin.

A. narrow-body　　B. wide-body　　C. fat-body　　D. thin-body

11. The largest civil airliner in service is ＿＿.

A. B747　　B. B787　　C. A380　　D. A340

12. The typical three-class cabin configuration is ＿＿.

A. first/business/economy　　　　B. high/medium/low

C. expensive/moderate/cheap　　　D. executive/business/economy

13. The "gentle giant" refers to ＿＿.

A. MD11　　B. B787　　C. A380　　D. A350

14. CRJ-200 is a popular regional airliner manufactured by ＿＿.

A. Boeing　　B. Airbus　　C. Bombardier　　D. Embraer

15. The airplane E190 crashed in Yichun airport is manufactured by ＿＿.

A. Boeing　　B. Airbus　　C. Bombardier　　D. Embraer

16. The major aircraft manufacturers in the world are ＿＿.

A. GE, RR and PW　　　　　　B. Boeing, Airbus, Bombardier and Embraer

C. Comac, Bae, Tupolev and Antonov　　D. Cessna, Piper, Cirrus and Mooney

Translations of Long and Difficult Sentences

1. Airplanes come in many different shapes and sizes depending on the mission of the aircraft, but all modern airplanes have certain components in common.

T：飞机不同的形状和尺寸取决于飞机的用途,但所有现代飞机都有一些共同的部件。

2. The engines, which are usually located beneath the wings, provide the thrust to push the airplane forward through the air.

T：发动机,通常安装在机翼下方,提供推力以推动飞机在空中向前飞行。

3. The planform shape of the wing (the shape of the wing as viewed from above) and placement of the wing on the fuselage (including the angle of incidence), as well as the airfoil section shape, depend upon the airplane mission and the best compromise necessary in the overall airplane design.

T：机翼的俯视形状(从上往下看到的机翼形状)和机翼在机身上的位置(包括安装角),以及机翼剖面的形状,取决于飞机用途和在飞机整体设计过程中必需的最好折中方案。

4. They include the tail assembly, the structures at the rear of the airplane that serve to control and maneuver the aircraft and structures forming part of and attached to the wing.

T：它们包括尾翼组件,在飞机后部用于控制和操纵飞机的结构,以及组成和连接到机翼的零部件结构。

5. Flaps are hinged or pivoted parts of the leading and/or trailing edges of the wing used to increase lift at reduced airspeeds, primarily at landing and takeoff.

T：襟翼是机翼前缘和/或后缘的铰接或者转动部件,用于在着陆和起飞阶段飞机速度减小时增大升力。

6. Usually the engines are located in cowled pods hung beneath the wings, but some aircraft, like fighter aircraft, will have the engines buried in the fuselage.

T：通常发动机安装在悬挂于机翼下方的整流罩吊舱里,但一些飞机,如战斗机,其发动机隐藏在机身里。

Questions

1. What components in common do all modern airplanes have?

2. How does the airplane produce lift?

3. What's the function of fuselage?

4. What do the shape and the placement of the wing depend upon?

5. What control surfaces does an airplane have? Please explain their functions respectively.

6. What are the main engine types?

7. Please retell the history of Boeing Company.

8. What effort will the Boeing Company make in the aspect of carbon emission?

9. Please give a brief introduction to Airbus Company.

10. What's the feature of the A380 aircraft?

11. Please give a brief introduction to Bombardier Company.

12. Please give a brief introduction to Embraer Company.

Extensive Reading

Major Manufacturers of General Aviation Aircraft

General aviation includes all non-scheduled civil flying, both private and commercial. General aviation can also include: business flights; private aviation; flight training; air charter; ballooning; parachuting; aerial photography; hang gliding; gliding; foot-launched powered hang gliders; air ambulance; crop dusting; charter flights; traffic reporting; police air patrols; and forest fire fighting.

The following small aircraft manufacturers are among a number of other manufacturers that serve the general aviation market with a focus on private aviation and flight training:

- Cessna
- Cirrus Design
- Diamond
- Mooney
- Piper

Cessna

Cessna Aircraft Company are the leading designer and manufacturer of light and midsize business jets, utility turboprops and single engine aircraft as they have sold and delivered more aircraft then anyone else (190,000 and counting) (2009). They started more than eight decades ago as a small aircraft company in Wichita, Kansas (USA) with an aim to build a monoplane that used a wing without struts or braces, and now they employ over 15,000 people worldwide (2009) The company is a subsidiary of the U. S. conglomerate Textron.

Cessna 152

(image embedded from Wikipedia on 13 September 2009)

Cirrus Design

Cirrus Design Corporation is an aircraft manufacturer and the worlds leading innovator of single-engine piston-powered aircraft, with their SR22 being the worlds best selling airplane in its class (2009). They began in 1984 as a kit airplane and design manufacturing company in Wisconsin, US with their VK-30 aircraft, before moving their headquarters in 1994 to Minnesota, US to begin research and development of the SR20 (four passenger, single-engine composite aircraft) with the help of over 950 employees (2009). Since they started they have also manufactured the fuselage, wings and tail section of a Tactical Unmanned Aerial Vehicle (TUAV) for the US Department of Defense using composite technology in all three components. Cirrus have also developed the SRV, SR20 and SR22 to incorporate flat-panel, multi-function display technology and state-of-the-art safety innovations, including a final level of protection known as the Cirrus Airframe Parachute System (CAPS) — a ballistic parachute deployed from the back of the aircraft, in most cases, that allows the entire aircraft to descend safely from an emergency (2009).

2003 model Cirrus SR22
(image embedded from Wikipedia on 1 October 2009)

Diamond

Diamond Aircraft Industries is an Austrian-based manufacturer of general aviation aircraft, motor gliders and simulators. They are a global manufacturer with offices in North America, Europe, Asia and Australia employing 1,200 people and producing over 3,500 aircraft (2009). There are two production facilities, one located in Austria (head office, research and development operations conducted) and one in Canada. At both of these facilities they produce aircraft for flight schools and private operators (2009).

Mooney

The Mooney Airplane Company (MAC) is a US manufacturer of single engine general aviation aircraft which was founded in 1929, and who have since delivered more than 11,000 aircraft worldwide (2009). Their headquarters are located in Kerrville, Texas (USA). Mooney serves 7,000 customers in the US and 1,000 internationally with a fleet

Diamond DA40 Diamond Star
(image embedded from Wikipedia on 1 October 2009)

Mooney M20T Acclaim
(image embedded from Wikipedia on 1 October 2009)

of aircraft that has flown more than 40 million hours (2009). During their involvement in the aviation industry so far, Mooney has accumulated a number of significant achievements including producing the first pressurized single-engine piston-powered aircraft (M22 Mustang); production of the fastest single-engine aircraft (Mooney Acclaim); first production aircraft to achieve 200 mph on 200 hp (M20J 201); and the fastest transcontinental flight in a single-engine piston-powered aircraft (M20K 231) (2009). All Mooney aircraft have the signature vertical stabilizer with its vertical leading-edge and swept trailing edge that gives the illusion of being forward-swept (2009).

Piper

Piper Aircraft, Inc., is a manufacturer of general aviation aircraft, located at the Vero Beach Municpial Airport in Vero Beach, Florida. Mr Piper introduced the Piper Cub in 1937, and since then Piper Aircraft have become the only general aviation manufacturer to offer a complete line of aircraft from rugged trainers to high-performance turbo-props, and the new PiperJet producing more than 144,000 aircraft—85,000 of which are still flying (2009). They currently manufacture Meridian (business and personal transportation); Mirage; Matrix; Seneca V; Seminole; Arrow; Warrior Ⅲ; PiperJet (2009).

Piper PA-28-161 Warrior Ⅱ

(image embedded from Wikipedia on 13 September 2009)

Questions for extensive reading

1. What's the definition of general aviation?

2. Please give a brief introduction to the major aircraft manufacturers of general aviation aircrafts.

Lesson 2

About the 737 Family

TOP 10 passenger
plane in 2021

Boeing 737

   The newest members of the Boeing 737 family—the 737-600/-700/-800/-900 models—continue the 737's pre-eminence as the world's most popular and reliable commercial jet transport. The 737 family has won orders for more than 6,000 airplanes, which is more airplanes than The Boeing Company's biggest competitor has won for its entire product line since it began business.

   The **737—a short-to-medium-range airplane**—is based on a key Boeing philosophy of delivering added value to airlines with reliability, simplicity and reduced operating and maintenance costs.

   The Next-Generation 737 models build on the strengths that made the 737 the world's most successful commercial airliner, while incorporating improvements and value-added technology designed for the 21st century.

   Advanced technology **winglets** allow airlines to save on fuel, extend its range, carry more **payload** and reduce engine maintenance costs. Blended winglets are wing tip extensions which provide several benefits to airplane operators. The winglet option increases the Next-Generation 737's lead as the newest and most technologically advanced airplane in its class. These new technology winglets are now available on 737-700s, 737-800s and 737-900ER as well as on the Boeing Business Jet (737-700 and 737-800).

Winglet

The passenger cabin on the Boeing Next-Generation 737s has a new look, providing passengers with comfortable, aesthetically pleasing surroundings. The Boeing 737-900ER is the newest member of the Next-Generation 737 airplane family. The higher capacity, longer-range derivative of the 737-900 was launched on July 18,2005 with an order for 30 airplanes from Indonesia's Lion Air.

737 Chronology

Did you know about 50 gallons of paint are used to paint an average 737? Once the paint is dry, it will weigh approximately 250 pounds.

You can learn more about the technologically advanced and economical 737 and the secret of its low-fare success. You can also learn how it provides a world of service, never sleeps, and provides more value than its competitor.

Also browse the 737 **chronology**(see Tab. 2-1), take a quick look at the 737 Program important dates and find out who has the newest single-aisle jetliners.

Tab. 2-1   737 chronology

Model	First Order	Rollout	First Flight	Certification	First Delivery	In Service	First Airline in Service	Last Delivery
737-100	02/15/65	01/17/67	04/09/67	12/15/67	12/28/67	02/10/68	Lufthansa	7/26/73 NASA

（Continued）

Model	First Order	Rollout	First Flight	Certification	First Delivery	In Service	First Airline in Service	Last Delivery
737-200	04/05/65	06/29/67	08/08/67	12/21/67	12/29/67	04/28/68	United	08/08/88 Xiamen Airlines
737-300	03/05/81 (go ahead 03/26/81)	01/17/84	02/24/84	11/14/84	11/28/84	12/07/84	Southwest （USA）	12/17/99 Air New Zealand
737-400	06/04/86	01/26/88	02/19/88	09/02/88	09/15/88	10/01/88	Piedmont	02/25/00 CSA Czech Air
737-500	05/20/87	06/03/89	06/30/89	02/12/90	02/28/90	03/02/90	Southwest （USA）	07/26/99 Air Nippon
737-600	03/15/95	12/08/97	01/22/98	07/98	09/19/98	10/25/98	SAS	
737-700	11/17/93 (go ahead 11/17/93)	12/08/96	02/09/97	FAA- 11/7/97 JAA- 2/19/98	12/17/97	01/18/98	Southwest （USA）	
737-800	09/05/94	06/30/97	07/31/97	FAA- 3/13/98 JAA- 4/9/98	04/22/98	04/24/98	Hapag-Lloyd （Germany）	
737-900	11/10/97	07/23/00	08/03/00	03/2001	05/16/01	5/27/01	Alaska （USA）	
737-900ER	07/18/05	08/08/06					Lion Air	

The Next-Generation 737 family is offered in four sizes, ranging from 110 to 220 seats in mixed-class configuration.

The 737-600 can carry 110 to 132 passengers.

• Scandinavian Airlines （SAS） became the launch customer for the 737-600 on March 15, 1995, when the airline ordered 35 airplanes.

• The 737-600 earned type certification from the U. S. Federal Aviation Administration （FAA） on Aug. 14, 1998, followed by **Europe's Joint Aviation Authorities** （**JAA**） validation on September 4, 1998.

• First delivery of the 737-600 went to SAS in the third quarter of 1998.

JAA

The 737-700 is capable of carrying 126 to 149 passengers.

• The 737-700 was launched in November 1993 with Southwest Airlines' order for 63 airplanes.

• First delivery occurred in December 1997.

• On Nov. 7, 1997, the 737-700 was awarded type certification by the FAA, clearing the airplane for passenger service within the United States.

• On Feb. 19, 1998, JAA—which comprises the aviation regulatory authorities of 27 countries—recommended type validation of the 737-700.

• On Jan. 31, 2006, the 737-700ER (Extended Range) was launched with an order conversion from ANA (All Nippon Airways) for two airplanes.

The 737-800 can seat 162 to 189 passengers.

• On Sept. 5, 1994, the 737-800 was launched with commitments from customers for more than 40 of the airplanes.

• On March 13, 1998, the 737-800 earned type certification from the FAA; JAA type validation followed April 9, 1998.

• The first delivery was to German carrier Hapag-Lloyd in spring 1998.

The 737-900ER can seat 180 to 220 passengers.

• A higher capacity, longer-range derivative of the 737-900, the 737-900ER (Extended Range), was launched on July 18, 2005 with an order for 30 airplanes from Indonesia carrier Lion Air.

• The first delivery was to Lion Air on April 27, 2007.

Next-Generation 737 Program Milestones

Next-Generation 737 program milestones see Tab. 2-2.

Tab. 2-2   Next-Generation 737 program milestones

Date	Milestones
May 5, 2009	The first painted P-8A Poseidon aircraft rolls out of the paint **hangar** displaying its new U. S. Navy livery.
April 28, 2009	Boeing unveils Next-Generation 737 performance improvements and The 737 Boeing Sky Interior.
April 27, 2009	The P-8A Poseidon completes its first flight.
April 16, 2009	Boeing delivers its 6,000th 737 to ILFC and operator Norwegian Air Shuttle.
Jan. 1, 2009	Boeing signs contract with Government of India to provide eight P-8Is, a derivative of the P-8A designed specifically for the Indian navy.
Aug. 12, 2008	Boeing celebrates design, build and completion of the first P-8A Poseidon during a commemorative event with Boeing employees and the U. S. Navy.

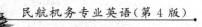

(Continued)

Date	Milestones
Aug. 2，2008	Boeing completes work on first BBJ 3 and delivers airplane to supplier to receive its long-range auxiliary fuel system and Head-up Display.
Aug. 1，2008	Boeing delivers first Next-Generation 737 with carbon brakes to Delta Air Lines on a 737-700.
July 16，2008	First P-8A Poseidon is factory complete.
March 31，2008	Final assembly begins on first P-8A Poseidon for U. S. Navy.
June 18，2007	Boeing surpasses 7,000 737 orders with an order placed by Next-Generation 737-900ER launch customer Lion Air. Boeing announced the order at the Paris Air Show. In August，737 employees commemorate the milestone by filling a giant "7,000" spanning an area about the length of two Next-Generation 737-700s.
April 27，2007	Launch customer Lion Air receives first 737-900ER.
April 20，2007	The 737-900ER earns type certification from the U. S. Federal Aviation Administration，and validated by the Indonesian regulatory agency April 26.
Feb. 14，2007	Boeing delivers the first 737-700ER to ANA. The second 737-700ER was delivered to ANA the following August.
Feb. 1，2007	The U. S. Federal Aviation Administration certifies the 737-700ER，with validation by the Japanese regulatory agency following closely.
Feb. 13，2006	Boeing delivers the 5,000th 737 to Southwest Airlines.
Jan. 31，2006	Boeing launches its longest-range Next-Generation 737，the 737-700ER（extended range），with an order from ANA.
Jan. 30，2006	Boeing offers efficiency enhancing carbon brakes for Next-Generation 737.
Jan. 26，2006	Boeing nears 737-900ER design completion.
Dec. 21，2005	Propelled by an order from Xiamen Airlines，the 737 surpasses the 6,000 sales mark.
July 18，2005	Boeing launches new higher capacity，longer range 737-900ER with an order for up to 60 airplanes from Lion Air.
May 12，2005	Boeing delivers revolutionary landing system on a Next-Generation 737. The system，called Global Positioning Landing System relies on data from satellites and ground stations to accurately pinpoint an airplane's position in the sky.
Jan. 24，2005	The first Next-Generation 737 without "eyebrow" windows rolled out of the Renton，Wash.，factory.
Jan. 17，2005	Final assembly time for Next-Generation 737 is cut to 11 days，making it the shortest final assembly time of any large commercial jet. The feat marks a 50 percent reduction in assembly time since the implementation of Lean tactics began in late 1999.
June 14，2004	The U. S. Navy awards The Boeing Company a System Development and Demonstration contract worth $3.89 billion for the Multi-mission Maritime Aircraft，which is based on the 737-800.
May 24，2004	A Boeing Business Jet completes the first North Atlantic flight by a business jet equipped with the advanced Future Air Navigation System（FANS），a system that streamlines communication between airplane crews and air-traffic controllers.

(Continued)

Date	Milestones
May 14, 2004	The 1,500th Next-Generation 737 is delivered to ATA Airlines. The Next-Generation 737 family reached this milestone delivery in less time than any other commercial airplane family, six years after the delivery of the first model. The Next-Generation 737 bested the previous record holder, the Classic 737 series, by four years.
Jan. 16, 2004	Fresh new redesigned lavatory debuts in Next-Generation 737.
June 13, 2003	The Next-Generation 737 fleet surpasses 10 million flight hours within five years of entering service, a record and a feat equal to one airplane flying more than 1,141 years nonstop.
Jan. 28, 2003	Boeing delivers a suite of three leading-edge display and flight management software for the 737. The new flight-deck technologies, which include the Vertical Situation Display (VSD), Navigation Performance Scales (NPS) and Integrated Approach Navigation (IAN), promise to reduce flight delays and enhance flight-crew efficiency.
Oct. 22, 2002	Boeing delivers first 737 with BigBins, which increase stowage capacity by more than 60 percent.
May 28, 2002	50 Boeing Business Jets completed and in service around the world.
March 19, 2002	Boeing introduces the Technology Demonstrator airplane, a 737-900 outfitted with a suite of new and emerging flight deck technologies to assess their value for enhancing safety, capacity and operational efficiency across the Boeing fleet of airplanes.
Nov. 2, 2001	Boeing delivers first Next-Generation 737-700 Convertible with Quick Change options.
Sept. 17, 2001	Boeing Business Jets adds Flight Dynamics' latest head-up guidance system to flight deck.
May 16, 2001	Boeing delivers the first 737-900 to launch customer Seattle-based Alaska Airlines.
May 8, 2001	"Blended" winglets make their world debut in revenue service with German carrier Hapag-Lloyd Flug.
April 19, 2001	The 737-900 receives validation by Europe's Joint Aviation Authorities (JAA).
April 17, 2001	The 737-900 earns type certification from the U.S. Federal Aviation Administration (FAA).
Feb. 14, 2001	The first shipset of "blended" winglets is installed during production of a Next-Generation 737 at the Renton, Wash., factory.
Jan. 12, 2001	First production 737 "blended" winglets arrive in Seattle, Wash.
Aug. 3, 2000	First flight of the Next-Generation 737-900. Flight-test program begins.
July 23, 2000	The first Next-Generation 737-900 stars in a ceremonial rollout at the Renton factory. Employees of launch customer Alaska Airlines and Boeing employees who worked on the 737-900 program attend the event.
May 15, 2000	The wings for the first 737-900 are joined to the fuselage at the Boeing factory in Renton, Wash.
April 27, 2000	The fuselage of the first Boeing Next-Generation 737-900 arrives at the Renton, Wash., plant by railcar from Wichita, Kan. The first 737-900 is scheduled for delivery to Alaska Airlines.
April 14, 2000	The Boeing 737-700C leaves on its first flight from Renton Municipal Airport in Renton, Wash.

（Continued）

Date	Milestones
Feb. 18，2000	Boeing announces availability of advanced technology "blended" winglets as an option on Next-Generation 737-800.
Feb. 14，2000	Aloha Airlines begins first 180-minute ETOPS service, introducing Nonstop service between Honolulu and Oakland, Calif.
Oct. 11，1999	Boeing launches a second Boeing Business Jet model, the BBJ-2, a modified version of the Next-Generation 737-800.
Sept. 1，1999	Next-Generation 737s are certified for 180 minute ETOPS Operation.
Feb. 5，1999	The 737-900 reaches firm design configuration, a key milestone in the development of the longest Next-Generation 737 model. Measuring 138 feet, 2 inches in length, the 737-900 model surpasses the 737-800 by nearly nine feet. The increased size will accommodate about 18 percent more cargo volume and about 9 percent more passenger cabin area than the 737-800.
Sept. 18，1998	Boeing delivers the first 737-600 to SAS.
Aug. 14，1998	The 737-600 earns type certification from the U. S. Federal Aviation Administration (FAA), formally recognizing that the aircraft has passed the stringent testing requirements of both Boeing and the FAA. The 737-600 now is ready to enter passenger service with Scandinavian Airlines (SAS).
April 22，1998	The first 737-800 is delivered to launch customer Hapag-Lloyd of Germany.
April 9，1998	Europe's Joint Aviation Authorities (JAA) recommends type validation of the 737-800.
March 13，1998	The 737-800 earns type certification from the U. S. Federal Aviation Administration (FAA). The certification formally recognizes that the 737-800 has passed all the rigorous testing requirements of both Boeing and the FAA, and is ready to enter passenger service with U. S. Airlines.
Feb. 19，1998	Europe's Joint Aviation Authorities (JAA), which comprise the aviation regulatory authorities of 27 countries, recommends type validation of the Boeing Next-Generation 737-700. The individual countries will award actual type certificates.
Jan. 22，1998	The Boeing 737-600—the smallest member of the Next-Generation 737 airplane family—makes its first flight.
Dec. 17，1997	Boeing delivers the first Next-Generation 737-700 to launch customer Southwest Airlines. The event is marked by a brief ceremony at Boeing Field. The airplane later departs for Love Field in Dallas, Texas.
Dec. 8，1997	Exactly a year to the date after the world premier of the first Next-Generation 737-700, the first 737-600 rolls out of the Renton factory. The ceremonial event marks the manufacturing completion of the 102-foot-6-inch airplane—the smallest member of the Next-Generation 737 airplane family. The airplane will be the first of three 737-600s that will participate in the 737-600 flight testing and certification program.

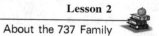
(Continued)

Date	Milestones
Nov. 10, 1997	Alaska Airlines announces an order for 10 737-900s and 10 options, launching the fourth model in the Next-Generation 737 family, the fastest-selling family of commercial jetliners in aviation history. This new model joins the already successful Next-Generation 737-600/-700/-800 family. The airplane now is the longest 737 built, with a length of 138 feet 2 inches.
Nov. 7, 1997	The newest member of the 737 family, the Next-Generation 737-700, earns type certification from the U. S. Federal Aviation Administration (FAA). The certification formally recognizes that the newest 737 airplane has passed all the stringent testing requirements mandated by the FAA and is ready to enter passenger service.
Sept. 3, 1997	Boeing launches the Next-Generation 737-700C with an order for two from the U. S. Navy. The Navy calls the model, a cargo version of the 737-700, the C-60.
Aug. 29, 1997	The first Boeing Next-Generation 737-600 arrives at the Renton, Wash., plant from Wichita. The airplane is 102 feet 6 inches long. The first 737-600 will be delivered to SAS.
July 31, 1997	The 737-800 makes its first flight, with Boeing Capts. Mike Hewett and Jim McRoberts at the airplane's controls. At 9 a. m. PDT, the 129-foot, 6-inch 737-800 takes off from Renton Municipal Airport in Renton, Wash., as Boeing employees cheer. After heading north over Lake Washington, the pilots fly north to the Straits of Juan de Fuca and conduct a series of flight tests between there and Tatoosh. Three hours and five minutes later, the airplane lands at Boeing Field in Seattle.
June 30, 1997	The first 737-800 debuts at a ceremonial rollout on the north end of the 737 final assembly factory. A crowd of several thousand Boeing Commercial Airplane employees are on hand to witness the premiere of the 129-feet-6-inch airplane—the longest 737 ever built. The first 737-800 is the 2,906th 737 built and the 6,508th commercial airplane built by Boeing in Renton.
April 22, 1997	YA001, the first 737-700, makes its 100th flight weighing 172,900 pounds—the highest Boeing 737 takeoff weight ever—and with an engine thrust of 27,000 pounds. During the flight the airplane conducts pre-certification flight testing to capture data for the 737-700 Increased Gross Weight (IGW) airplane, also referred to as the Boeing Business Jet. Commenting on the flight, Capt. Mike Hewett said the airplane's wings performed exceptionally well and "the stability control data points looked very good for the flight-test conditions."
April 11, 1997	The first 737-800 rolls to final assembly for airplane systems, horizontal stabilizer and vertical tail installation.
April 1, 1997	The last 737-700 flight-test airplane makes its first flight at 10:55 a. m. and lands 1 hour and 47 minutes later at Boeing Field in Seattle, Wash.
March 28, 1997	Employees attach the wings on the first 737-800 airplane in the Renton manufacturing plant.

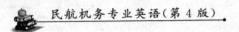
(Continued)

Date	Milestones
March 15, 1997	The Next-Generation 737-700 reaches an altitude of 41,000feet, flying higher than any other 737 in aviation history. Flying up to speeds of 0.81 Mach (464 knots or 535 mph), Boeing Capts. Mike Carriker and Paul Desrochers fly the second 737-700 flight-test airplane to its new altitude during certification testing for climb and descent.
March 14, 1997	The fuselage of the first 737-800, destined for German-carrier Hapag-Lloyd, arrives in Renton from Boeing Wichita, after traveling 2,190 miles by railcar. At 129 feet 6 inches in length, the 737-800 is 19 feet 2 inches longer than the 737-700.
March 11, 1997	The No. 3 737-700 makes its first flight from the Municipal Airport in Renton, Wash.
Feb. 27, 1997	The No. 2 737-700 makes its first flight from Renton Municipal Airport in Renton, Wash. The maiden flight lasts 2 hours and 4 minutes.
Feb. 9, 1997	The first Boeing 737-700 makes its maiden flight, with Boeing Capts. Mike Hewett and Ken Higgins at the airplane's controls. At 10:05 a.m. PST, the airplane—painted in the Boeing red, white and blue livery—takes off from Renton Municipal Airport in Renton, Wash., as hundreds of Boeing employees and their families watch and cheer. After heading north over Lake Washington, the pilots fly the newest member of the 737 family north over Tattoosh, east to Spokane and then back to Western Washington before landing at Boeing Field in Seattle.
Dec. 8, 1996	The first 737-700 is introduced to the world at The Boeing Company's Renton, Wash., plant. Nearly 50,000 guests attend the Next-Generation 737 celebration.
Dec. 2, 1996	The first 737-700 rolls out of the Renton factory and advances into the paint hangar.
Nov. 29, 1996	The No. 3 737-700 arrives in Renton from the Boeing Wichita plant.
Oct. 26, 1996	The first CFM56-7 engine is attached to the right wing of the first 737-700. The left-hand engine is installed the next day.
Oct. 20, 1996	The second 737-700 fuselage arrives in Renton from the Boeing Wichita plant.
Oct. 10, 1996	Employees attach the horizontal stabilizers to the first 737-700, completing the installation of all major airplane structures.
Oct. 7, 1996	The 23-foot, 5-inch vertical tail is installed on the first 737-700. The vertical tail weighs approximately 1,500 pounds.
Oct. 6, 1996	The first 737-700 fuselage rolls on its own landing gear to the final assembly area, where flight control surfaces, engine and systems are installed.
Sept. 18, 1996	Employees attach the wings to the first 737-700 fuselage in the Renton, Wash., 737 factory.
Sept. 3, 1996	The first completed 737-700 fuselage arrives in Renton, Wash., after traveling nearly 2,200 miles from the Boeing Wichita plant. The first pair of CFM56-7 engines arrive at Propulsion Systems Division in Seattle for engine buildup.
Aug. 24, 1996	The first 737-700 one-piece fuselage leaves Wichita, Kan., bound for Renton, Wash.
Aug. 12, 1996	Assembly begins in Wichita, Kan., on the nose section of the first 737-800.

(Continued)

Date	Milestones
July 26, 1996	The last major body structure for the first 737-700 fuselage is loaded into the integration tool in Wichita, Kan.
July 15, 1996	Employees at the Boeing Renton, Wash., factory unload the No. 1, left-hand 737-700 wing out of its tooling and move the approximately 50-foot-long structure to its next manufacturing position.
July 2, 1996	The Boeing Company launches a Boeing Business Jet, derived from the Next-Generation 737-700 model. The jet will offer customers new dimensions in corporate travel.
June 17, 1996	Assembly begins in Wichita, Kan., on the No. 1 nose, or cab, section for the first Boeing 737-700.
April 30, 1996	The first Common Display System for the 737-600/-700/-800 flight deck arrives at the Boeing Integrated Aircraft Systems Laboratory in Seattle. The programmable software display unit allows airlines to easily maintain the flight deck and to tailor it to their specifications.
April 22, 1996	The first 737-700 machined wing ribs arrive from Kawasaki Heavy Industries in Japan. Boeing 737 wing ribs were previously built-up assemblies. The single-pieced machined ribs increase quality and decrease weight.
March 20, 1996	The 737-700 program reaches its 90 percent product definition release, marking a major engineering milestone for the new 737 family. The milestone signifies the transition from the development phase to production phase of the program.
Jan. 16, 1996	The new engine for the Next-Generation 737 family, the CFM56-7, makes its first flight attached to the left-hand wing of a General Electric 747 flying test bed in Mojave, Calif.
Dec. 1, 1995	Major assembly begins on the No. 1 737-700 model when a 55-foot-long spar, or horizontal wing structure, is loaded into an automated assembly tool in the Renton, Wash., factory. Assembly also begins in Wichita, Kan., on the first 737-700 fuselage Section 43 panel (an upper fuselage section).
April 28, 1995	The new engine for the Next-Generation 737 family, the CFM56-7, powers up for its first ground test at the Snecma test facility in Villaroche, France.
Nov. 17, 1995	The Next-Generation 737 program sets a new aviation record by selling more in the first two years they have been offered than any other commercial jetliner.
March 15, 1995	Scandinavian Airlines System (SAS) places an order for 35 of the 737-600 model, launching the last of the three newest 737 versions.
Sept. 5, 1994	The Next-Generation 737-800 is launched at the Farnborough Air Show in England. German carrier Hapag-Lloyd will take delivery of the first 737-800 in early 1998.
Nov. 17, 1993	The Boeing Company board of directors authorizes the Next-Generation 737-600/-700/-800 program. Southwest Airlines launches the -700 program, with an order for 63 of the newest 737 aircraft.

New Words & Phrases

737—a short-to-medium-range airplane 737 中短程飞机

winglet 翼梢小翼

payload 有效载荷

chronology 年表

Europe's Joint Aviation Authorities (JAA) 欧洲联合航空局

hangar 机库

Choose the Best Answer

1. 737 is a ____ airplane.

A. medium-to-long range
B. short-to-medium range
C. short range
D. long range

2. 737-600/700/800/900 are categorized to ____.

A. Boeing 737CL
B. Boeing 737NEW
C. Boeing 737NG
D. Boeing 737-6789

3. Winglet was introduced by NASA，while blended winglet was invented by ____.

A. Boeing
B. Airbus
C. Bombardier
D. Embraer

4. ____ is a modified version of 737-700 or 737-800.

A. ACJ
B. BBJ
C. ARJ
D. ERJ

5. The newest member of 737 family is ____.

A. 737-800
B. 737-900
C. 737-900ER
D. 737-1000

6. ____ is short for Europe's Joint Aviation Authorities.

A. FAA
B. JAA
C. CAAC
D. JAA

7. The first airlines to order a new type of airplane is called ____.

A. new customer
B. launch customer
C. delivering customer
D. receiving customer

8. "ER" is short for ____.

A. longer range
B. extended range
C. expensive range
D. extended runway

9. On Jan. 24，2005，the first 737 without ____ windows rolled out.

A. eye
B. brow
C. eyebrow
D. eyelid

10. Advanced technology winglets allow airlines to save on fuel and carry more ____.

A. workload
B. download
C. payload
D. upload

Translations of Long and Difficult Sentences

1. The newest members of the Boeing 737 family — the 737-600/-700/-800/-900 models — continue the 737's pre — eminence as the world's most popular and reliable commercial jet transport.

T：波音737家族的最新成员——737-600/700/800/900延续了737飞机作为世界上最受欢迎和最可靠的商用喷气式交通工具的卓越性能。

2. The 737 — a short-to-medium-range airplane — is based on a key Boeing philosophy of delivering added value to airlines with reliability, simplicity and reduced operating and maintenance costs.

T：737飞机，一种中短程飞机，它成功的关键在于波音公司的理念——给航空公司提供附加值，即可靠性、操作简单和降低其运营及维护成本。

3. The Next-Generation 737 models build on the strengths that made the 737 the world's most successful commercial airliner, while incorporating improvements and value-added technology designed for the 21st century.

T：新一代737机型的卓越性能使737成为了世界上最成功的商用航线运输机，同时它融合了面向21世纪所做的改进和附加值技术。

Questions

1. What's the Boeing philosophy of delivering of B737 aircraft?
2. What's the function of winglet?
3. Give a brief introduction to B737 family.
4. Please memorize the important B737 aircraft milestones.

Extensive Reading

Boeing 737 Next Generation

Prompted by the modern Airbus A320, Boeing initiated development of an updated series of aircraft in 1991. After working with potential customers, the 737 Next Generation (NG) program was announced on November 17, 1993. The 737NG encompasses the -600, -700, -800, and -900, and is to date the most significant upgrade of the airframe. The performance of the 737NG is, in essence, that of a new aircraft, but important commonality is retained from previous 737 models.

Boeing 737NG fuselage

The wing was redesigned with a new airfoil section, greater chord, increased wing span by 16 ft (4.9 m) and area by 25%, which increased total fuel capacity by 30%. New, quieter, more fuel-efficient CFM56-7B engines were used. The wing, engine, and fuel capacity improvements combined increase the 737's range by 900 nautical miles to over 3,000 nautical miles (5,600 km), now permitting transcontinental service. With the increased fuel capacity, higher maximum takeoff weight (MTOW) specifications are offered. The 737NG included redesigned vertical stabilizers, and winglets were available on most models. The flight deck was upgraded with modern avionics, and passenger cabin improvements similar to those on the Boeing 777, including more curved surfaces and larger overhead bins than previous-generation 737s. The Next Generation 737 interior was also adopted on the Boeing 757-300.

The first NG to roll out was a-700, on December 8, 1996. This aircraft, the 2,843rd 737 built, first flew on February 9, 1997. The prototype -800 rolled out on June 30, 1997 and first flew on July 31, 1997. The smallest of the new variants, the -600s, is the same size as the -500. It was the last in this series to launch, in December 1997. First flying January 22, 1998, it was given certification on August 18, 1998. A flight test program was operated by 10 aircrafts: 3 -600s, 4 -700s, and 3 -800s.

Air Berlin 737-700 in Boeing livery, showing blended winglets available on the Next Generation 737 models

In 2004, Boeing offered a Short Field Performance package in response to the needs of Gol Transportes Aéreos, which frequently operates from restricted airports. The enhancements improve takeoff and landing performance. The optional package is available for the 737NG models and standard equipment for the 737-900ER. The CFM56-7B Evolution nacelle began testing in August 2009 to be used on the new 737 PIP (Performance Improvement Package) due to enter service mid-2011. This new improvement is said to shave at least 1% off overall drag and have some weight benefits. Overall, it is claimed to have a 2% improvement on fuel burn on longer stages. In 2010, new interior options for the 737NG included the 787-style Boeing Sky Interior.

Boeing delivered the 5,000th 737 to Southwest Airlines on February 13, 2006. Boeing delivered the 6,000th 737 to Norwegian Air Shuttle in April 2009. The Airbus A320 family has outsold the 737NG over the past decade, although its order totals include the A321 and

A318, which have also rivaled Boeing's 757 and 717, respectively. The 737NG has also outsold the A320 on an annual basis in past years, with the next generation series extending the jetliner's run as the most widely sold and commonly flown airliner family since its introduction.

Questions for extensive reading

1. What's the reason of Boeing 737 next generation development?
2. What's the function of the blended winglet of B737NG aircraft?

Lesson 3

B787 Dreamliner

New future
airplane

Boeing 787

Everett, Wash., Jan. 15, 2010—Boeing has completed **initial airworthiness** testing on the 787 **dreamliner**. This milestone will enable more crew members to take part in flights and will allow more airplanes to join the flight test program.

"This is an important step forward," said Scott Fancher, vice president and general manager of the 787 program, Boeing Commercial Airplanes. "We are very pleased with the results we have achieved so far. The airplane has been performing as we expected."

Since the first flight in mid-December, the program has conducted 15 flights, achieving several key accomplishments. Pilots have taken the airplane to an altitude of 30,000 feet (9,144 meters) and a speed of Mach 0.65. Nearly 60 hours of flying have been completed. Initial **stall tests** and other **dynamic maneuvers** have been run, as well as an extensive check-out of the airplane's systems. Six different pilots have been behind the controls of the 787.

B787 Interior Flight Test

"The pilots have told me the results we are seeing in flight match their expectations and the simulations we've run. That's a real tribute to Boeing's expertise and the international team that helped develop and build the airplane," said Fancher.

Flight testing will continue in the months ahead. First delivery is planned for the fourth quarter of this year.

"This airplane is specifically configured to test the passenger experience elements of the airplane," said Tom Galantowicz, director of 787 Interiors, Commercial Airplanes. "Our engineers and flight-test team use a disciplined process to certify the various elements of the interior and conduct airplane-level verifications."

The interior includes 135 seats, multiple lavatories and two crew rests. Certifying the interior components involves analyses and testing of the lighting, lavatories, **stowage bins**, dimmable windows and galleys.

Passengers will be welcomed onto the 787 by sweeping arches, dynamic lighting, larger lavatories, more spacious luggage bins and electronic window shades whose transparency they can change during flight.

Sweeping arch

"Our team is making great progress and is looking forward to getting this airplane in the air later this month," Galantowicz added.

Flight testing will continue in the months ahead. Delivery of the first 787 to **launch customer ANA (All Nippon Airways)** of Japan is planned for the fourth quarter of this year.

B787 Power On

The Boeing Company has completed the Power On sequence for the first 787 dreamliner, marking the completion of the next major milestone on the path to the first flight later this year.

B787 dreamliner

Power On is a complex series of tasks and tests that bring electrical power onto the airplane and begin to exercise the use of the electrical systems. The 787 is a more-electric airplane with the pneumatic, or bleed air, system being totally replaced by electronics.

"The team has made great progress in bringing the bold innovation of the 787 to reality," said Pat Shanahan, vice president and general manager of the 787 program. "There is plenty of work to be done between now and first flight, but with every step forward we grow more and more confident."

Responding to the overwhelming preference of airlines around the world, Boeing Commercial Airplanes' new airplane is the Boeing 787 dreamliner, a super-efficient airplane. An international team of top aerospace companies is developing the airplane, led by Boeing at its **Everett facility** near Seattle, Wash.

Unparalleled Performance

The 787-8 dreamliner will carry 210—250 passengers on **routes** of 7,650 to 8,200 nautical miles (14,200 to 15,200 kilometers), while the 787-9 dreamliner will carry 250—290 passengers on routes of 8,000 to 8,500 nautical miles (14,800 to 15,750 kilometers). A third 787 family member, the 787-3 dreamliner, will accommodate 290—330 passengers and be optimized for routes of 2,500 to 3,050 nautical miles (4,600 to 5,650 kilometers).

In addition to bringing big-jet ranges to mid-size airplanes, the 787 will provide airlines with unmatched fuel efficiency, resulting in exceptional environmental performance. The airplane will use 20 percent less fuel for comparable missions than today's similarly sized airplane. It will also travel at speeds similar to today's fastest **wide bodies**, Mach 0.85. Airlines will enjoy more cargo revenue capacity.

Passengers will also see improvements with the new airplane, from an interior environment with higher humidity to increased comfort and convenience.

Advanced Technology

The key to this exceptional performance is a suite of new technologies being developed by Boeing and its international technology development team.

Boeing has announced that as much as 50 percent of the primary structure—including the fuselage and wing—on the 787 will be made of **composite materials.**

GE engine for B787

An open architecture will be at the heart of the 787's systems, which will be more simplified than today's airplanes and offer increased functionality. For example, the team is looking at incorporating **health-monitoring systems** that will allow the airplane to self-monitor and report maintenance requirements to ground-based computer systems.

Boeing has selected **General Electric** and **Rolls-Royce** to develop engines for the new airplane. It is expected that advances in engine technology will contribute as much as 8 percent of the increased efficiency of the new airplane, representing a nearly **two-generation jump** in technology for the middle of the market.

Another improvement in efficiency will come in the way the airplane is designed and built. New technologies and processes are in development to help Boeing and its supplier partners achieve unprecedented levels of performance at every phase of the program. For example, by manufacturing a one-piece fuselage section, we are eliminating 1,500 aluminum sheets and 40,000—50,000 **fasteners.**

Continuing Progress

The Boeing board of directors granted authority to offer the airplane for sale in late

2003. Program launch occurred in April 2004 with a record order from All-Nippon Airways. Since that time, 55 customers from six continents of the world have placed orders for 840 airplanes valued at $140 billion, making this the most successful launch of a new commercial airplane in Boeing's history. The 787 program opened its final assembly plant in Everett in May 2007.

All Nippon Airways

The program has signed on 43 of the world's most capable **top-tier** supplier partners and together finalized the airplane's configuration in September 2005. Boeing has been working with its top tier suppliers since the early detailed design phase of the program and all are connected virtually at 135 sites around the world. Eleven partners from around the world completed facility construction for a total of 3 million additional square feet to create their major structures and bring the next new airplane to market.

In the weeks ahead, the team will continue to expand the **flight envelope** at which the 787 will operate to reach an altitude of more than 40,000 feet (12,192 meters) and a speed of Mach 0.85. Subsequent testing will push the airplane beyond expected operational conditions.

New Words & Phrases

initial airworthiness　初始适航
dreamliner　梦想飞机,即 B787 飞机
stall test　失速测试
dynamic maneuver　动态机动
stowage bin　储物箱
launch customer　启动客户
ANA＝All Nippon Airways　全日空航空公司
Everett facility　埃弗里特工厂

route　航程

wide bodies　宽体客机

composite material　复合材料

health-monitoring systems　健康监控系统

General Electric　美国通用电气公司

Rolls-Royce　英国劳斯莱斯公司

two-generation jump　跨越两代的

fastener　紧固件

top-tier　顶级

in the weeks ahead　在未来几个星期

flight envelope　飞行包线

Choose the Best Answer

1. The launch customer of 787 is ____.

A. UA　　　　　B. ANA　　　　　C. AA　　　　　D. Air France

2. ____ is to bring electrical power onto the airplane and begin to exercise the use of electrical system.

A. Power on　　B. Electricity on　　C. Power off　　D. Turn on

3. 787 is a more electronic airplane with the ____, or bleed air system being totally replaced by electronics.

A. pneumatic　　B. electrical　　C. hydraulic　　D. air

4. A half of the primary structures of 787 are made of ____ materials.

A. complex　　B. composite　　C. alloy　　D. plastic

5. ____ and ____ supply engines to 787.

A. PW, R. R　　B. PW, CFM　　C. GE, RR　　D. GE, CFM

6. Which one is not a fastener?

A. Nut.　　　　B. Bolt.　　　　C. Rivet.　　　　D. Sensor.

7. B787 is a ____ airplane.

A. wide-body　　B. fat body　　C. narrow body　　D. thin body

8. One ____ is just the speed of sound.

A. mach　　　　B. mile　　　　C. nautical mile　　D. foot

9. Dreamliner refers to ____.

A. 777　　　　B. 787　　　　C. 380　　　　D. 350

10. Which one of the following statements about 787 is wrong?

A. Its pneumatic system is replaced by electronics.

B. A half the primary structure of it is made of composite materials.

C. It brings big-jet range to mid-size airplanes.

D. The cabin humidity is decreased.

Translations of Long and Difficult Sentences

1. Initial stall tests and other dynamic maneuvers have been run, as well as an extensive check-out of the airplane's systems.

T：包括一项飞机系统的广泛检查在内，初始失速测试和其他动态操纵已经完成。

2. Passengers will be welcomed onto the 787 by sweeping arches, dynamic lighting, larger lavatories, more spacious luggage bins and electronic window shades whose transparency they can change during flight.

T：旅客通过大拱门登上 787 飞机，787 飞机内有动态照明、更宽敞的厕所、更大空间的行李箱和在飞行中旅客可以自己调整亮度的电子式窗户遮光板。

3. The Boeing Company has completed the Power On sequence for the first 787 dreamliner, marking the completion of the next major milestone on the path to the first flight later this year.

T：波音公司已经完成了第一架 787 梦想飞机的通电程序，这标志着今年年底实现第一次飞行的又一个主要里程碑的完成。

4. In addition to bringing big-jet ranges to mid-size airplanes, the 787 will provide airlines with unmatched fuel efficiency, resulting in exceptional environmental performance.

T：除了中型飞机实现远航程的飞行外，787 也提供给航空公司无可比拟的燃油燃烧效率，这将表现出突出的环保性能。

5. For example, the team is looking at incorporating health-monitoring systems that will allow the airplane to self-monitor and report maintenance requirements to ground-based computer systems.

T：例如，开发团队正研制健康监控系统，这将使飞机能够自行检测并把维护要求报告给地面计算机系统。

Questions

1. What materials are used to make as much as 50% of the primary structure of B787?

2. What is the Boeing international technology development team looking at?

3. How do the advances inengine technology benefit B787?

4. What features does the B787 aircraft interior have?

5. What's the meaning of B787 Power On?

6. How do you understand the unparalleled performance of B787 aircraft?

Extensive Reading

B787 and Its Competitor

The B787 is often compared against the A380 jumbo jet as the time that these concept were released were relatively close, and it was thought by many that it is Boeing's competing weapon against the A380 to regain Boeing market position. After the not so successful launch of the 747-X supersonic concept, Boeing had realized that it needed an aircraft that would meet airliners needs. The B787 was the opposite of the A380 in the sense that Boeing saw the need for efficiency and cost saving in airlines, instead of aggressive expansion and optimistic forecasting in travel demand. Apart from the many technical innovations, the B787 is also sold at a fraction less than the A380.

In 2005, Airbus launched the maiden flight of its jumbo jet — the A380. The capacity was even greater than the previous jumbo jet B747. This revolutionary aircraft had totally changed the possible ways of operation in the commercial airline industry, as it would allow airlines to meet their rapid growing demand in a much more efficient and effective way— by carrying more passengers per flight. The aircraft could travel longer distances, allowing less stopover and transits, more direct point-to-point routing, and the extra room in the cabin to develop a more comfortable travel experience for travelers. At the point of development, it was commented by many that it would be the trend of future travel.

In contrary, the B787 was a downsized aircraft from Boeing's previous model B747; it promoted the spokes-and-hub system instead of encouraging long-haul point to point services; the cabin was not designed to carry more passengers at once, but to more efficiently carry existing demand as Boeing saw the aviation market to be diminishing in demand due to various environmental reasons such as the slowdown in economy; many markets being mature and have settled down in the flying population; the raise of low-cost carriers that encourage use of smaller airports which do not accommodate for larger aircraft, etc.

Here the two aircraft are not compared against each other for it specifications or performance, as they are totally different aircraft categories and sizes; the comparison is to the different perspectives that the two manufacturers have taken against the future traveling trends in the airline industry. Where the Airbus has taken the optimistic expansion approach to the airline industry's future; Boeing has approached their near future with a perspective closer to reality, where airlines can use this aircraft as a tool to improve their product on current services without breaking the bank. Boeing is seeing the next period of air travel to be more of a recovering period for most airlines, and more importantly adapting their designs to current market needs with some creative innovations more than trying to create a new market all together.

B787's Technical difficulties

Apart from the late delivery, the B787 also failed to offer as much as they had promised with the new aircraft making technologies. It appeared that the major reason of delay was because the aircraft had difficulty achieving its weight target and the increased efficiency did not make a significant difference. Although there were massive reductions in fastens and aluminum sheers, it did not seem to help. As a result, the manufacturer proposed to its customers a 10%—15% reduction in the aircraft range for early deliveries, and the aircraft would still be 8% overweight.

In addition, the composition factor had promised the first major structural examination to be at the aircraft's 12th anniversary, as it had less concerns over corrosion. However, as suggested by Lawrence and Thornton a more severe matter is that corrosion in metal is easy to be noticed, and much more is known about the fracture mechanics of metal pieces than composition; and the complexity of investing to evaluation composite structures will be a labor-intensive and expensive job for its customers. However if the composite material proves to be a more enduring and reliable material, it is likely that there will be increase usage of the material and the above concerns should gradually diminish as the knowledge to maintenance improves.

Despite the multiple technical problems that had struck the delivery roll out of the B787 Dreamliner, its innovative and ground breaking technology that promotes to enhance cost saving for airlines is still a major advantage of the aircraft. The global economical downturn had also favored the concept further as airlines struggled financially and needed methods to cut costs. The trend is obvious that airlines are turning towards a more cost-effective way of operation, and is likely to stay so at least for the foreseeable future. Therefore, here it is concluded that the Dreamliner has gained itself an important contribution to future air travel trends. The B787 has secured it's position to both low-cost and conventional airline business modes by offering a flexible configuration in favor to fully utilize the aircraft to meet their market needs on top of cost-saving, be it the customers wish to carry more cargo or passengers, have three cabins or one.

Questions for extensive reading
1. Why is the B787 compared against the A380 jumbo jet?
2. Why does the B787 fail to deliver on time?

Lesson 4

Autopilot System

Flight controls

Airplane cockpit

Introduction

The thrust management system does two functions. It moves the **throttles** and calculates the thrust limit for the EICAS display.

The Yaw damper/Stabilizer trim Module (**YSM**) combines these functions: yaw damper; stabilizer trim; rudder ratio changer; speed brake; elevator feel limit; **elevator feel shift**; BITE.

The autoflight lesson will only cover the yaw damper, stabilizer trim, and BITE functions of the YSM. The yaw damper function controls the rudder to decrease yaw **oscillations** due to **Dutch roll** or **gust-induced** sideslips.

The automatic stabilizer trim and **mach trim** system controls stabilizer position as a

EICAS

function of these: mach at high speeds; autopilot trim commands when the autopilot is **engaged**.

The BITE section provides **troubleshooting** for the functions of the YSM.

The autopilot flight director system provides automatic control to these control systems to operate the selected mode: aileron; elevator; stabilizer; rudder. It also provides pitch and roll flight director commands, system warnings, and annunciations.

The maintenance monitor system provides a centralized flight and ground faults readout and ground test capability for these systems: autopilot flight director system; thrust management system; flight management system.

Yaw Damper Function

The yaw dampers move the rudder to dampen Dutch roll to improve ride quality. They also provide **turn coordination**.

Each of two YSMs moves a servo. The servos operate independently and their outputs combine to move the rudder. There is no **feedback** to the rudder pedals from yaw damper operation.

The YSM outputs supply corrective rudder action through the yaw damper actuators. The YSM calculates the commands with inputs from these: Air Data Computers (**ADC**); Inertial Reference Units (**IRU**); **modal suppression accelerometers**; **FMCs**.

The YSM receives yaw inputs from the IRU inertial reference data. They provide corrective rudder action through the yaw damper servos. The output of each servo is mechanically limited. These outputs add together to provide the total rudder response to yaw damper commands. These commands are adjusted by an airspeed input from the ADC air data which decreases rudder commands for an increase in airspeed.

You do a test of the YSM on the ground from the flight compartment. You see proper operation by the **INOP** annunciation and rudder movement. The INOP lights on the yaw damper control panel show disengagement of the yaw damper. Bite is also available from the front panel BITE control module.

Automatic Stabilizer Trim Function

The autopilot and the yaw damper/stabilizer trim modules (YSMs) make the commands to automatically trim the stabilizer. **A/P** stabilizer trim commands occur when there is an elevator deflection command from the autopilot that is beyond the trim **threshold** and stays for a long time. The change of stabilizer position decreases elevator **deflection** and drag.

Mach trim commands improve pitch attitude control. These commands adjust for changes in mach.

Mach trim can only operate if the A/P is not engaged and there is no manual electric trim command. As mach increases, the stabilizer leading edge moves down. The pilot can **override** any automatic trim command with an opposite column force.

Two stabilizer position indicators are on the **aisle stand**. An **UNSCHEDULED STAB TRIM** (amber) light shows when the stabilizer moves without a command to trim.

Autopilot Flight Director System

The autopilot flight director system (**AFDS**) supplies automatic control of these flight control systems: ailerons; elevators; rudder (autoland).

The AFDS also does the calculations for the flight director commands. You use the AFCS mode control panel to select autopilot and flight director modes and for autopilot engagement.

Each electronic attitude director indicator (**EADI**) shows flight director commands and the AFDS flight mode annunciator (**FMA**). The FMA shows AFDS status and roll/pitch **arm** and engaged modes.

The autoland status annunciator (**ASA**) shows the system capability and limitation status for autoland operations.

The AFDS mode control panel has **mode selector** switch annunciation and reference displays.

A red A/P **DISC** light or an amber AUTOPILOT caution light give visual alerts for A/P warnings and cautions.

Thrust Management Computer System

The thrust management computer (**TMC**) does the thrust limit calculation and the **autothrottle** calculation.

MCP

These functions each have different modes that are selected and show in different places.

The thrust limit modes are selected on the thrust mode select panel (**TMSP**) or by the FMC in the **VNAV** mode. The thrust limit modes show on EICAS display. The thrust limit shows on the EICAS display and is used as an upper limit for autothrottle calculations.

The thrust limit function is always active.

The autothrottle modes are selected on the AFCS mode control panel (**MCP**) or by the FMC in VNAV mode. The autothrottle modes show on the EADI. The autothrottle does not engage in a mode unless the AFCS MCP is in the **A/T** ARM position, and a mode is selected on the AFCS MCP. This mode is used to control the throttles.

Maintenance Monitor System

The maintenance monitor system combines flight fault storage and ground test functions for these systems: autopilot flight director system; thrust management system; flight management computer system.

There is one maintenance control and display panel (**MCDP**). It is connected to these computers: flight control computers (FCCs); thrust management computer (TMC); flight management computers (FMCs).

Through these computers, you can do tests of many avionics systems.

The MCDP is usually off. It turns on automatically after touchdown and the autoflight computers transmit messages for any failures which occurred during the flight. The MCDP can store up to five faults from each of the computers. The MCDP can also be used for ground maintenance. You can look at the stored in-flight faults or do the ground test function for troubleshooting or system verification.

This page may show in flight below 10,000 feet if the EICAS flight test switch is in the flight test position. Above 10,000 feet, the ADCs supply the discrete that lets the **MAINT** page show.

CDU

Flight Control Inputs

All flight control surfaces are moved by hydraulic power control actuators (PCAs). Mechanical inputs control the PCAs. These inputs are from manual controls or autopilot servos.

Manual inputs are supplied from these components: **control wheels**; **control columns**; rudder **pedals**; **nose wheel steering** through the rudder pedals.

The nosewheel steering **tiller** does not move the rudder. Only nosewheel steering through the rudder pedals moves the rudder.

These controls connect to a system of quadrants and rods that supply movement to the PCAs. Manual control of the ailerons is helped by lateral central control actuators (LCCAs) which drive the mechanical system in the wings. Because there is no aerodynamic pressure feedback, the feel and trim system supplies pressure feedback to the flight crew.

The autopilot system provides electrical commands to control servo actuators. The actuators provide mechanical input to the PCAs and back drive the manual control source (wheel, column, or pedals). The position feedback information is by electrical signals from the servo actuators.

The yaw damper supplies another input to the rudder control. This input is down stream of the feel system through a summation device. There is no back-drive to the manual control source for this input. Position feedback is by electrical signals from the servo actuator.

Flight Control Computer

The FCC supplies the input, output, monitor and calculation functions for the autopilot flight director system.

The FCC contains modules, subassemblies, and a **chassis** assembly housed in an **ARINC** 600 size 8 unit. The FCC has front hold-down hooks to mount in a standard ARINC rack. A handle is on the front panel to help removal and handling of the unit.

The case contains two removable side covers which gives access to all circuit cards and modules. The top and bottom covers are the outside parts of the air plenum chambers. cooling air enters at the bottom and exits at the top.

A single three-section connector on the back of the box connects with a rack mounted receptacle.

These are the three types of software in the FCC: operational program software (**OPS**); operational configuration files (**OPC**); resident operational software (**RPS**).

The FCC has resident operational software (RPS) that is embedded as part of the FCC hardware and is only changed when the hardware part number changes.

The OPS is the core software and the application software for the FCC. There is a software part number for the OPS. The OPC sets the configuration information for the FCC.

This configuration information used with hardware program pins tells the FCC how to use the OPS. There is a software part number for the OPC.

The portable data loader connection lets you load software into the FCC.

Maintenance Control and Display Panel

The maintenance control and display panel (MCDP) is the primary component of the AFDS maintenance system operation. After each flight, it collects and stores flight fault data found by the FCC, TMC, and FMC during the flight. It makes this data available for display during FLT FAULT mode operation. During the **GRD** TEST mode, it allows display of ground fault data and fault information from ground tests. It also provides operator instructions and test control necessary to do ground tests of AFDS related devices.

The MCDP also supplies information about FCC software. It can show the FCC software and hardware part numbers and software loading faults.

Go-around Mode

The **go-around** mode is a combined autopilot (or **F/D**) and autothrottle mode provided for **climbout** after an aborted approach. Go-around may be entered from a single channel, multi-channel, or F/D only approach.

Go-around is armed when **glideslope** is captured or flaps are not up. Go-around is inhibited in the take-off mode. Push either of the go-around switches on the throttles to enter the mode.

Pitch control for go-around is a speed-through-elevator mode with **windshear** protection. At an altitude rate less than 600 ft/minute, the autopilot control is a pitch attitude con-

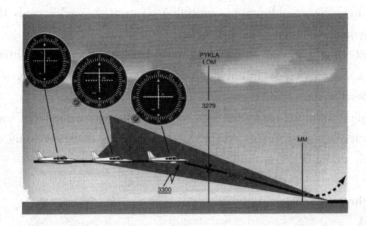

PYKLA
LOM

3279

MM

3300

Glideslope

trol. When the altitude rate is more than 1,200 ft/minute, the control is to MCP speed or the existing airspeed at go-around start. For an altitude rate between 600 and 1,200 ft/minute, the control is a combination of airspeed and attitude.

For a flight director go-around, the control is the same as the autopilot when the altitude rate is more than 1,200 ft/minute. At a negative altitude rate, the control is to pitch attitude.

The pitch go-around mode provides limits that keep the airplane within maximum and minimum airspeeds. Pitch mode annunciation is go-around on both FMAs. No pitch modes show on the MCP.

The AFDS roll command maintains track hold. If localizer was captured before go-around, the airplane maintains runway track (**ILS** course). Current ground track is maintained in all other situations. The roll mode annunciation is GA on both FMAs. No roll modes show on the MCP.

The go-around thrust limit mode shows on the upper EICAS display. The thrust reference target cursor changes to a go-around thrust limit and the thrust limit mode display changes to GA. At engagement, the autothrottle system controls the airplane within the go-around thrust limits established by the TMC.

The autothrottle mode annunciation is GA on both FMAs. No autothrottle modes show on the MCP. At go-around, the autothrottle system maintains the airplane vertical speed to 2,000 feet/minute within the go-around thrust limits from the TMC.

The go-around mode for approach is armed at glideslope capture or flaps not up. The thrust mode display on EICAS shows GA and both thrust target cursors move to go-around thrust limits.

Go-around starts by a push of one or both of the thumb operated switches on the thrust levers. Roll, pitch, and autothrottle modes show GA. ILS approach guidance stops.

The AFDS status stays the same. If multichannel engaged, the AFDS stays multichannel engaged until the go-around mode is cancelled. If multichannel armed，the engaged autopilot stays engaged while the others disarm.

The AFDS roll controls the airplane to maintain track and the pitch controls to maintain a MCP selected airspeed after an initial pitch up command. The autothrottle maintains airplane vertical speed within FMC thrust limits.

After the airplane is more than 400 feet radio height，go-around for each axis is cancelled by selection of another mode. Autothrottle go-around is cancelled by selection of another autothrottle mode or pitch mode.

New Words ＆ Phrases

throttle 油门

YSM＝Yaw damper/Stabilizer trim Module 偏航阻尼器/安定面配平组件

elevator feel shift 升降舵感觉漂移

oscillation 振荡

Dutch roll 荷兰滚

gust-induced 由阵风所引起的(风切变)

mach trim 马赫配平

engage 接通

troubleshooting 排故

turn coordination 转弯中的协调

feedback 反馈

ADC＝Air Data Computer 大气数据计算机

IRU＝Inertial Reference Unit 惯性基准组件

modal suppression accelerometer 模式抑制加速计

FMC＝Flight Management Computer 飞行管理计算机

INOP＝inoperation 失效

A/P＝Autopilot 自动驾驶

threshold 门槛值

deflection 偏转

override 超控

aisle stand 边台

UNSCHEDULED STAB TRIM 非计划(无指令)的安定面配平

AFDS＝Autopilot Flight Director System 自动驾驶飞行指引系统

EADI＝Electronic Attitude Director Indicator 电子姿态指引指示仪

FMA＝flight mode annunciator 飞行模式报警器

arm 预位

ASA＝autoland status annunciator 自动着陆状态报警器

mode selector 模式选择器

DISC＝Disconnect 断开；脱开

TMC＝thrust management computer　推力管理计算机

autothrottle　自动油门

TMSP＝thrust mode select panel　推力模式选择面板

VNAV＝Vertical Navigation　垂直导航

MCP＝mode control panel　模式控制面板

A/T＝autothrottle　自动油门

MCDP＝maintenance control and display panel　维修控制与显示面板

MAINT＝maintenance　维护；保养

control wheel　驾驶盘

control column　驾驶杆

pedal　脚蹬

nose wheel steering　前轮转弯

tiller　舵柄

chassis 底盘

ARINC＝Aeronautical Radio Incorporation　美国航空无线电公司,该缩写代表航空无线电的通信标准

OPS＝operational program software　操纵程序软件

OPC＝operational configuration file　操纵配置文件

RPS＝resident operational software　保留操纵软件

GRD＝ground　地面

go-around　复飞

F/D＝Flight Director　飞行指引仪

climbout　急剧爬升

glideslope　下滑道

windshear　风切变

ILS＝Instrument Landing System　仪表着陆系统

Choose the Best Answer

1. The thrust management system does two functions. It moves the ＿＿ and calculates the thrust limit for the EICAS display.

A. control column　　B. flaps　　　C. rudder pedals　　D. throttles

2. Go-around is armed when ＿＿ is captured or flaps are not up.

A. glideslope　　　B. localizer　　　C. NDB　　　D. VOR

3. AFDS in this passage is an acronym for ＿＿.

A. autopilot flight data system

B. autopilot flight director system

C. automatic flight descent system

D. automatic flight data system

4. All flight control surfaces are moved by ＿＿ power control actuators.

A. electrical   B. mechanical   C. hydraulic   D. pneumatic

5. Mechanical inputs control the hydraulic power control actuators. These inputs are from manual controls or ____.

A. electrical controls   B. electric controls

C. electronic controls   D. autopilot servos

6. Manual inputs are supplied from these components: control wheels; control columns; rudder pedals; ____ through the rudder pedals.

A. main wheel steering   B. nose wheel steering

7. Go-around is inhibited in the ____ mode.

A. landing   B. RTO   C. cruising   D. take-off

8. ILS is short for ____.

A. instrument landing system

B. integrated logistic support

C. integrated instrument system

D. integrated lodging service

9. The yaw dampers move the rudder to dampen Dutch roll to improve ride quality. They also provide ____ coordination.

A. yaw   B. pitch   C. roll   D. turn

10. The go-around mode is a combined autopilot and auto throttle mode provided for ____ after an aborted approach.

A. landing   B. cruising   C. climbout   D. gliding

Translations of Long and Difficult Sentences

1. The yaw damper/stabilizer trim module (YSM) combines these functions: yaw damper; stabilizer trim; rudder ratio changer; speed brake; elevator feel limit; elevator feel shift; BITE.

T: 偏航阻尼器/安定面配平组件组合了这些功能: 偏航阻尼器; 安定面配平; 方向舵比例变换器; 速度刹车; 升降舵感觉限制; 升降舵感觉偏移; 自检测试设备。

2. A/P stabilizer trim commands occur when there is an elevator deflection command from the autopilot that is beyond the trim threshold and stays for a long time.

T: 当有一个来自自动驾驶的升降舵偏转指令且偏转超过了配平限度并长时间持续时, 自动驾驶安定面配平指令会发出。

3. The FCC has resident operational software (RPS) that is embedded as part of the FCC hardware and is only changed when the hardware part number changes.

T: 飞行控制计算机保留有一个操作软件, 该软件是嵌入到硬件里面的, 并作为硬件的一部分, 只有当硬件件号更换时才会跟着变换。

Questions

1. What's the function of thrust management system?

2. What's the function of YSM?
3. What control systems does the autopilot flight director system provide automatic control to?
4. Please retell the yaw damper's function.
5. How do you understand UNSCHEDULED STAB TRIM?
6. What's the function of AFDS?
7. How do we use the MCDP to maint the aircraft?
8. Please explain the meaning of go-around.

Extensive Reading

Modern Autopilots

Not all of the passenger aircraft flying today have an autopilot system. Older and smaller general aviation aircraft especially are still hand-flown, and even small airliners with fewer than twenty seats may also be without an autopilot as they are used on short-duration flights with two pilots. The installation of autopilots in aircraft with more than twenty seats is generally made mandatory by international aviation regulations. There are three levels of control in autopilots for smaller aircraft. A single-axis autopilot controls an aircraft in the roll axis only; such autopilots are also known colloquially as "wing levellers," reflecting their limitations. A two-axis autopilot controls an aircraft in the pitch axis as well as roll, and may be little more than a "wing leveller" with limited pitch oscillation-correcting ability; or it may receive inputs from on-board radio navigation systems to provide true automatic flight guidance once the aircraft has taken off until shortly before landing; or its capabilities may lie somewhere between these two extremes. A three-axis autopilot adds control in the yaw axis and is not required in many small aircraft.

Autopilots in modern complex aircraft are three-axis and generally divide a flight into taxi, takeoff, ascent, cruise (level flight), descent, approach, and landing phases. Autopilots exist that automate all of these flight phases except the taxiing. An autopilot-controlled landing on a runway and controlling the aircraft on rollout (i. e. keeping it on the centre of the runway) is known as a CAT Ⅲ b landing or Autoland, available on many major airports' runways today, especially at airports subject to adverse weather phenomena such as fog. Landing, rollout, and taxi control to the aircraft parking position is known as CAT Ⅲ c. This is not used to date, but may be used in the future. An autopilot is often an integral component of a Flight Management System.

Modern autopilots use computer software to control the aircraft. The software reads the aircraft's current position, and then controls a Flight Control System to guide the aircraft. In such a system, besides classic flight controls, many autopilots incorporate thrust control capabilities that can control throttles to optimize the airspeed, and move fuel to different tanks to balance the aircraft in an optimal attitude in the air. Although autopilots handle new or dangerous situations inflexibly, they generally fly an aircraft with a lower fuel-consumption than a human pilot.

The autopilot in a modern large aircraft typically reads its position and the aircraft's attitude from an inertial guidance system. Inertial guidance systems accumulate errors over time. They will incorporate error reduction systems such as the carousel system that rotates once a minute so that any errors are dissipated in different directions and have an overall nulling effect. Error in gyroscopes is known as drift. This is due to physical properties within the system, be it mechanical or laser guided, that corrupt positional data. The disagreements between the two are resolved with digital signal processing, most often a six-dimensional Kalman filter. The six dimensions are usually roll, pitch, yaw, altitude, latitude, and longitude. Aircraft may fly routes that have a required performance factor, therefore the amount of error or actual performance factor must be monitored in order to fly those particular routes. The longer the flight, the more error accumulates within the system. Radio aids such as DME, DME updates, and GPS may be used to correct the aircraft position.

Questions for extensive reading

1. What types of aircraft do not have an autopilot system?

2. What's the difference among three levels of control in autopilots for smaller aircrafts?

Lesson 5

Aircraft Electrical Power

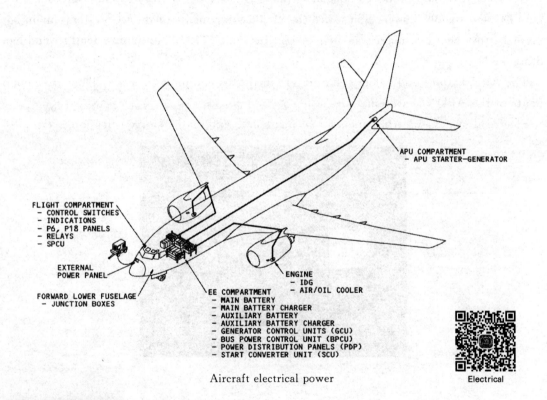

Aircraft electrical power

Electrical

Introduction

The electrical power system makes, supplies, and controls electrical power to the airplane. The system has these subsystems: external power; generator drive system; **AC** generation; AC electrical load distribution; **DC** generation.

General Description

The electrical power system supplies AC and DC power to airplane systems. The power sources can not be put in parallel. These are the major components of the AC system: generator control unit (**GCU**); bus power control unit (**BPCU**); power panels in the main equipment center.

For airplane ground operations, AC power comes from one of these sources: external power panel; auxiliary power unit (**APU**) generator. For in-flight operations, power comes from an integrated drive generator (**IDG**) on each engine or from the APU generator.

A hydraulic motor generator (**HMG**) system operates as a back-up source if there is a loss of all main electrical power. The HMG does not have a time limit for operation.

AC/DC conversion produces normal airplane DC power. Battery systems provide alternate DC and **standby power**. These are the major components of the DC system: main battery; battery charger; main transformer rectifier unit (**TRU**); **static inverter**; ground handling TRU.

The APU battery and battery charger are in the aft equipment center. They are components of the APU DC system.

Electrical system control panels allow manual or automatic source selection.

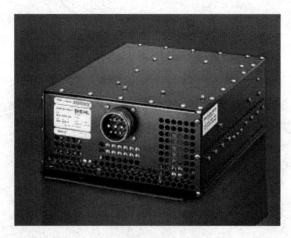

Static inverter

Distribution

Electrical power is supplied through the AC and DC distribution systems. The AC distribution system has these buses: left and right AC buses; ground handling bus; ground service **bus**; flight instrument transfer buses; center AC bus; AC standby bus; utility buses.

The DC distribution system has these buses: DC ground handling; left and right DC buses; center DC bus; DC standby bus; APU battery bus; battery bus; main hot battery bus.

The left and right AC buses get power from these sources: IDGs; APU generator; external power.

The IDG connects to its bus through the closed generator circuit breaker (**GCB**). The power output of the APU generator or external power cart can also connect to the AC buses through the closed auxiliary power breaker (**APB**) or external power contactor (**EPC**). Parallel operation of the IDGs or any two sources on the main buses is inhibited by the operation of the related bus tie breaker (**BTB**).

The ground handling bus gets power from either the APU generator or external power through the ground handling relay (**GHR**). The bus gets power when external power or APU power is available. If APU and external power are available, external power supplies power to the bus. The ground handling bus does not have power in flight.

The ground service bus gets power from the right main AC bus when the right bus has power. If the right bus is off, the ground service bus may get power from external power or the APU generator when the ground service switch is pushed. If external and APU power are available, external power supplies power to the bus.

There are two transfer buses, the **captain** and the **first officer**. The captain transfer bus usually gets power from the left AC bus. If the left AC bus does not have power, the instrument transfer bus switches to the right AC bus. The first officer transfer bus usually gets power from the right AC bus but switches to the left AC bus if the right AC bus loses power.

The left and right transfer buses usually get power from their related main bus.

The center AC bus usually gets power from the left main bus. During autoland operations, the center AC bus supplies the static inverter. This makes sure that the autopilots get power from three independent AC sources.

The standby AC bus gets power from the left transfer bus, but changes to the static inverter when these are all true: left transfer bus does not have power; battery **switch** is on; standby power switch is in AUTO. To remove power from the standby bus, put the standby power switch to the OFF position.

Two utility buses get power from their main AC bus through a utility bus relay (**UBR**). If the electrical load is more than generation capacity, the UBRs open and remove utility loads from the generators.

The DC ground handling bus gets power from the ground handling TRU when the AC ground handling bus has power. Power to left and right DC buses is supplied by two TRUs. The DC buses are separated by the DC tie relay. The DC tie relay is normally open, but closes if DC power is lost on either the left or right DC bus. The DC tie relay may be opened by un-latching any BTB switch.

The center DC bus is supplied by the left DC bus. During autoland operations, the center bus transfers to the hot battery bus. This makes sure that the autopilots are on three separate DC sources.

The battery bus gets power from either the left DC bus or the hot battery bus. The left DC bus supplies the battery bus. If the bus loses power, the battery bus transfers and gets power from the hot battery bus.

The DC standby bus usually gets power from the battery bus. If the standby power switch is in the OFF position, the DC standby bus loses power.

The main hot battery bus gets power from the main battery. When the ground service bus has power, the battery charger supplies power to the hot battery bus and charges the main battery. If both main AC buses lose power in flight, the HMG becomes the power source for the hot battery bus as well as the transfer buses.

The APU battery bus gets power from the APU battery. When the ground service bus has power, the battery charger supplies power to the APU battery bus and charges the battery.

The APU TRU supplies DC power to start the APU when the right main bus has power.

During engine start, when external or APU power supplies the load, the engine generator takes over the correct load bus. When manually selected, external power has priority over all other sources. When the APU generator operates and a failure of either IDG, the APU generator automatically powers the correct load. If external or APU generator power is not available and there is a failure of either engine generator, the generator that remains supplies power to the two main load buses. During autoland, the center DC bus gets power from the hot battery bus and the center AC bus is supplied from the static inverter. The flight instrument transfer buses supply power to selected captain and first officer flight instruments. When the primary power source fails, an alternate is selected automatically.

Electrical Power System Control Panel

The electrical panel is on the P5 overhead panel. The panel has three momentary-action switches and eight alternate-action switches. You use these to operate most of the electrical system. These are the momentary-action switches: external power; drive disconnect.

These are the alternate-action switches: battery; APU generator; Bus tie; generator control; utility bus.

The standby power has a three-position rotary switch. You use it to manually control standby power.

The battery switch connects the hot battery bus to the battery bus. ON is a mechanical indication. It shows that the switch is in the latched-in position. OFF is an amber light that shows when the switch is out and the airplane has ac power.

The APU generator switch arms the APU GCU to control APU generator electrical power. ON is a mechanical indication that shows the switch is in the latched-in position. OFF is an amber light that shows when the switch is out. If the APU is running, the light

B737—NG

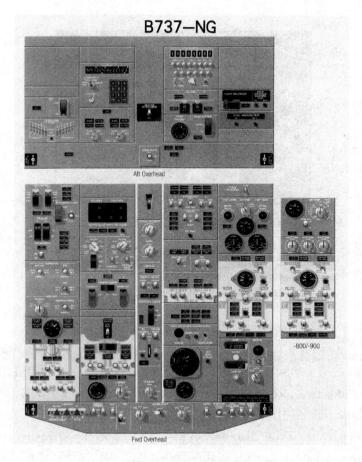

Aft Overhead

-800/-900

Fwd Overhead

P5 overhead panel

also comes on when the auxiliary power breaker (APB) opens when the external power contactor (EPC) is also open. The switch is usually on.

Each bus tie switch controls the operation of its related BTB. AUTO is a mechanical indication that shows the switch is in the latched-in position. ISLN is an amber light that shows when the switch is out and the BTB is open. The isolation (ISLN) light also comes on if the switch is in AUTO and the GCU opens the BTB for a fault. The switches are usually in AUTO.

The external power switch controls the operation of the external power contactor (EPC). **AVAIL** is a white light that shows good power quality at the ground power source. ON is a white light that shows a closed EPC.

Each generator control switch arms its GCU to control IDG electrical power. ON is a mechanical indication that shows the switch is in the latched-in position.

OFF is an amber light that shows that the related generator circuit breaker (GCB) is open. The switches are usually on.

The latching utility bus switches allow manual control of the power to the utility and galley buses. The On legend shows the switch position and is hidden when the switch is

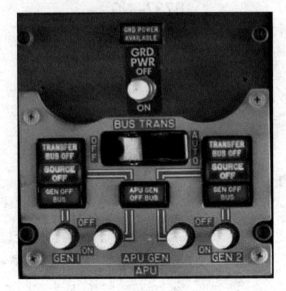

Electrical power control panel

unlatched. The amber OFF light is on if the associated utility bus relay is open.

The drive disconnect (DISC) switch removes gearbox power from the IDG. When you push the switch, the two-piece IDG input shaft moves apart. DRIVE is an amber light that shows that the related IDG has a fault.

Plastic guards cover the drive **disconnect** switches to prevent accidental operation.

The standby power switch has these three positions: OFF; AUTO; BAT.

The off position turns the standby buses off.

The automatic (AUTO) position lets the standby buses receive power from their normal or backup sources. The switch is usually in AUTO.

When AC power is on the airplane and the switch is in the battery position (BAT), the battery supplies power to the standby system. A circuit automatically does checks of the operation of the switching relays.

Generator Drive

The generator drive system usually supplies electrical power to all of the electrical loads while the engines operate. The integrated drive generators (IDGs) are the primary sources of electrical power. The APU generator is a secondary source of electrical power.

The generator drive system usually supplies electrical power to all of the electrical loads while the engines operate. The integrated drive generators (IDGs) are the primary sources of electrical power. The APU generator is a secondary source of electrical power.

Each engine mechanically turns its IDG. The IDGs change the mechanical power to constant-frequency AC electrical power. Drive disconnect switches on the electrical panel con-

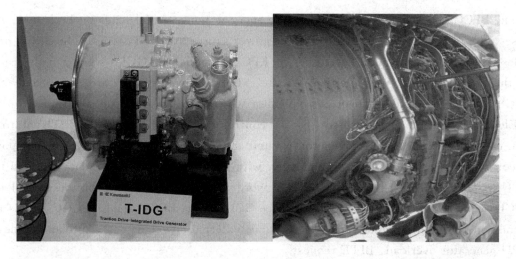

IDG

trol the IDG disconnect operations.

AC Generation

The AC generation system supplies 115 V AC power to the airplane. The AC generation system has these subsystems: power and regulation; control; fault sensing; hydraulic motor generator system; AC generator annunciation; AC meters.

The AC power system makes 115 V AC power and provides control and protection for airplane electrical loads.

The primary AC system is a three-phase, four-wire, **wye** connected system that operates at a voltage of 115/200 V AC, a frequency of 400 Hz and is rated at 90 kVA. The system has left and right main AC channels. Each channel consists of a main AC bus supplied by an integrated drive generator (IDG). An APU-driven auxiliary generator provides dispatch capability if one primary source IDG is inoperative and also provides an independent power source for ground operation. An external power source can be connected to the AC tie bus through the external power receptacle and the external power contactor (EPC).

Both main AC buses can be supplied from any one of four isolated power sources (left and right IDG, auxiliary generator and external power) through the AC tie bus when the appropriate GCB, APB, EPC, and BTBs are closed. Operation of these contactors is controlled automatically by the generator control units (GCUs) and bus power control unit (BPCU) to maintain power on the buses from any available source. Also, the two main AC buses can be supplied independently from two different sources.

The three GCUs provide automatic control and protection functions for each channel by monitor of IDG output, BPCU status information and control switch positions.

The GCU provides protective trip commands to the GCB and/or BTB to prevent load and source equipment damage if faults or failures occur in the system.

The BPCU sends load shed signals to de-energize nonessential loads on both main AC buses if an in-flight generator shutdown or power source overload occurs. The BPCU provides tie bus fault protection by trip of the EPC and signals to GCUs when a fault occurs on the tie bus. Protective functions for the external power system are provided by the BPCU when unacceptable power is supplied or when there are overload conditions.

Electrical system status, protection, and control information, as well as **BITE** information is sent between the bus power control unit and generator control units. The bus power control unit has two way communication with each GCU. It sends a data word to the GCU first. The GCU then returns a data word to the BPCU. This continues until the BPCU sends and received data from all three GCUs. The BPCU sends the GCUs this information: differential faults; breaker position; external power request; autoland request; APU generator overload; BITE request.

The GCU sends this information: generator differential protection and overload information; breaker position and status; ground mode data; dead tie bus data; underspeed data; APU available data; BITE code data.

Each GCU and the BPCU has built-in test equipment (BITE) with self-check and fault diagnosis capability. The BITE display and controls are on the BPCU. During operation with two generators, the electrical power system can supply all necessary electrical power.

Each generator is rated for 90 kVA (measured at the generator terminals) continuous operation. The capacity available at the load bus for an IDG is 86 kVA and for the auxiliary generator is 83.2 kVA. This allows for feeder losses of 4 and 6.8 kVA respectively, at 90 kVA.

With one generator, the total airplane load demands can exceed the continuous rated capacity of one generator.

There are automatic **load shedding circuits** which de-energize the left and right utility and galley buses to prevent generator overload. However, the APU generator can be used as a power source and the galley loads can be applied again.

New Words & Phrases

AC＝Alternating Current 交流电

DC＝Direct Current 直流电

GCU＝Generator Control Unit 发电机控制组件

BPCU＝Bus Power Control Unit 汇流条电源控制组件

APU ＝Auxiliary Power Unit 辅助动力装置

generator 发电机

IDG＝Integrated Drive Generator 整体驱动发电机

HMG＝Hydraulic Motor Generator 液压马达发电机

standby power 备用电源

TRU＝Transformer Rectifier Unit 变压整流器

static inverter　静变流机

bus　汇流条

GCB＝Generator Circuit Breaker　发电机电路断路器

APB＝Auxiliary Power Breaker　辅助电源断路器

EPC＝External Power Contactor　外电源接触器

BTB＝Bus Tie Breaker　汇流条连接断路器

GHR＝Ground Handling Relay　地面处理继电器

captain　机长

first officer　副驾驶

switch　电门

UBR＝Utility Bus Relay　可用汇流条继电器

AVAIL＝available　有用的

disconnect　脱开

wye　Y字；Y字形物

BITE＝Built-in Test Equipment　机内自检设备

load shedding circuit　负载屏蔽电路

Choose the Best Answer

1. AC in this passage is short for ____.

A. alternate current

B. alternating current

C. alternative current

D. alternated current

2. The power sources ____ be put parallel.

A. can　　　　　　　　　　　　B. can't

3. AC power comes from one of these sources：external power panel；____ generator.

A. IDG　　　　B. GCU　　　　C. BPCU　　　　D. APU

4. For in—flight operations，power comes from ____ on each engine，or from APU generator.

A. GCU　　　　B. PCU　　　　C. IDG　　　　D. TRU

5. TRU in this passage is short for ____.

A. transformer rectifier unit

B. transmit receive unit

C. true

D. transport rectifier unit

6. The AC generation system supplies ____ V AC power to the airplane.

A. 28　　　　B. 15　　　　C. 400　　　　D. 220

7. BITE is an acronym for ____.

A. built in test equipment

B. built in test electronics

C. built in testing equipment

D. build in test equipment

8. IDG in this passage is short for ____.

A. integrated drive generator

B. integration drive generator

C. integrating drive generator

D. integrated driven generator

9. BPCU in this passage refers to ____.

A. bus power control unit

B. bite panel control unit

C. bottom plug control unit

D. barometric pressure control unit

10. ____ are the primary sources for electrical power.

A. APU generator

B. Ground power

C. IDG

D. Battery

Translations of Long and Difficult Sentences

1. These are the major components of the AC system: generator control unit (GCU); bus power control unit (BPCU); power panels in the main equipment center.

T：这些是交流电源系统的主要部件：发电机控制组件（GCU）；汇流条电源控制组件（BPCU）；在主设备中心的电源面板。

2. The power output of the APU generator or external power cart can also connect to the AC buses through the closed auxiliary power breaker (APB) or external power contactor (EPC).

T：通过闭合辅助电源断路器或者外电源接触器，也能把 APU 发电机和外电源车的输出电源连接到交流汇流条上。

3. If the right bus is off, the ground service bus may get power from external power or the APU generator when the ground service switch is pushed.

T：若右汇流条断开，当地面勤务电门闭合时，地面勤务汇流条可以从外电源或者 APU 发电机获得电源。

4. The standby AC bus gets power from the left transfer bus, but changes to the static inverter when these are all true: left transfer bus does not have power; battery switch is on; standby power switch is in AUTO.

T：备用交流汇流条从左转换汇流条获得电源，但当如下情况都发生时，变换到静变流机：左转换汇流条没有电；电瓶电门接通；备用电源电门在自动位。

5. If external or APU generator power is not available and there is a failure of either engine generator, the generator that remains supplies power to the two main load buses.

T：如果外电源或者 APU 发电机电源无效并且有任何一台发动机的发电机失效，剩下的发电机供电给两个主负载汇流条。

6. The primary AC system is a three-phase, four-wire, wye connected system that operates at a voltage of 115/200 V AC, a frequency of 400 Hz and is rated at 90 kVA.

T：主交流电系统是一个三相、四线、Y 字形连接的系统，其工作电压为 115/200 伏特，频率 400 赫兹，额定功率为 90 千伏安。

7. Protective functions for the external power system are provided by the BPCU when unacceptable power is supplied or when there are overload conditions.

T：当没有有效的电源供电或者当出现过载现象时，外电源系统的保护功能由 BPCU 提供。

Questions

1. What's the function of electrical power system?
2. Why can not the power sources be put in parallel?
3. What power can the electrical power system supply?
4. Please enumerate the buses of electrical power system.
5. What's the quality of the aircraft electrical power?
6. When do we use the APU electrical power?
7. How does the GCU control the circuit?

Extensive Reading

Aircraft Electrical System

Most aircraft are equipped with either a 14- or a 28-volt direct current electrical system. A basic aircraft electrical system consists of the following components：

- Alternator/generator
- Battery
- Master/battery switch
- Alternator/generator switch
- Bus bar, fuses, and circuit breakers
- Voltage regulator
- Ammeter/loadmeter
- Associated electrical wiring

Engine-driven alternators or generators supply electric current to the electrical system. They also maintain a sufficient electrical charge in the battery. Electrical energy stored in a battery provides a source of electrical power for starting the engine and a limited supply of electrical power for use in the event the alternator or generator fails.

Most direct-current generators will not produce a sufficient amount of electrical current at low engine rpm to operate the entire electrical system. During operations at low engine rpm, the electrical needs must be drawn from the battery, which can quickly be depleted.

Alternators have several advantages over generators. Alternators produce sufficient current to operate the entire electrical system, even at slower engine speeds, by producing alternating current, which is converted to direct current. The electrical output of an alternator is more constant throughout a wide range of engine speeds.

Some aircraft have receptacles to which an external ground power unit (GPU) may be connected to provide electrical energy for starting. These are very useful, especially during cold weather starting. Follow the manufacturer's recommendations for engine starting using a GPU.

The electrical system is turned on or off with a master switch. Turning the master switch to the ON position provides electrical energy to all the electrical equipment circuits except the ignition system. Equipment that commonly uses the electrical system for its source of energy includes:

- Position lights
- Anticollision lights
- Landing lights
- Taxi lights
- Interior cabin lights
- Instrument lights
- Radio equipment
- Turn indicator
- Fuel gauges
- Electric fuel pump
- Stall warning system
- Pitot heat
- Starting motor

Many aircraft are equipped with a battery switch that controls the electrical power to the aircraft in a manner similar to the master switch. In addition, an alternator switch is installed which permits the pilot to exclude the alternator from the electrical system in the event of alternator failure.

With the alternator half of the switch in the OFF position, the entire electrical load is placed on the battery. All nonessential electrical equipment should be turned off to conserve battery power.

Questions for extensive reading

1. What components does a basic aircraft electrical power system consist of?
2. What's the function of batteries in an aircraft?

Lesson 6

Hydraulic Power

Hydraulics

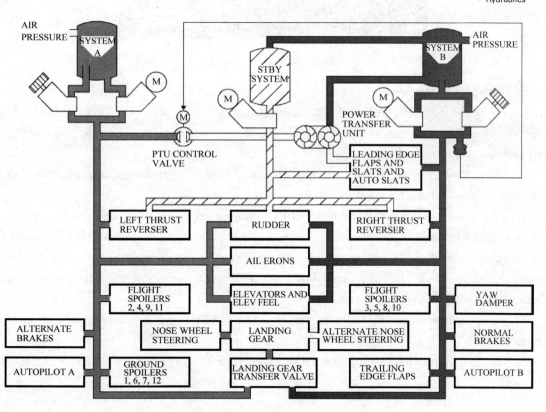

Hydraulic power system for B737 aircraft

Introduction

Hydraulic systems give power to operate these items: **landing gear**; flight controls; other aircraft systems. Acceptable BMS 3-11, Type Ⅳ fluids such as **skydrol** can be used.

The three hydraulic systems are identified by the location of the primary components. They are the left, right, and center systems. The left system components are in the left

Hydraulic system of A380

engine **strut**. The left system has 17 gallons of hydraulic fluid. The right system components are in the right engine strut. The right system has 20 gallons of hydraulic fluid. The center system components are in or near the right main wheel well. The center system has 40 gallons of hydraulic fluid.

The three systems have no connections with each other. They have different color-codes on their related tubing for identification.

There are two engine-driven pumps (**EDPs**), one on each engine. These are the primary pumps in the left and right systems. There are four ac motor pumps (**ACMPs**). Two are the primary pumps in the center system, and one each is the demand pump in the left and right systems. An air-driven pump (**ADP**) is the demand pump in the center system. Air comes from the pneumatic system.

These are the sources for this air: engine bleed; APU; ground source such as an air cart.

A ram air turbine (**RAT**) pump in the center system is an emergency source of hydraulic pressure.

Pressure Source

The primary source of power for the left and right systems is engine-driven pumps (EDPs) rated at 37 **GPM** at takeoff power.

The primary source of power for the center system is two alternating current motor pumps (ACMPS) rated at 7 GPM each.

Secondary (demand) pumps come on when the primary pumps cannot keep sufficient pressure.

RAT

The left and right systems have an ACMP demand pump.

These are identical to and interchangeable with the center system primary pumps. The center system uses an air-driven pump (ADP) rated at 37 GPM as a demand pump. The center system also has an emergency ram air turbine (RAT) pump rated at 11. 3 GPM.

Primary flight control actuators and **autopilot servos** get hydraulic power from all three hydraulic systems.

The **spoiler** system also uses power from all three systems. Dual system power is supplied to these systems: **stabilizer**; **yaw dampers**; **elevator feel system**; brakes.

These systems get hydraulic power from one source: high lift devices; landing gear; **rudder ratio changer**; hydraulic generator option.

Systems Distribution

Primary and some secondary flight controls get power from the left and right systems. **Thrust reversers** also get power from these systems. The right system supplies power to the normal brakes.

A **pitch enhancement system**, power transfer unit (**PTU**) between the left and right systems, supplies a third source of power for the horizontal stabilizer.

The center system supplies hydraulic power for primary and secondary flight controls. These systems get hydraulic power from the center system: landing gear; **nose wheel steering**; alternate and **reserve brakes**; hydraulic motor generator option.

Three independent systems give aircraft hydraulic power. Each system has a **reservoir** that stores and supplies hydraulic power to the pumps. Eight pumps pressurize the hydraulic systems. Each pump has a filter module with pressure and case drain line filters.

Each system has a return filter module to filter fluid that returns to the reservoir. One **heat exchanger** in each system cools pump case drain fluid before it returns to the reservoir.

Thrust reverser

A central fill location lets you service all three systems from one place.

Flow Path

Fluid goes to the engine-driven pump (EDP) through a reservoir **standpipe**. A supply shutoff valve operated by the fire switch is in this supply line. It closes to stop fluid to the engine-driven pump if there is an engine shutdown due to fire.

The EDP provides 3000 psi hydraulic fluid to operate left system components. EDP case drain fluid is used to lubricate and cool the pump. Pressure and case drain outputs are filtered in the same module. Case drain fluid is cooled in a heat exchanger in the left wing.

An electric pump (ACMP) is a demand source of system pressure. A separate filter module filters ACMP case drain and pressure output. Pump pressures and system pressure are monitored by pressure switches. System pressure is also monitored by a pressure transducer and transmitted to the **EICAS** computers. System fluid that returns to the reservoir goes through a return filter. A power transfer unit pump pressurizes left system return fluid and provides it to the stabilizer **trim** control module when the PTU is on.

Loads

The left hydraulic system supplies power for these functions: primary flight controls; some secondary controls; thrust reversers.

The hydraulic lines to the tail (**empennage**) area and the wing units have isolation valves for maintenance use. **Check valves** and **fuses** are in the left system rudder and elevator pressure and return lines to protect the left hydraulic system if there is a failure of the hydraulic lines in the horizontal or vertical stabilizer.

Fuses

The right hydraulic system is similar to the left system. Right system pressure is provided to these components: ailerons; spoilers; rudder and elevator autopilots **LCCAs** and **PCAs**; normal brake system; thrust reverser; power transfer unit motor.

Reservoir Fill

You service the left system reservoir through a servicing fitting and selector valve in the right fairing area aft of the right main **wheel well.**

Ground service disconnects (quick disconnects) are on the EDP and return filter modules in the aft part of the engine strut.

Reservoir

Each reservoir is pressurized to make sure there is fluid supply to the pumps. The pressure is controlled to 40 psi with air from the **pneumatic** system. The air goes through the pressurization module which contains these components: two filters; two check valves; manual **bleed valve; capped test port.**

The reservoirs are aluminum **weldments.** A standpipe supplies fluid to the EDP and the ACMP draws fluid from the bottom of the reservoir.

The reservoir holds eight gallons, but is serviced to 4. 77 gallons to allow for air volume necessary for head pressure.

A hydraulic quantity indicating system gives reservoir fluid level data for each system. A capacitance probe in each reservoir measures the fluid level. As the fluid level changes, the amount of the probe in fluid changes. This changes the probe capacitance. Probes in the left and right reservoir are interchangeable. A larger probe is used in the center system reservoir. A variable resistance temperature transmitter is on each hydraulic reservoir.

Reservoir

The EICAS computer shows the temperature on the lower EICAS display.

The reservoir service station is in the right aft body **fairing** area aft of the **RH** wheel well. The reservoir service station gives single point servicing for checks and for maintenance of fluid levels in all three hydraulic reservoirs.

A four-position selector valve and switch is controlled by one lever that selects the reservoir to be serviced and to show on the hydraulic quantity indicator.

NOTE: To get a proper fluid level in the reservoirs, the reservoirs must be serviced with all landing gears down, gear doors closed, steering and flight controls neutral. When servicing the right system, the brake accumulator pressure indicator must read at least 2500 psi.

The hydraulic quantity indicator is calibrated in percent of full increments (110 percent =1. 1) with a green band between 0. 80 and 1. 1.

Two sight glasses are on each reservoir. The lower REFILL sight glass gives indication to replenish reservoir. The upper OVERFILL sight glass gives indication to drain reservoir to FULL level. A pressure-fill port, service filter, and a hand pump with handle and suction hose are also in the reservoir service station.

WARNING: DO NOT OVERFILL THE HYDRAULIC RESERVOIR. AN OVERFILL CAN CAUSE HYDRAULIC FLUID TO ENTER THE PNEUMATIC DUCTING AND THE AIR CONDITIONING PACKS RESULTING IN SMOKE AND NOXIOUS FUMES ENTERING THE FLIGHT DECK AND PASSENGER CABIN.

REPEATED HYDRAULIC CONTAMINATION OF THE PNEUMATIC SYSTEM CAN ALSO RESULT IN DAMAGE TO TITANIUM DUCTS.

CAUTION: DO NOT EXCEED 150 PSI FILL PRESSURE WHEN SERVICING HYDRAULIC RESERVOIR. EXCESSIVE PRESSURE COULD DAMAGE RESERVOIR.

EDP Shutoff Valve

When the engine driven pump (EDP) supply shutoff valve closed, it shuts off the supply of hydraulic fluid to the EDP.

The two-position valves are electrically operated and are normally open. Valve position is controlled by the engine fire switch. Electrical power is 28 V DC from the battery bus. When the valve is selected closed, the EDP depressurization **solenoid** is also energized.

A red valve position indicator extends from the side of the valve/motor drive housing to show valve position. The valve cannot be manually operated.

New Words & Phrases

landing gear   起落架

skydrol   （防护及润滑用）特种液压工作油

strut   吊架

EDP＝Engine-Driven Pump   发动机驱动泵

ACMP＝AC Motor Pump   交流电动泵

ADP＝Air-Driven Pump   空气驱动泵

RAT＝Ram Air Turbine   冲压空气涡轮

GPM ＝Gallons Per Minute   每分钟加仑数；加仑

autopilot servo   自动驾驶伺服机构

spoiler   扰流板

stabilizer   安定面

yaw damper   偏航阻尼器

elevator feel system   升降舵感觉系统

rudder ratio changer   方向舵比例变换器

thrust reverser   反推装置

pitch enhancement system   俯仰增强系统

PTU＝Power Transfer Unit   动力转换组件

nose wheel steering   前轮转弯

reserve brake   备用刹车

reservoir   油箱

heat exchanger   热交换器

standpipe   竖管；管体式水塔

EICAS＝Engine Indication and Crew Alert System   发动机指示与机组警告系统

trim   配平

empennage   尾翼

check valve   单向活门

fuse   液压保险

LCCA＝Lateral Central Control Actuator　侧向中央控制作动筒

PCA＝Power Control Actuator　动力控制作动筒

wheel well　轮舱

pneumatic　气源的

bleed valve　引气活门

capped test port　封盖的测试端口

weldment　焊接件

fairing　整流

RH＝right　右

solenoid　电磁线圈

Choose the Best Answer

1. There are ＿＿ hydraulic systems in B737.

A. 3　　　B. 4　　　C. 5　　　D. 6

2. The left and right system components are in the engine ＿＿.

A. nacelle　　B. fairing　　C. strut　　D. fan

3. The center system components are in or near the ＿＿ main wheel area.

A. right　　B. left

4. EDP in this passage means ＿＿.

A. electronic data processing

B. engine driven pump

C. embedded data processor

D. engineering design plan

5. ＿＿ are the primary pumps in the left and right systems.

A. EDP　　B. ADP　　C. ACMP　　D. BDP

6. A ＿＿ pump in the center system is an emergency source of hydraulic pressure.

A. RAT　　B. EDP　　C. ADP　　D. ACMP

7. The hydraulic lines to the tail area and the wing units have ＿＿ valves for maintenance use.

A. isolation　　B. check　　C. lock　　D. shut off

8. Power transfer unit motor is powered by ＿＿.

A. left hydraulic system　　B. right hydraulic system

9. Each reservoir is pressured to make sure there is fluid supply to the pumps. The pressure is controlled to ＿＿ psi with air from the pneumatic system.

A. 35　　　B. 40　　　C. 45　　　D. 1850

10. EICAS is short for ＿＿.

A. engine indication and crew alerting system

B. electronic indication and crew alerting system

C. engine indication and cockpit alerting system

D. engine indication and crew alternating system

Translations of Long and Difficult Sentences

1. A pitch enhancement system, power transfer unit (PTU) between the left and right systems, supplies a third source of power for the horizontal stabilizer.

T：一套俯仰增强系统，在左右液压系统之间的动力转换组件，将提供给水平安定面第三种动力源。

2. A power transfer unit pump pressurizes left system return fluid and provides it to the stabilizer trim control module when the PTU is on.

T：一台动力转换组件泵给左系统回流液压油增压，并且当动力转换组件接通时把增压后的液压油供给安定面配平控制组件。

3. A four-position selector valve and switch is controlled by one lever that selects the reservoir to be serviced and to show on the hydraulic quantity indicator.

T：一个四位选择活门和电门被一个手柄所控制，可以选择使用中的液压油箱，并在液压油油量指示器上显示油量。

Questions

1. What's the function of hydraulic system?
2. What kind of fluid can be used in the aircraft?
3. What subsystems does the hydraulic power system include?
4. What's the difference between EDP and ACMP?
5. When can a ram air turbine be used?
6. What systems does the center system supply hydraulic power to?
7. How does the hydraulic fluid flow?
8. What systems does the left hydraulic system supply hydraulic power to?
9. What systems does the right hydraulic system supply hydraulic power to?
10. How does the EDP shutoff valve work?

Extensive Reading

Aircraft Hydraulic System

As aircraft performance increased in mid-20th century, the amount of force required to operate mechanical flight controls became excessive, and hydraulic systems were introduced to reduce pilot effort. The hydraulic actuators are controlled by valves; these in turn are operated directly by input from the aircrew (hydro-mechanical) or by computers obeying control laws (fly by wire).

Hydraulic power is used for other purposes. It can be stored in accumulators to start an auxiliary power unit (APU) for self-starting the aircraft's main engines. Many aircraft equipped with the M61 family of cannon use hydraulic power to drive the gun system, permitting reliable high rates of fire.

The hydraulic power itself comes from pumps driven by the engines directly, or by electrically driven pumps. In modern commercial aircraft these are electrically driven pumps; should all the engines fail in flight the pilot will deploy a propeller-driven electric generator called a Ram Air Turbine (RAT) which is concealed under the fuselage. This provides electrical power for the hydraulic pumps and control systems as power is no longer available from the engines. In that system and others electric pumps can provide both redundancy and the means of operating hydraulic systems without the engines operating, which can be very useful during maintenance.

Aircraft hydraulic fluids fall under various specifications:

(1) Common petroleum-based.

• Mil-H-5606: Mineral base, flammable, fairly low flashpoint, usable from $-65\,℉$ ($-54\,℃$) to $275\,℉$ ($135\,℃$), red color.

• Mil-H-83282: Synthetic hydrocarbon base, higher flashpoint, self-extinguishing, backward compatible to -5606, red color, rated to $-40\,℉$ ($-40\,℃$) degrees.

• Mil-H-87257: A development of -83282 fluid to improve its low temperature viscosity.

There are no military specifications for Skydrol hydraulic fluids. The list below contains most of the existing industry specifications and approvals:

• S. A. E. -Ac974

• S. A. E. -AS1241

• Boeing Seattle-BMS3-11

• Boeing Long Beach-DMS2014

• Boeing Long Island-CDS5478

• Lockheed-LAC C-34-1224

• Airbus Industrie-NSA307110

• British Aerospace-BAC M. 333. B

• Bombardier-BAMS 564-003

(2) Below are some of the more common aircraft Phosphate-ester based hydraulic fluids.

• Skydrol 500B-4 (Type Ⅳ class 2): The Skydrol 500 series of fluids has the longest service history among phosphate ester products. The first version, Skydrol 500, was introduced in 1952. Steady improvements to the formulation led in 1978 to the current version, Skydrol 500B-4 which contains the same breakthrough anti erosion additive and acid scavenger found in Skydrol LD-4 . Skydrol 500B-4 is the most worker friendly of the aviation phosphate esters; it is least irritating to skin and less prone to form mists which can be irritating to the respiratory tract. This has given the product enormous popularity for use in work shops and indoor test stands.

• Skydrol LD-4 (Type Ⅳ class 1): Was also introduced in 1978, and is today the largest selling aviation phosphate ester fluid in the world. At the time of its introduction it was a breakthrough product, solving problems of valve erosion and thermal stability common in earlier fluids. Its excellent thermal stability under real world conditions has given it a reputation as the gold standard among Type Ⅳ fluids. In recent years it has received an additional qualification of 5000 psi approval under Boeing BMS 3-11 (Type Ⅴ, Grade B and Grade C). Skydrol LD-4 features low density, excellent thermal stability, valve erosion prevention, and deposit control.

• Skydrol 5 (Type Ⅴ): Introduced in 1996, Skydrol 5 was the first Type Ⅴ fluid qualified under the Boeing BMS 3-11 specification. Skydrol 5 offers higher temperature capability than Type Ⅳ fluids, the lowest density, and better paint compatibility. Skydrol 5 does not have universal air frame manufacturer approval.

• Skydrol PE-5 (Type Ⅴ): Skydrol PE-5, introduced in 2010, has full approval from Airbus and Boeing for use in all of their aircraft models. Skydrol PE-5 was developed to meet and exceed the more demanding Type Ⅴ fluid requirements. It features the longest fluid life of any commercially available fluid, low density and low viscosity at low temperature; an unbeatable combination of the best features for optimum fluid performance.

• Exxon HyJet Ⅳ-A plus (Type Ⅳ): Exxon HyJet Ⅳ-A plus is a fire-resistant phosphate ester hydraulic fluid designed for use in commercial aircraft. It is the best-performing Type Ⅳ fluid and approaches to a great extent many of the performance capabilities of Type Ⅴ fluids, including high temperature stability, fluid life, low density, and rust protection. It is superior to all other Type Ⅳ fluids in these respects. Exxon HyJet Ⅳ-A plus meets the specifications of all major aircraft manufacturers and SAE AS1241.

• Exxon Hyjet Ⅴ (Type Ⅴ): Exxon HyJet Ⅴ is a Type Ⅴ fire-resistant phosphate ester hydraulic fluid, which is superior in thermal and hydrolytic stability to commercially available Type Ⅳ hydraulic fluids. Better stability means the extent of fluid degradation in aircraft systems will be less than Type Ⅳ fluids, in-service fluid life will be longer, and aircraft operator maintenance costs will be lower. HyJet Ⅴ provides excellent high and low temperature flow properties (kinematic viscosities) and rust protection. HyJet Ⅴ has also demonstrated an improvement over the erosion protection performance afforded by Type Ⅳ fluids.

Questions for extensive reading

1. Which type of hydraulic fluid is often used in the modern large comercial airplanes?
2. When does the pilot use Ram Air Turbine (RAT)?

Lesson 7

Auxiliary Power Unit

Engines and APU

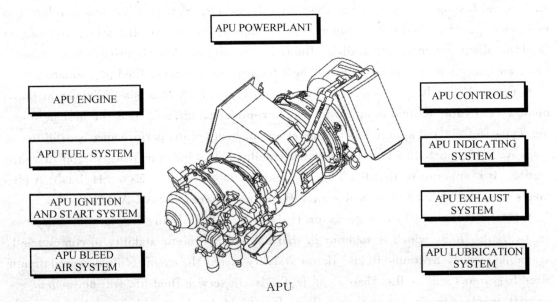

APU POWERPLANT

APU ENGINE

APU FUEL SYSTEM

APU IGNITION AND START SYSTEM

APU BLEED AIR SYSTEM

APU CONTROLS

APU INDICATING SYSTEM

APU EXHAUST SYSTEM

APU LUBRICATION SYSTEM

APU

Introduction

The **Allied Signal** GCTP 331-200ER gas **turbine** APU supplies the auxiliary power system with electric and pneumatic power. This lets the airplane operate independently of ground external power sources or the main engines. Auxiliary power is also available in the air.

The APU generator supplies 90 **kVA** electrical power at any altitude. Pneumatic pressure is available up to an altitude of 17,500 feet (5,300 m). The APU can operate at 100 or 101 percent. The APU operates at 101 percent during these modes: in the air; **ECS** demand; main engine start (**MES**).

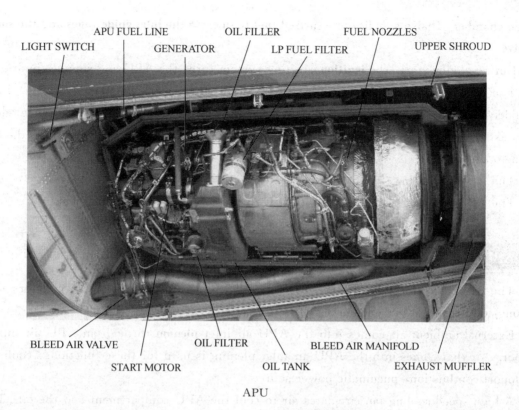

LIGHT SWITCH   APU FUEL LINE   OIL FILLER   FUEL NOZZLES   UPPER SHROUD

GENERATOR   LP FUEL FILTER

BLEED AIR VALVE   OIL FILTER   BLEED AIR MANIFOLD

START MOTOR   OIL TANK   EXHAUST MUFFLER

APU

General Description

The APU system contains these subsystems: control system; power plant; engine; APU and generator lubrication system; oil indicating system; fuel system; ignition/starting system; air system; indicating system; **exhaust** system.

An APU controller controls APU system functions and is an **interface** with other airplane systems.

The APU is a single shaft gas turbine engine which drives an electric generator and a **load compressor**. A **gearbox** on the front of the APU supplies power to APU **accessories**.

The **power plant** has these systems and components: auxiliary power unit; APU mounts; APU **wire harness**; APU air **intake**; APU **drains** and **vents**.

The APU engine has these components: two-stage **centrifugal** flow compressor; reverse flow annular **combustion chamber**; three-stage **axial flow** turbine.

The APU and generator lubrication system lubricates and cools these components: APU bearings; gearbox; electric generator.

The APU oil indicating system supplies this data about the APU oil to **flight deck** displays: temperature; pressure; quantity.

The APU engine fuel system supplies pressurized and metered fuel to the APU combustion chamber. It also supplies pressurized fuel to operate the **inlet guide vanes** and the **surge valve**.

During engine start, the **ignition**/starting system turns the APU and supplies ignition.

The APU air system supplies pressurized air to the airplane pneumatic system. Inlet guide vanes control the amount of air supplied to the load compressor. A surge valve releases excess bleed air overboard. A cooling system cools the APU compartment and the engine oil.

The APU indicating system supplies APU **EGT** data for flight deck displays.

The APU exhaust system sends the APU exhaust gases out of the **tail cone**.

APU Interfaces

The APU has interfaces with these systems that have information in other chapters/sections: electrical power; pneumatics; fire protection; EICAS.

External ambient air comes into the APU air inlet **plenum** through an APU air intake door. Air that comes into the APU air inlet plenum is used for these functions: cooling; support combustion; pneumatic power source.

A high speed cooling fan circulates air to cool the APU compartment and the oil. The inlet guide vane (IGV) actuator controls the pneumatic output of the APU. The IGVs open and close to regulate the amount of air that comes into the load compressor section of the APU. They are controlled in response to aircraft pneumatic demand. A flow sensor measures pneumatic output. The ECU uses this information to move a surge valve to prevent a load compressor surge.

The APU uses a common oil system to cool and lubricate these components: bearings; gearbox; generator.

The APU generator has a separate, non-bypass oil filter. If the generator fails, the filter protects the remaining APU components from damage.

A de-oil system permits easier start at cold temperatures.

The low oil pressure switch signals the **ECU** when there is low oil pressure in the pressure supply line. The oil temperature sensor supplies oil temperature information to the ECU. The gearbox **pressure regulating valve** controls gearbox pressurization. At lower altitudes, the gearbox vents to ambient. At higher altitudes, high pressure air is used to pressurize the gearbox. This prevents oil foam in the oil pump. The gearbox shutoff valve controls the input of high pressure air to pressurize the gearbox above 18,000 feet. The shuttle valve selects the source of buffer air for the compressor and cooling fan bearings.

The APU engine fuel system regulates and distributes fuel for engine combustion and inlet guide vane control.

The fuel control unit (**FCU**) does these functions for the fuel supply: shuts off; filters; pressurizes; meters.

The fuel control unit is electrically controlled by the ECU. The flow divider and solenoid valve separate fuel flow into primary and secondary flows. The solenoid valve prevents excessive fuel flow into the combustion chamber during start. Fuel manifolds and nozzles give even distribution of primary and secondary fuel flows into the combustion chamber.

The APU starts with a 28 V DC electric motor. A single ignition unit sends a high voltage to the igniter plug that causes ignition.

All operations of the APU are controlled and monitored by the APU electronic control unit (ECU). Two APU **monopoles** supply redundant speed (RPM) signals to the ECU. The APU inlet pressure and temperature sensors send signals of inlet air conditions to the ECU. The ECU uses this information for fuel flow schedule and surge protection.

Operation conditions of the auxiliary power unit go to the EICAS computers for display. EICAS shows this information: APU RPM; EGT; oil status messages; fault messages.

Oil level information goes from the oil quantity sensor directly to EICAS. EGT **thermocouples** measure exhaust gas temperature.

APU Control

These are the APU flight deck controls: APU selector; APU maintenance switch; APU fire switch.

The APU selector on the APU control panel is used to start and shut down the APU. The APU maintenance switch causes engine and APU data to show on the lower EICAS Display. The APU fire switch, on the cargo fire/engine control panel, will shutdown the APU when pulled. Turn the handle to discharge the extinguisher bottle.

You can shutdown the APU from outside the airplane with the APU fire **shutdown** switch. This switch is on the P40 APU remote shutdown panel on the **nose landing gear** strut. If this switch is operated, the battery switch must be recycled to reset the system.

EICAS shows this data: APU exhaust gas temperature (EGT); APU speed; oil status. Alert, status and maintenance messages can also show.

APU Installation and Removal

The APU is removed with two **fishpole** hoists or a single hydraulic lift. Either method, the installation of an APU **cradle**, that supports the APU during installation and removal, is necessary. The cradle attaches to the left forward and both right side mounting brackets.

To remove the APU, disconnect these items: APU harness; **ground jumper cables**; generator and starter motor electrical connections; APU fuel line; drain tank air pressure line; three air ducts (pneumatic system air supply duct, oil cooling air discharge duct and the exhaust duct).

Install these items: APU cradle; fishpole hoists; ground support equipment. You may install a ground support saddle assembly and clip assemblies to support the exhaust duct and secure the tubular supports during APU removal. The fishpole hoists install in keyhole slots permanently attached to the bottom of the APU air inlet plenum.

With the hoist installed, the APU weight can be removed from its support installation. Disconnect the APU from its tubular support and lower it out of the airplane.

If the APU is removed, and the generator is not installed, installation of 78 pounds of ballast weight mounted on the cradle is necessary.

APU Drains and Vents

Waste fuel, oil, and water are removed from the APU by gravity-fed drains and vents.

Rainwater that leaks into the intake plenum drains overboard on the right side of the APU compartment through the APU plenum drain.

An air intake housing and duct drain sends rainwater leakage overboard on the right side of the airplane. Water that collects in the inlet plenum drains into the APU compartment through the inlet plenum drain.

An APU drain mast removes waste fluid that collects in the APU. The drain mast exits through the right APU access door.

APU Exhaust

The APU exhaust system sends the APU exhaust overboard through the exhaust duct. The exhaust system prevents APU compartment damage from high exhaust gas temperatures and it decreases exhaust noise levels.

The exhaust duct is an 11.5-inch diameter. A bellows assembly attached to the turbine exhaust end of the duct allows movement between the APU and exhaust duct. The exhaust duct attaches to the APU with a V-band clamp. The aft end of the duct is supported by a leaf spring support ring attached to the airplane tail cone. A two-piece, 0.9-inch thick stainless steel foil insulation blanket is wrapped around the duct. The blanket is held on with safety wire lacings and is sealed to keep out fluids.

APU exhaust

New Words & Phrases

Allied Signal　联信公司（APU 制造商）

turbine　涡轮

kVA　千伏安

ECS＝Engine Control System　发动机控制系统

MES＝Main Engine Start　主发动机起动

exhaust　排气

interface　交互

load compressor　负载压气机

gearbox　齿轮箱

accessory　附件

power plant　动力装置

wire harness　导线保护管（套）

intake　吸入

drain　排泄

vent　排气

centrifugal　离心的

combustion chamber　燃烧室

axial flow　轴流式的

flight deck　驾驶舱

inlet guide vane　进口导向叶片

surge valve　喘振活门

ignition　点火

EGT＝Exhaust Gas Temperature　发动机排气温度

tail cone　尾锥

plenum　集气室

ECU＝Electronic Control Unit　电子控制组件

pressure regulating valve　压力调节活门

FCU＝Fuel Control Unit　燃油控制组件

monopole　电极

thermocouple　热电偶

shutdown　关断

nose landing gear　前起落架

fishpole　钓鱼竿

cradle　支架

ground jumper cable　搭铁线

Choose the Best Answer

1. APU is an acronym for ____.

A. audio processing unit

B. auxiliary power unit

C. auto processing unit

D. auto power unit

2. The APU generator in this passage supplies ____ kVA electrical power at any altitude.

A. 90　　　　　　B. 115　　　　　C. 28　　　　　D. 40

3. The APU operates at 101 percent during these modes except ____.

A. in the air　　　　　　　B. on the ground

C. ECS demand　　　　　　D. main engine start

4. EGT is short for ____.

A. exhaust gas temperature

B. exhaust gas turbine

C. engine gas temperature

D. exhausted gas temperature

5. The ____ actuator controls the pneumatic output of the APU.

A. OGV　　　　B. IGV　　　　C. ECU　　　　D. FCU

6. The ____ does these functions for the fuel supply: shuts off; filters; pressurizes; meters.

A. ECU   B. APU   C. FCU   D. ECS

7. All operations of the APU are controlled and monitored by the APU _____.

A. ECU   B. APU   C. FCU   D. ECS

8. The P40 APU remote shutdown panel is on the _____ landing gear strut.

A. nose   B. main

9. The APU is a single shaft gas turbine engine which drives an electric generator and a _____.

A. axial flow compressor   B. centrifugal compressor

C. load compressor   D. turbine

10. Which of the following companies is not an APU manufacturer?

A. Allied Signal   B. Honeywell

C. Boeing   D. Hamilton

Translations of Long and Difficult Sentences

1. The IGVs open and close to regulate the amount of air that comes into the load compressor section of the APU.

T：进口导向叶片的开和关用来调节进入到 APU 负载压气机部分的空气量。

2. Either method，the installation of an APU cradle，that supports the APU during installation and removal，is necessary.

T：用于在 APU 安装和拆除期间支撑 APU 的 APU 支架,其安装的任何一种方法都是必需的。

3. You may install a ground support saddle assembly and clip assemblies to support the exhaust duct and secure the tubular supports during APU removal.

T：你可以安装一个地面支撑底座和夹具来支撑排气管,并确保在 APU 拆除时管状支撑物的安全。

4. The exhaust system prevents APU compartment damage from high exhaust gas temperatures and it decreases exhaust noise levels.

T：排气系统防止 APU 舱受到排出气流高温的损坏并且能降低排气的噪声水平。

Questions

1. What's the function of APU?
2. When does the APU operate at 101 percent?
3. What subsystem does the APU system contain?
4. What systems does the APU have interfaces with?
5. What's the function of FCU?
6. How do you install or remove the APU?
7. How are the waste fuel，oil and water removed from the APU?
8. How does the APU exhaust?

Extensive Reading

APU

APS3200 APU for Airbus 318, 319, 320, and 321

The primary purpose of an aircraft APU is to provide power to start the main engines. Turbine engines must be accelerated to a high rotational speed in order to provide sufficient air compression for self-sustaining operation. Smaller jet engines are usually started by an electric motor, while larger engines are usually started by an air turbine motor. Before engines are to be turned, the APU is started, generally by a battery or hydraulic accumulator. Once the APU is running, it provides power (electric, pneumatic, or hydraulic, depending on the design) to start the aircraft's main engines.

APUs are also used to run accessories while the engines are shut down. This allows the cabin to be comfortable while the passengers are boarding before the aircraft's engines are started. Electrical power is used to run systems for preflight checks. Some APUs are also connected to a hydraulic pump, allowing crews to operate hydraulic equipment (such as flight controls or flaps) prior to engine start. This function can also be used, on some aircraft, as a backup in flight in case of engine or hydraulic failure.

Aircraft with APUs can also accept electrical and pneumatic power from ground equipment when an APU has failed or is not to be used.

APUs fitted to extended-range twin-engine operations (ETOPS) aircraft are a critical safety device, as they supply backup electricity and compressed air in place of the dead engine or failed main engine generator. While some APUs may not be startable in flight, ETOPS-compliant APUs must be flight-startable at altitudes up to the aircraft service ceiling. Recent applications have specified starting up to 43,000 ft (13,000 m) from a complete cold-soak condition such as the Hamilton Sundstrand APS5000 for the Boeing 787 Dreamliner. If the APU or its electrical generator is not available, the aircraft cannot be released for ETOPS flight and is forced to take a longer non-ETOPS route.

APUs providing electricity at 400 Hz are smaller and lighter than their 50/60 Hz counterparts, but are costlier; the drawback being that such high frequency systems suffer from voltage drops.

History

The Riedel 2-stroke engine used as the pioneering example of an APU, to turn over the central shaft of the World War Ⅱ-era German Junkers Jumo 004 jet engine.

The intake diverter in a Jumo 004 engine which housed the Riedel APU unit, complete with its D-shaped pull handle at the diverter's center.

The first military use of an APU of any sort was the Riedel opposed-twin cylinder 2-stroke engine used to start a Junkers Jumo 004 jet engine, used in the first combat jet of any type worldwide, the Messerschmitt Me 262A fighter.

The first American military aircraft to use an APU unit was the USAF Douglas Globe-master.

The Boeing 727 in 1963 was the first jetliner to feature a gas turbine APU, allowing it to operate at smaller airports, independent from ground facilities. The APU can be identi-fied on many modern airliners by an exhaust pipe at the aircraft tail.

Sections

A typical gas turbine APU for commercial transport aircraft comprises three main sec-tions:

(1) Power section

The power section is the gas generator portion of the engine and produces all the shaft power for the APU.

(2) Load compressor section

The load compressor is generally a shaft-mounted compressor that provides pneumatic power for the aircraft, though some APUs extract bleed air from the power section com-pressor. There are two actuated devices: the inlet guide vanes that regulate airflow to the load compressor and the surge control valve that maintains stable or surge-free operation of the turbo machine. The third section of the engine is the gearbox.

(3) Gearbox section

The gearbox transfers power from the main shaft of the engine to an oil-cooled generator for electrical power. Within the gearbox, power is also transferred to engine accessories such as the fuel control unit, the lubrication module, and cooling fan. In addition, there is also a starter motor connected through the gear train to perform the starting function of the APU. Some APU designs use a combination starter/generator for APU starting and electrical power generation to reduce complexity.

On the Boeing 787 more-electric aircraft, the APU delivers only electricity to the aircraft. The absence of a pneumatic system simplifies the design, but high demand for electricity requires heavier generators.

Onboard solid oxide fuel cell (SOFC) APUs are being researched.

Manufacturers

Two main corporations compete in the aircraft APU market: United Technologies Corporation (through its subsidiaries Pratt & Whitney Canada, Hamilton Sundstrand and the recently acquired Goodrich Corporation), and Honeywell International Inc. Hodyon is an ISO-certified company in Cedar Park, Texas that manufacturers Dynasys APUs for heavy trucks and military vehicles.

Questions for extensive reading

1. What main components does a typical gas turbine APU for commercial transport aircraft have?

2. How many APU manufactruers are there in the world today?

Lesson 8

How Can I Be an Aircraft Mechanic?

Engine check

How to become
a pilot

What Is a Mechanic Job Like?

You work in hangars, out on the field on the **"flight lines"** where aircraft park, or in repair stations. You use hand and power tools as well as sophisticated test equipment. Maintenance is performed **around the clock**, seven days a week. New **mechanics** and technicians should expect to work nights and weekends. The noise level both indoors and on the flight line could be very high. Sometimes your work requires physical activity, from climbing ladders to crawling. You work under **deadline** to make sure an airplane is ready to fly.

Do I Need a License to Be An Aircraft Mechanic?

Not necessarily. However, if you don't have a mechanic's certificate from FAA, you can work only when supervised by someone who does have a certificate. You cannot approve equipment for return to service. Without a certificate, you are less likely to advance to the top of the career field.

The FAA issues mechanic and repairman certificates. Mechanics can get either an airframe cer-

Aircraft mechanic

tificate or a powerplant certificate—most mechanics get both. Repairmen get certificates to perform only one or two specific tasks, and they must be supervised by FAA-approved Repair Stations, commercial operators, or air carriers where these specific tasks are done daily.

Do I Need Any Other Certificate to Work on Avionics Equipment?

If you have an airframe certificate you don't need any other certificate, but you must be properly trained and qualified and have the proper tools and equipment. You can even work on avionics equipment without a certificate if you have avionics repair experience from the military or from working for avionics manufacturers and related industries.

How Do I Get a Repairman's Certificate?

Requirements to Become an Aircraft Mechanic
- Basic Requirements;
- Experience Requirements;
- Oral, Practical, & Written Tests.

To get a repairman's certificate, you must be recommended by a repair station, commercial operator, or air carrier.

Basic Requirements

You must
- be at least 18 years old;
- be able to read, write, speak, and understand English;
- be qualified to perform maintenance on aircraft or components;
- be employed or have a specific job requiring special qualifications by an FAA-certified Repair Station, commercial operator, or air carrier;
- be recommended for the repairman certificate by your employer;

- have either 18 months practical experience in the specific job or complete a formal training course acceptable to FAA.

Experience Requirements

You can get the experience you need to become a certified power plant or airframe mechanic in one of three ways.

(1) You can attend one of the 170 **FAR part 147** Aviation Maintenance Technician Schools nationwide. These schools offer training for one mechanic's certificate or both. Many schools offer avionics courses that cover electronics and instrumentation.

You need a high school diploma or a General Education Diploma (GED) to get in to most schools. The schooling lasts from 12 months or 24 months, generally less than required by FAA for **on-the-job** training. When you graduate, you are qualified to take FAA's exams. Graduates often get higher starting salaries than individuals who got their required experience in one of the other two ways.

(2) You can work an FAA Repair Station or **FBO** under the supervision of a certified mechanic for 18 months for each certificate, or 30 months for both. You must document your experience with pay receipts, a log book signed by your supervising mechanic, a notarized statement from your employer, or other proof you worked the required time.

(3) You can join one of the armed services and get training and experience in aircraft maintenance. Make sure you are in a military occupational specialty for which FAA gives credit. You can get a current list of acceptable specialties from the local FAA **Flight Standards District Office (FSDO)**.

You must present an official letter from your military employer certifying your length of service, the amount of time you worked in each specialty, the **make** and model of the aircraft or engine on which you got practical experience, and where you got the experience. You cannot count time you spent training for the specialty, only the time you spent working in the specialty.

With both types of on-the-job training you should set aside additional study time to prepare for the written and oral/practical tests. The FAA will give you credit for your practical experience only after we review your paperwork and you have a satisfactory interview with an FAA **airworthiness inspector.**

Oral, Practical, & Written Tests

To become an aircraft mechanic, you must take oral and practical tests as well as written tests. There is a fee for the test. A Designated Mechanic Examiner gives you the oral and practical test. You can get a list of these examiners at the local FAA office. The oral and practical tests cover 43 technical subjects. Typically tests for one certificate—airframe or power plant—takes about 8 hours.

To apply to take the written test, you must present your proof of experience to an FAA inspector at the local FAA office. There are separate tests for airframe and power plant mechanic certificates, as well as a general test covering both. If the inspector decides you meet the requirements to take one of the tests, you may make an appointment for testing at one of the many computer testing facilities world-wide. You can get a list of sample general, airframe, and power plant test questions.

If you fail part of a test, you have to wait 30 days before you can take it again, unless you give a letter to the Examiner showing you've gotten additional training in the areas you failed.

You must pass all the tests within a 24-month period. The FAA will then issue you a certificate.

Repair station

America's Oldest Public Aviation Mechanic School—Harvard H. Ellis Technical School—Turns 70

The Harvard H. Ellis Technical School located in Danielson, **CT** is home to a historic aviation maintenance technician school. The AMT program began in Putnam, CT in September of 1930 has been in continuous operation since that. For over seventy years thousands of graduates have worked for major and regional airlines, corporate aviation, and manufactures such as Sikorsky, Pratt and Whitney, and Kaman Aerospace. Robert W. Conry was an instructor in the AMT program at Ellis Tech. This is the story of this historic program.

The Putnam (CT) Trade School was established in 1915 to provide free trade education for boys. Trade school curriculum was designed to meet the needs of local industry. Northeastern Connecticut's main industry at the turn of the century was textiles. Putnam's textile mills had a dependable source of waterpower in the Quinebaug and French Rivers to run the looms. The region saw an increasing labor pool as many immigrated for local jobs. The new Putnam Trade School provided skilled tradesmen for the local mills.

Mr. Harvard H. Ellis became the Putnam Trade School's director in 1920. Ellis was a tool and dye maker by training. He apprenticed and worked as a tool and dye maker for a typewriter company. The late 1920's saw the decline of the textiles in Connecticut. The textile industry moved south where cotton was grown saving transportation costs. A new trade was needed as the mills closed. Harvard Ellis was a visionary who saw the future in the fledgling aviation industry. Ellis began an aggressive campaign to expand the school's trade programs with an aviation mechanic school. Ellis supervised and recommended the first aircraft mechanic curriculum. He persuaded the State Board of Education to approve such a program Ellis went to Washington, D. C. to procure federal assistance for the mechanic program. The Vocational Training Division of the State Board of Education approved the **Aviation Maintenance Technician (AMT)** School on September 17, 1930. The State of Connecticut's approval makes the Ellis Tech the oldest public aviation mechanic school in continuous operation in the United States.

Classes were held on the second floor of the Putnam Trade School. The school building was a former textile mill, typical of those found in Eastern Connecticut. Original power for the mill was provided by water from the river next to the building. Overhead shafts ran belts which powered the weaving machinery. Waterpower was converted to electricity but the overhead shaft and belt system was kept to run **lathes, drill presses,** and milling machines in the aircraft shop. There was no airport at the school. The Civil Aeronautics Authority had an emergency landing strip located nearby in Pomfret, CT, which the school used. The Pomfret airport had a hangar available for the school's use. Airplanes were flown into Pomfret's field, disassembled, and trucked to Putnam. The first instructor hired by Ellis was Mr. Frank C. Hannam of Woodstock, CT. Hannam had served as a flight mechanic with the British Royal Flying Corps during World War I.

Training was free to Connecticut boys. A student was required to have a minimum two years of satisfactory high school. Today all students are required to be high school graduates or equivalent. Students began the program with a probation lasting 500 hours. They began their academic and shop training with courses in machine shop and electrical shop. Successful completion of these shops and probation allowed students to continue on to airframe and engine classes. Over the next ten years the school would graduate thirty-four students; all but one would find employment as aviation mechanics.

Ellis was able to procure surplus military engines from the federal government. Some of these engines were taken from the first American military planes built for service in France. The Liberty engine was among the first received. To obtain additional operating funds the school decided to buy old airplanes to overhaul, restore, and sell. The first was purchased on April 25, 1931. It was a Curtis Fledgling powered by a Challenger engine. The Fledgling was flown from Hartford to the Pomfret airport, dismantled and taken to the school. The airframe and engine were completely overhauled. In July of 1932 the Civil

Aeronautics Administration relicensed the craft. Captain Harry Generous and Captain George Kane, National Guard **aviators**, took the ship aloft on its first flight. They proclaimed her "airworthy" after the first test flight, to the delight of the students and instructor.

View of the hangar at the back of the Putnam Trade School.
Students are seen working on a Stearman biplane.

The school received repair station license No. 113 from the Civil Aeronautics Administration on March 17, 1932. The certificate was the first of its kind issued to a vocational school. "So far as we know, yours is the only strictly mechanics training school which has been issued a repair station certificate," wrote Mr. George M. Gardner, acting Chief of the U.S. Department of Commerce Inspection Service, in a letter to Director Ellis.

With repair station approval the school could now perform maintenance on privately owned airplanes. The first work performed on a privately owned airplane was the complete overhaul of a DeHavilland Gypsy Moth owned by Charles Maynard of Putnam. The work was completed on May 23, 1932. Other airplanes restored by the shop were: Curtis Robin, Eaglerock, Buhl Pup, Gypsy Moth, Spartan Warrior, Fleet Biplane, Stinson Reliant Monoplane, Curtis Junior, Stinson Lycoming Monoplane, pusher-type Curtis Wright, Monocoupe with a Lambert Engine, Fairchild Warner 22C7E, Stearman with a Wright J-67, Travelair, and J-2 Cub. The school obtained a D-17 Staggerwing Beech. The D-17 was purchased for around seven thousand dollars. Jigs and fixtures had to be made to replace spars and ribs. The Jacobs engine was completely overhauled. An unusual feature of the Jacobs was both battery and magneto ignition. After a completion the D-17 was sold for over twice the purchase price.

The use of outside production with a repair station was and still is a unique feature of the school. Hands on training is obtained in both airframe and engine repair. Airframe skills were taught including fabric, wirework, wood working, metal working, welding, and rigging. Engine skills included complete inspection, overhaul including machine tools in fitting of new parts, and wood and metal propellers. These skills were learned first in theory class then applied as aircraft were overhauled and repaired in the shop. By 1939 the program required 4800 hours of theory and shop instruction. Approximately 60% of the hours required were operative experience, the rest in related technical instruction. The school day ran from 8:00 AM to 5:00 PM with one hour for lunch. Instructors worked an additional half day on Saturday to plan lessons and grade work. The students kept time cards. When a student attained his 4800 hours the School's Director was called to the shop and the student graduated on the spot. He received his diploma and a handshake. Students did practical testing for the A&E license with a C. A. A. inspector.

In July of 1936 Wendell L. Russell succeeded Frank Hannam as instructor in the aircraft shop. Over the next two years the program filled to the limit of twenty students as set by the terms of the repair station license. In January of 1937 the C. A. A. granted the school approval for mechanics school license No. 91. An additional instructor, Mr. John Rogers, was hired the same year and the enrollment was raised to forty students.

In March of 1937 a grant for $3,100 was sought from the state to build a hangar, dope shed, and engine test cell. Construction was begun in June of 1937 with the trade school students performing the work. The structures were located at the rear of the school. The hangar was large enough to house three thirty-foot planes at any one time. It was completed in June of 1938.

Two views of the engine shop. Overhead shafts and drive belts which ran the machines can be seen, as well as the original Magniflux test machine.

In May of 1939 Louis deFlorez of Pomfret and New York, a pilot, engineer, and aviation enthusiast gave the aircraft school its first scholarship endowment of $200. Kostak Koleda was the first recipient of the deFlorez award and used his grant to complete flight training.

Mr. William B. Simmons was hired as an instructor in 1939 replacing John Rogers. Simmons graduated as an A&E mechanic in 1932 from the Curtis-Wright School at Hadley Airport, in Brunswick, NJ. Simmons was the first graduate of the Curtis-Wright School and the first person in the state of New Jersey to receive an aviation mechanic's license. After graduating Simmons went to work for Curtis-Wright as an instructor. Simmons was also a Private Pilot. He learned to fly in a Curtis Fledgling in the early 1930's. While working at Hadley, Simmons met Ellis who recruited him to teach in Putnam. Three months after Simmons started working for Ellis, Russell left to work for the National

Guard making Simmons department head. A second instructor, Mr. Huss, was hired.

The outbreak of World War II brought change to the school. The two instructors were issued deferments. Only four maintenance students were issued deferments. The aircraft shop contributed to the war effort by training students from Pratt and Whitney at night. P&W students commuted from East Hartford to Putnam to receive their engine training. These students received engine theory, applied engine shop, and welding. The instructors were given one month off during the summer for the duration of the war. As soon as a class completed the engine school a new one would begin immediately.

Security was tight at the school. Simmons recalls he had bought a Lugar pistol. Ironically he carried it to defend the school and airplanes against German espionage. For additional security the rudders were always removed from the airplanes. They were kept under lock and key separate from the planes. Fortunately no incidents occurred, but all were vigilant for the duration of the war.

Post-war prosperity brought a need for trained mechanics as the aviation industry returned. The return of AI's and the **AI** bill brought many new students to the school. Major airlines, Pratt and Whitney, Kaman, and Sikorsky hired most of the graduates. Virtually all found work in the aviation industry. As class sizes increased an addition was needed. The rapidly advancing aviation technology required more lab space and shop floor space.

The original building was built in 1915 and expanded in the 1920's. By 1941 an expansion of the shop and the construction of an airport proposed. The cost would be $180,000. There were plans for the addition of a dormitory at the school. The Pomfret airport was to be paved and a crosswind runway added. This was never accomplished, as it was defeated in a referendum by the voters of Putnam. The need for a new building and hangar was crucial as the aviation program grew. Sparked by the defeat by the voters of Putnam it was decided to move the entire trade school including the aircraft shop into a new building. Enough land would be obtained in nearby Danielson to build the new school building and construct a new airport.

The 1950's saw the school, including the aircraft shop, move into the new building in Danielson. The airport design was begun. In 1950 the aircraft program was showcased in the Connecticut exhibit of the Eastern States Expo in Springfield, MA. The shop received praise in 1952 by aeronautics inspector Mr. P. S. Lovering, a supervising agent for the C. A. A. The school narrowly escaped disaster in 1955 with flooding from two hurricanes. Over one third of the Putnam Trade School was damaged by floodwaters from the swollen Quinebaug and French Rivers. Damage to the school was estimated at $150,000. The aircraft shop escaped major damage from the storm. The test cell was washed away into the river, but the hangar and dope shed were saved. This disaster proved a benefit to the school as it prompted the decision to build a new centrally located school.

Harvard H. Ellis died on July 17, 1956. He never saw his dreams of expansion ful-

Four aircraft students and Mr. William Simmons, Sr. (far right). The second student
from the left is Mr. Delton Briggs from Lebanon, CT. Briggs was able to identify the biplane
as a 1928 Kitty Hawk Viking built in New Haven, CT. The Viking was repaired at the school
after a landing accident damaged the landing gear and lower wing. The students were from high
school and attended the aircraft shop during the War. The photo was taken in the spring of 1944.

filled. His successor, Alton Aldrich, was an enthusiastic supporter of aviation. With
Aldrich's support the state built an airport and new school building that included the aviation maintenance school. The new technical school building was built first. Construction
of the $2.5 million dollar school began in Danielson in late winter of 1958. The building
opened officially on July 1, 1959 with a dedication on Sunday, November 8, 1959. The
school was renamed Harvard H. Ellis Technical School to honor the work and dedication
of Mr. Ellis.

Although the Danielson Airport was to be built solely for the school, Aldrich pushed for
a municipal airport to be shared between the school and the Danielson region. In January
of 1961 John Dempsey, the former mayor of Putnam, was inaugurated governor. Dempsey supported the building of the Danielson Airport. Governor Dempsey signed for the airport construction on March 24, 1961. Ground breaking was held on Monday, July 10,
1961. The $500,000 airport was completed and dedicated on July 4, 1962. Over 10,000
people attended the dedication ceremony with Charles Kaman of Kaman Aircraft the principal speaker.

Until the 1970's the aircraft program had only two instructors and averaged thirty
students. Many applicants to the program were not accepted due to the lack of space and
instructors. Thomas Meskill succeeded Governor Dempsey. Governor Meskill was a pilot
and aviation enthusiast. He often would fly the state airplane to the school to visit. The
new governor supported additional hangar, classroom, and lab space for the maintenance
school. In 1974 an addition was completed bringing the shop to its present size. With the
addition, two additional instructors were hired. Class sizes ranged from 65 to 75 students
with several years having as many as 80.

In June of 1976 William Simmons, Sr. retired as department head. William (Bill) Jr.
replaced his father. The program continued to prosper and received many accolades for the
work and restorations performed. Bill Simmons Jr. retired in 1994. On June 9, 1995 Mr.

William Simmons, Sr. was awarded the Charles Taylor Master Mechanic Award from the F. A. A. for a lifetime of achievement in aviation maintenance.

At the end of the Connecticut Legislative Session in 2001 the State Legislature approved $10 Million Dollars to construct a new facility to house the Ellis AMT School. Plans include a new hangar and classrooms to be located at the Brainard Airport in Hartford. One of the difficulties attracting AMT students to Ellis Tech has been its location. Access from the Hartford area is difficult due to the lack of interstate highways connecting east to west. Most of Connecticut's major aerospace employers and its main airport (Bradley Field) are located in the central part of the state. Most graduates are employed here. Many students intern or work part-time in this region. By relocating the AMT program closer to employers and a more central location enrollment will increase. Tuition for the program remains very affordable for Connecticut residents. College credit is awarded at several Community Colleges for completion of the program.

Over 1,000 airframe and powerplant mechanics have graduated from the program since its inception in 1930. This makes the aircraft shop one of the most successful trade programs in the state's vocational-technical system. As the shop enters its seventh decade it continues as the nation's oldest public Aviation Maintenance Technician School. Unlike the textile industry of the 1920's aerospace continues at the cutting edge of technology. The Aviation Maintenance Technician School at Ellis Tech has made a lasting mark on this industry in the United States.

New Words & Phrases

flight line　航线

around the clock　全天候

mechanic　机械工(指机务,即飞机维修人员)

deadline　截止日期

FAR part 147　(美国)联邦航空规章(Federal Aviation Rules)147 部

on-the-job　在职

FBO＝Fixed Base Operator　固定基地运营商

Flight Standards District Office (FSDO)　飞行标准区域办公室

make　牌子

airworthiness inspector　适航检查员

CT＝Connecticut　美国康涅狄格州

Aviation Maintenance Technician (AMT)　航空维修技术员

lathe　车床

drill press　钻床

aviator　飞行员

AI＝Aviation Industry　航空工业

Choose the Best Answer

1. FAA issues ____ and repairman certificate.

A. mechanics   B. technicians   C. maintenance man   D. mechanical

2. Mechanics can get either an ____ or a powerplant certificate.

A. fuselage   B. airframe   C. mainbody   D. aircraft

3. If you have an airframe certificate you ____ any other certificate to work on avionics equipment.

A. need   B. don't need

4. Aircraft mechanics usually work in hangars, out on the field on the "flight lines" where aircraft park, or in ____.

A. repair stations   B. gas station   C. office   D. runways

5. The two largest repair stations in China are ____.

A. STARCO and AMECO   B. AMECO and TAECO

C. AMECO and GAMECO   D. STARCO and TAECO

6. Aviation maintenance technician schools in America are regulated by FAR part ____.

A. 121   B. 61   C. 25   D. 147

7. Aircraft mechanics can work in a repair station or FBO. FBO is short for ____.

A. fixed base operator   B. flights between overhauls

C. fan blade off   D. federal budget outlays

Translations of Long and Difficult Sentences

1. Repairmen get certificates to perform only one or two specific tasks, and they must be supervised by FAA-approved Repair Stations, commercial operators, or air carriers where these specific tasks are done daily.

T：修理人员获得证书以完成一或两项具体的任务，并且在日常完成这些具体任务时，他们必须受到 FAA 所批准的修理站、商用运营商或者航空承运人的监督。

2. You can even work on avionics equipment without a certificate if you have avionics repair experience from the military or from working for avionics manufacturers and related industries.

T：在没有证件的情况下，如果你有在军队修理航电的经验或者给航电厂家和相关单位在航电设备上工作的经验，你甚至能在电子设备上工作。

3. You must document your experience with pay receipts, a log book signed by your supervising mechanic, a notarized statement from your employer, or other proof you worked the required time.

T：你必须用付款收据，你的监督机务（师傅）签字的记录本，你单位（雇佣人）的证明，或者其他你工作了所需时间的证明，作为你学习经历的证明。

4. You must present an official letter from your military employer certifying your length of service, the amount of time you worked in each specialties, the make and model of the

aircraft or engine on which you got practical experience, and where you got the experience.

T：你必须提供一封来自你所在部队的证明信,它要能证明你的服役时间、你在每一种设备上的工作时间、你曾经获得实践经验的飞机或发动机的构造和型号及获得实践经验的地点。

5. If the inspector decides you meet the requirements to take one of the tests, you may make an appointment for testing at one of the many computer testing facilities world-wide.

T：如果检查者断定你达到了参加一种测试的要求,你可以在全世界任何一台计算机测试设备上预约测试。

Questions

1. In your opinion, What's a mechanic job like?
2. What is the difference between the mechanic certificate and the repairman certificate?
3. What condition do you have to reach if you want to work on avionic equipment?
4. What requirements do you have to meet if you want to get a repairman's certificate?
5. What tests do you have to take for a FAA certificate?

Extensive Reading

Becoming a Licensed Aircraft Maintenance Engineer in New Zealand

Becoming a Licensed Aircraft Maintenance Engineer usually takes between 4—5 years. To gain the license you have to be 21 years of age or older. There are four options of study you can undertake or four paths in order to become a LAME in New Zealand.

Option One

Work with a specific aircraft maintenance company and learn on the job under the guidance of an already licensed engineer. This kind of training will require five years, on which you will also undergo exams. Once the five years are up you can apply for a license. Not every aircraft maintenance company will take a trainee so the trainee has to find a company and approach them. In New Zealand they are about fifty certified maintenance organisations. A list of these organisations can be sort at [http://www.caa.govt.nz] under "personnel Licensing/Engineer".

Option Two

This options is for individuals who have worked in an apprentice engineering field that is not aviation related such as an automotive mechanic . To become a Licensed Aircraft Maintenance Engineer, they have to undergo three years of aviation engineering experience and sit the required exams.

Option Three

This option is for those who have already gone through a traineeship in an aviation related field such as military aircraft engineering. As long as they have four years experience as an aircraft engineer they only have to sit the LAME exams and pass in order to receive their certificate.

Option Four

Train through a certified training organisation. In New Zealand, Air New Zealand's Training School is the only organisation approved to provide LAME training. The course is offered to anyone even a school leaver as long as you are over 17 years of age. With Air New Zealand it takes 4 years and the total fees for the period is more than 60,000. Study link can cover up to 6,500 a year but you have to cover the difference which also includes Safety Equipment and text books.

Whichever of the four options you choose the exams you sit for your LAME license are the same. The exams comprise of:

- Aircraft Engineering
- Aeronautical Science
- Avionics
- Air Law/ Civil Aviation Legislation
- Aeroplanes 1 or Rotorcraft
- Human Factors and Supervision
- Aircraft Materials.

At the end of training the maintenance engineer will have attained:

- Tertiary Education
- Competence in IT
- Technical knowledge & skills
- English Communication-Oral and written
- Conversant with Aviation Laws
- Human Factors.

Today added to the training is:

- Simulators
- Less trade demarcation
- Technology-based learning methods
- Recurrent training.

Challenges Faced in Training Maintenance Personnel

The biggest challenge in aircraft maintenance training is attaining the correct mix of skills, technical knowledge and system knowledge. These skills are so closely intertwined in every maintenance task that often it is impossible to break them up for several people to perform the task.

Questions for extensive reading

1. How could you become a licensed aircraft maintenance engineer in New Zealand?
2. What is the biggest challenge in aircraft maintenance training?

Lesson 9

Airplane Health Management

Aircraft health management

Managing Information to Improve Operational Decision Making

Airplane Health Management (AHM) is a decision support capability provided via the My-BoeingFleet. com portal. Airplane Health Management uses real-time airplane data to provide enhanced fault forwarding, troubleshooting and historical fix information to reduce **schedule interruptions** and increase maintenance and operational efficiency. It delivers valuable information when and where it's needed.

AHM integrates the remote collection, monitoring and analysis of airplane data to determine the status of an airplane's current and future **serviceability** or performance. It converts the data into information that you can use to make the operational or "fix-or-fly" decisions that can make the difference between profit and loss.

Airplane Health Management is part of the Boeing commitment to providing its customers with the solutions they need to improve profitability. Airplane Health Management is a component of Boeing's effort to provide lifecycle solutions which enhance operational performance to the aerospace industry.

AHM is a system for reducing delays, cancellations, air **turn-backs**, and diversions through the innovative use of existing aircraft data. Boeing is actively developing and ex-

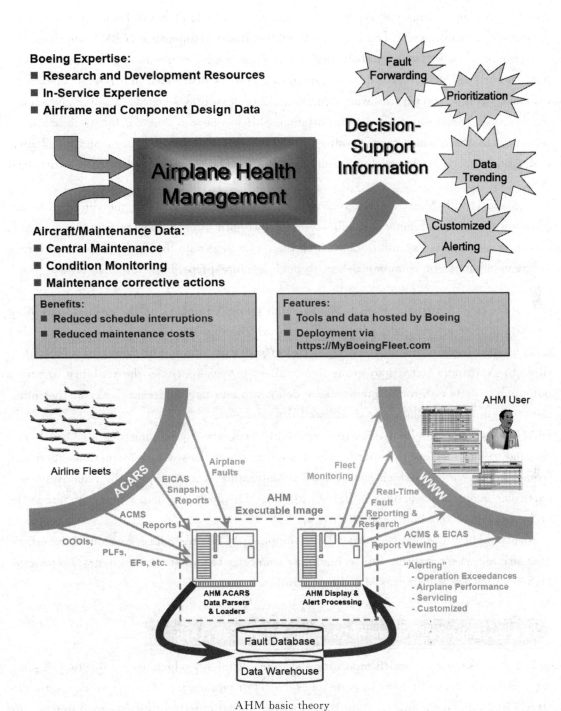

Boeing Expertise:
- **Research and Development Resources**
- **In-Service Experience**
- **Airframe and Component Design Data**

Airplane Health Management

Decision-Support Information

Fault Forwarding

Prioritization

Data Trending

Customized Alerting

Aircraft/Maintenance Data:
- **Central Maintenance**
- **Condition Monitoring**
- **Maintenance corrective actions**

Benefits:
- **Reduced schedule interruptions**
- **Reduced maintenance costs**

Features:
- **Tools and data hosted by Boeing**
- **Deployment via https://MyBoeingFleet.com**

AHM User

Airline Fleets

ACARS

EICAS Snapshot Reports

Airplane Faults

ACMS Reports

OOOIs, PLFs, EFs, etc.

AHM Executable Image

Fleet Monitoring

Real-Time Fault Reporting & Research

ACMS & EICAS Report Viewing

"Alerting"
- Operation Exceedances
- Airplane Performance
- Servicing
- Customized

WWW

AHM ACARS Data Parsers & Loaders

AHM Display & Alert Processing

Fault Database

Data Warehouse

AHM basic theory

panding its AHM offering to provide more opportunities to convert airplane-generated data into value-added decision support information. **SMI（Scientific Monitoring Inc.）**will be developing enhanced aircraft system monitoring software which will be used in future releases of AHM. AHM is part of the Boeing commitment to providing its customers with the solutions they need to improve profitability. Information on AHM and other services provided by Boeing Commercial Aviation Services are available at www. boeing. com.

Scientific Monitoring Inc. is a leader in **Condition Based Maintenance（CBM）** solutions. The company provides software products and services for condition monitoring and decision support for turbines and other industrial equipment. SMI's **distributed** and remote monitoring technology can be applied to a wide range of industries such as aerospace, power generation, manufacturing, and ground/sea transportation. SMI has been recognized for its technical excellence in NASA Achievement Award（2002）, Tibbetts Award（2001）, and Small Business Administrator's Award for Excellence（2000）. The company is located in Scottsdale, Ariz.

Airplane Health Management gives airlines significant insight as to the condition of airplanes in the sky, providing in-flight access to **fuel-burn** information so airlines can identify and correct problems that might be wasting fuel, as well as data that allow preparation for the airline to minimize or eliminate delays through advance preparation for maintenance procedures.

In some cases, Airplane Health Management allows engineers on the ground to monitor the health of an aircraft while it is in the air, which allows airlines to take action before a fault occurs, leading to a more reliable, **cost-effective** operation. For example, a fault identified by AHM and relayed to ground controllers provides airlines the visibility to turn a potentially costly on-ground maintenance delay into an easily addressable repair that minimizes or eliminates scheduling problems for passengers.

AHM also supports long-term fleet-reliability programs by helping airlines identify and respond to faults before they occur. The system provides fleet-wide information aggregated from other operators, which can be used to determine, for example, the effectiveness of particular maintenance actions in fixing problems. The goal is to help airlines operate at the highest levels of reliability and efficiency.

Airplane Health Management is a key component in Boeing's larger vision of the e-Enabled airline, where information technology, connectivity and strategic integration promise greater efficiency and improved airline operations.

Other Monitoring System or Methods for the Aircrafts

The various on-wing health monitoring systems of today, which are a collection of separate, unrelated technologies, provide a basic level of monitoring. Their capabilities are relatively limited and the information they provide is used mostly to initiate maintenance actions, not for real-time decision-making.

Current engine vibration monitoring systems sample at a relatively low frequency—too low to capture much significant or useful information on the vibratory modes of the system. They check the vibration magnitude to determine that it is within a normal range. Magnitudes that are too high might indicate a bearing failure or engine imbalance, magnitudes that are too low might indicate a faulty sensor or seized engine.

Lubrication system monitoring is performed using a **magnetic chip** detector to determine the existence of ferrous debris in oil. This is an indication of part wear.

Life cycle counts are performed on-wing. Engine parts, especially those in the hot section, may experience a maximum number of severe thermal transients before they must be retired. Each time the engine goes through a start-up transient, the life cycle count for each of the critical components is incremented. This way, part life is tracked as a function of use to facilitate scheduled maintenance.

Using internal and externally-funded resources, SMI has devoted considerable R&D efforts and resources focused on analyzing and applying **cutting-edge** technologies to create unique software algorithms, methodologies, tools, and processes which enable Condition Based Maintenance systems. The following are examples of the solutions created through the application of these technologies:

Electrical Power System Diagnostics and Health Management

Typical failure modes for **aircraft electrical power systems (EPS)** include bearing and winding failures in generators and failed GCU circuitry. These failures can lead to significant losses in mission capability and high maintenance and repair costs. The current electrical system health management techniques lack the capability for early detection of system degradation in order to develop mission performance life remaining predictions and enable proactive actions to prevent component and system failures.

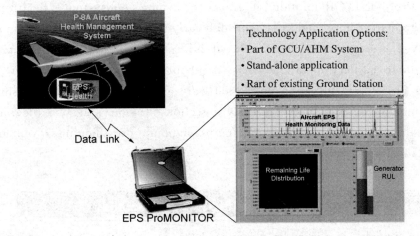

Diagnostics for aircraft electrical power system

EPS ProMONITOR solution improves aircraft power system health management, reduces unscheduled maintenance events, unnecessary scheduled maintenance, and the time required to isolate and repair faults. Minimized in-flight component failures can improve safety. Reduced and timely maintenance actions can provide increased aircraft availability,

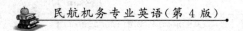

increasing mission readiness.

EPS ProMONITOR is an open, software application, capable of using existing equipment monitoring data to enable early detection of electrical power system degraded health state and mission performance life remaining predictions—providing improvement in maintenance, readiness, safety and cost.

Aircraft Avionics Health Management System

The avionics systems in both military and commercial aircraft are critical for the operation and effectiveness of the aircraft's mission. Avionics are essentially the brain of the aircraft. Avionics systems include the communication navigation and identification system; global positioning system (GPS) inertial navigation systems (INS), identification friend or foe system (IFF), radar altimeter and voice and data communications systems. In today's modern aircraft, many of the electronics within these avionics units are **commercial-off-the-shelf (COTS)** parts. Affordability of leading edge technologies mandates that the avionics industry be largely dependent on COTS electronic components (modules and assemblies) that were not originally designed for avionics. That is, they were designed primarily for computers and telecom use. The result is that when it comes to avionics systems, the problem of No-Fault-Found (NFF) continues to plague the aviation industry. The repair and rework, and maintaining the supply chain with spare units, continue to be quite costly. For example, on average, removals of avionics boxes result in No-Fault-Found 35%—50% of the time.

Avionics ProMONITOR solution integrates the avionics subsystem's health monitoring capabilities to deliver improved safety through early fault detection, prevention and recovery, improved system availability, reduced NFF rates, reduced avionics maintenance costs, and improved fleet operations decision support.

Avionics ProMONITOR is an open, software application, capable of using existing equipment monitoring data to enable early detection of avionics systems degraded health state and mission performance life remaining predictions—providing improvement in maintenance, readiness, safety and cost.

British Airways to Roll Out the AHM for Its Long-haul Fleets

Boeing and British Airways today announced that the airline will feature Boeing's Airplane Health Management (AHM) system to monitor the in-flight condition of more than 100 Boeing twin-aisle jetliners. AHM will be used on the airline's current 777 and 747-400 fleets and future deliveries, including 787 Dreamliners.

Through the MyBoeingFleet.com portal, British Airways will be able to track in-flight faults and make real-time operational decisions regarding maintenance, in order to **deploy**

the necessary people, parts and equipment to address the issue before the airplane arrives at the gate.

"We are always looking for the most innovative and effective tools for improving our management and maintenance of BA's fleet, "said Garry Copeland, engineering director, British Airways. "The Boeing AHM system will allow us to continuously improve aircraft downtime, minimize delays and analyse aircraft performance trends. The system has proved very effective during our testing, so we are pleased to be rolling it out across the **long-haul** fleet. "

Air China to Expand Boeing Airplane Health Management Coverage

Air China Cargo is included in coverage of Boeing 777 and 747-400 fleets.

Seattle, March 3—Boeing, in conjunction with Air China and Air China Cargo, announced today that the airlines will expand the use of Boeing's Airplane Health Management (AHM) system to monitor the in-flight condition of the carriers' Boeing 777 and 747-400 fleets.

The new agreement adds 42 in-service and **on-order** airplanes to a previous agreement to monitor 117 Air China 737s that are in service and on order. Air China is Boeing's first Chinese customer for AHM and the 33rd commercial customer overall.

"We are certain that Boeing's Airplane Health Management will benefit our passengers and cargo customers who count on Air China and Air China Cargo meeting our schedules," said Air China Chief Engineer Zhong Detao. "This will improve our entire operation. "

Airplane Health Management captures and evaluates critical real-time in-flight flying condition data and relays the information to maintenance controllers. That allows the airline to turn a potentially time-consuming and costly maintenance delay into a well-planned and more easily accomplished repair. Airlines are better able to meet flight schedules, benefiting the airline, passengers and other cargo customers.

The AHM system helps airlines identify and respond to problems proactively while accessing a multiple operator knowledge base, so repair decisions are more reliable and the airplane is available for service more quickly.

"Airplane Health Management is a key tool in working with our customers in our mutual pursuit of greater efficiency," said Dennis Floyd, vice president, Technical Services for Commercial Aviation Services at Boeing. "The expansion of AHM coverage at Air China and Air China Cargo will provide them an advantage in the highly competitive Chinese aviation market."

AHM is a component in Boeing's larger vision of Lifecycle Solutions—improving airline efficiency with digital productivity tools, product and industry expertise and the power of aviation's leading integrated supply chain, supporting Boeing airplanes from order placement through retirement.

Air China operates 10 Boeing 777-200s and 10 747-400s. Air China Cargo operates seven 747-400 freighters, including two Boeing converted freighters.

Air France Adopts Boeing's Airplane Health Management System

Air France has adopted Boeing's Airplane Health Management (AHM) system for its 42 B-777s and 21 B-747s.

AHM uses real-time airplane data to provide enhanced fault forwarding, troubleshooting and historical fix information to reduce maintenance-caused schedule interruptions and to increase maintenance efficiency.

In September, Air France announced its decision to put Boeing's class-3 **EFBs (electronic flight bags)** on its entire fleet of 777s. Since a class-3 EFB is an integrated part of an airplane's avionics system, it can serve as a direct communications gateway for passing fault and other aircraft status information between the airplane and an airline's operations and maintenance centers on the ground.

Air France was a developmental partner for the original AHM release, and it is the first Europe-based AHM customer.

Boeing to Provide Airplane Health Management System to Qantas

Seattle, March 24, 2008—The Boeing Company today announced that Qantas Airways' fleet of 747-400 airplanes will be monitored by Boeing's Airplane Health Management (AHM), a software system that helps airlines improve the management of unscheduled maintenance events. In addition, Qantas will use Airplane Health Management for future 787 Dreamliner deliveries. Qantas has 65 Boeing 787s on order.

Qantas'30 747-400s will use Airplane Health Management to gather and evaluate critical in-flight data on the real-time flying condition of its airplanes, information that can be used across the enterprise to identify and address overall efficiency.

"This system will help improve our 747-400 maintenance operations and greatly assist in meeting our customers'expectations for punctuality and serviceability," said David Cox,

Qantas executive general manager, Engineering.

"Qantas demonstrates a strong commitment for efficiency with the decision to subscribe to AHM to monitor its 747-400 fleet," said Dan da Silva, vice president of Sales and Marketing for Boeing Commercial Aviation Services. "In addition, the use of AHM on its 747 fleet will increase Qantas'experience with the system, which will also be used for the 787."

Qantas joins more than 20 operators from around the world that have committed to Boeing's AHM. More than 44 percent of the world's combined 777 and 747-400 fleet use the technology.

New Words & Phrases

Airplane Health Management (AHM)　飞机健康管理

schedule interruption　航班中断

serviceability　可用性;可维修性

fix-or-fly　修理或是放飞

turn-back　返航

SMI(Scientific Monitoring Inc.)　一家软件公司

Condition Based Maintenance (CBM)　视情维修

distributed　分布式的

fuel-burn　油耗

cost-effective　有成本效益的；划算的

magnetic chip　磁屑

cutting-edge　最前沿的

aircraft electrical power systems (EPS)　飞机电源系统

commercial-off-the-shelf (COTS)　商业成品零件

No-Fault-Found (NFF)　无故障被检查到(指送修的零部件没有检测到故障.)

deploy　调动

long-haul　长途运输的

on-order　订购的

EFBs (electronic flight bags)　电子飞行包

Choose the Best Answer

1. AHM in this passage is short for ____.

A. airplane health management

B. aircraft handling manual

C. APU health monitoring

D. airport handling manual

2. ____ are essentially the brain of the aircraft.

A. Electronics　　B. Avionics　　C. Hydraulics　　D. Pneumatics

3. Avionics systems include ____ and identification system; global positioning system, inertial navigation systems, identification friend or foe system, radar altimeter and voice and data communication systems.

A. communication navigation

B. electrical power

C. pneumatic

D. hydraulic

4. Lubrication system monitoring is performed using a ____ detector to determine the existence of ferrous debris in oil.

A. debris chip   B. iron chip   C. metal chip   D. magnetic chip

5. ____ is Boeing's first Chinese customer for AHM.

A. Air China   B. China Eastern   C. China Southern   D. Hainan Airlines

6. EFB in this passage is an acronym for ____.

A. erbium fiber bragg

B. electronic flying bag

C. electronic flight bag

D. electrical flight bag

Translations of Long and Difficult Sentences

1. Airplane Health Management uses real-time airplane data to provide enhanced fault forwarding, troubleshooting and historical fix information to reduce schedule interruptions and increase maintenance and operational efficiency.

T：飞机健康管理使用实时的飞机数据提前提供故障信息、排故方法和历史修理信息以减少航班计划的中断并增强了维修和运营效率。

2. AHM integrates the remote collection, monitoring and analysis of airplane data to determine the status of an airplane's current and future serviceability or performance.

T：飞机健康管理集成了飞机数据的远程收集、监控和分析，由此决定了一架飞机当前和未来的可用性或者性能状态。

3. Airplane Health Management gives airlines significant insight as to the condition of airplanes in the sky, providing in-flight access to fuel-burn information so airlines can identify and correct problems that might be wasting fuel, as well as data that allow preparation for the airline to minimize or eliminate delays through advance preparation for maintenance procedures.

T：飞机健康管理使航空公司能观察在空中飞行的飞机状态，提供空中通道以获取燃油消耗信息，从而使航空公司能识别和纠正浪费燃油的问题，也使航空公司获得数据，从而通过提前做好维修程序的准备工作以最小化或减少航班延误。

4. In some cases, Airplane Health Management allows engineers on the ground to monitor the health of an aircraft while it is in the air, which allows airlines to take action before a fault occurs, leading to a more reliable, cost-effective operation.

T：在一些情况下，飞机健康管理允许地面的工程师在飞机还在空中时就能监控飞机的健康状态，这就使得航空公司能够在故障发生前采取措施，从而获得一个更加可靠、经济效益好的运行操纵。

5. Airplane Health Management is a key component in Boeing's larger vision of the e-Enabled airline, where information technology, connectivity and strategic integration promise greater efficiency and improved airline operations.

T：飞机健康管理是波音公司电子化航线长远战略里的一个关键部分，在这个战略里，信息技术、网络连接和战略整合将获得更高的效益以及提高航线运营的能力。

Questions

1. What's AHM?

2. What's the function of AHM?

3. What can the British Airways do through the MyBoeingFleet. com portal?

4. How many airplanes will the Boeing AHM be applied into for Air China and Air China Cargo?

5. Please explain the Lifecycle Solutions of Boeing's larger vision.

6. Please introduce all kinds of aircraft monitoring system in detail.

Extensive Reading

Boeing to Provide Airplane Health Management System to Qantas

Seattle, March 24 — The Boeing Company today announced that Qantas Airways fleet of 747-400 airplanes will be monitored by Boeing's Airplane Health Management (AHM), a software system that helps airlines improve the management of unscheduled maintenance events. In addition, Qantas will use Airplane Health Management for future 787 Dreamliner deliveries. Qantas has 65 Boeing 787s on order.

Qantas 747-400s will use Airplane Health Management to gather and evaluate critical in-flight data on the real-time flying condition of its airplanes, information that can be used across the enterprise to identify and address overall efficiency.

"This system will help improve our 747-400 maintenance operations and greatly assist in meeting our customers expectations for punctuality and serviceability", said David Cox, Qantas Executive General Manager.

Airplane Health Management gives airlines significant insight as to the condition of airplanes in the sky, providing in-flight access to fuel-burn information so airlines can identify and correct problems that might be wasting fuel, as well as data that allow preparation for the airline to minimize or eliminate delays through advance preparation for maintenance procedures.

In some cases, Airplane Health Management allows engineers on the ground to monitor the health of an aircraft while it is in the air, which allows airlines to take action before a fault occurs, leading to a more reliable, cost-effective operation. For example, a fault identified by AHM and relayed to ground controllers provides airlines the visibility to turn a potentially costly on-ground maintenance delay into an easily addressable repair that minimizes or eliminates scheduling problems for passengers.

"Qantas demonstrates a strong commitment for efficiency with the decision to subscribe to AHM to monitor its 747-400 fleet," said Dan da Silva, vice president of Sales and Marketing for Boeing Commercial Aviation Services. "In addition, the use of AHM on its 747 fleet will increase Qantas experience with the system, which will also be used for the 787."

Qantas joins more than 20 operators from around the world that have committed to Boeing's AHM. More than 44 percent of the world's combined 777 and 747-400 fleet use the technology.

AHM also supports long-term fleet-reliability programs by helping airlines identify and respond to faults before they occur. The system provides fleet-wide information aggregated from other operators, which can be used to determine, for example, the effectiveness of particular maintenance actions in fixing problems. The goal is to help airlines operate at the highest levels of reliability and efficiency.

Airplane Health Management is a key component in Boeing's larger vision of the e-Enabled airline, where information technology, connectivity and strategic integration promise greater efficiency and improved airline operations.

Questions for extensive reading

1. What's the Airplane Health Management?
2. Do you think the AHM would play an important role in the flight safety? And why?

Lesson 10

Aviation Material Management

15 future conceptal
aircrafts

Aviation materials

Boeing Aviation Material Management

We are pleased to present an easy and efficient way for you to research, **quote**, order and track parts from Boeing Spares.

To provide more value and better service to our customers, we have developed a website on the World Wide Web to give customers direct access to our extensive part information and ordering system. You can order parts and view part information through the award winning Boeing PART Page website(Part Analysis & Requirement Tracking).

Through the Boeing PART Page, current data such as part **inventories**, prices, **part interchangeability**, quotes and purchase order status are at your fingertips.

The system is simple and accessible to any authorized Boeing customer.

Parts: View up-to-date part information such as prices, availability and interchangeability. Partial part number search is available.

Orders: Order as many as 25 items at a time, change an existing order, or check the status of your orders. View multiple purchase orders at once by entering selection criteria, such as "all open purchase orders".

Quotes: Request a price quote or view existing price quotes. Receive quote information back via email.

Contacts: Instantly retrieve information on how to contact us at Boeing Spares.

Help: Get answers to your questions in our "Help" and "Frequently Asked Questions" sections.

Accuracy and speed: Customers who are currently telephoning, faxing, telexing or emailing orders benefit from more accurate orders. In addition, orders are processed and acknowledged in seconds.

Cost savings: The Boeing PART Page may prove to be less expensive than other communication methods, depending on your local cost of Internet access.

Minimal training: We designed the Boeing PART Page to be intuitive for even the first-time user. The screens and data entry fields are uncomplicated and easy to navigate.

Security: The Boeing PART Page has built-in safeguards to allow only authorized customer personnel access.

Hardware and Software Requirements: All you need to access the Boeing PART Page is one of the following browsers with JavaScript, cookies and SSL 2.0 enabled:
- Netscape Communicator/Navigator 4.06 (or higher)
- Microsoft Internet Explorer 4.0 (or higher)

Proprietary Parts

Genuine Boeing proprietary parts are those for which Boeing owns the engineering drawings. These parts, available for both in and out of production aircraft, are built in accordance with Boeing's quality system and come with full traceability documentation.

Boeing Part Page: Easy and efficient way for you to research, quote, order and track parts from Boeing Spares.

Parts Leasing and Redistribution Services

To provide customers with better access to surplus spares, in 1999 Boeing granted Volvo Aero Services exclusive rights to market and sell Boeing commercial aircraft surplus inventory. By working together, our strategic team offers customers the highest quality Boeing parts, the most complete service possible, and market pricing. In some instances, we also can provide certified overhauled and serviceable inventory. The unique program is managed by Boeing and Volvo Aero Services out of facilities in Kent, Washington, minutes from Seattle-Tacoma International Airport.

Parts leasing and redistribution services

Spares Engineering and Provisioning

You make decisions about how much to spend on spares, which parts are necessary, and how many of each to purchase. Spares Engineering and Provisioning Services can make your choices easier. We help you develop a comprehensive spare parts list customized to your fleet, and we create a provisioning schedule so you receive parts as your maintenance plan requires them. We offer technical expertise on a broad range of spares issues, such as part interchangeability and **substitutions**, providing ways for you to use your inventory and budget more effectively. By working to develop a level of materials management that suits your needs, we help you reduce inventory-holding costs without **jeopardizing** flight and maintenance schedules.

24-Hour AOG Parts Support

When your Boeing 7-series or MD-series airplane is disabled, we stand ready to help you return it to revenue service, wherever in the world it happens to be, with 24-hours-a-day, seven-days-a-week dispatch availability. We have a long track record of reacting swiftly to any customer need, including an aircraft-disabling incident. We not only work to **repair the aircraft to as-new condition** as quickly as possible, using Boeing data and expertise, but we also provide you with total support.

We handle diagnosis, repairs, logistics, parts procurement, warranty and certification issues, and more. Our goal is to get you back in the air with as little disruption to your schedules as possible and to **streamline** your communication with all departments of Boeing, as well as with applicable regulatory agencies.

Embraer Aviation Material Management

Embraer has become one of the largest aircraft manufacturers in the world by focusing on specific market segments with high growth potential in commercial, defense, and executive aviation. We develop and adapt successful aircraft platforms and judiciously introduce new technology whenever it creates value by lowering acquisition price, reducing direct operating costs, or delivering higher reliability, comfort, and safety.

As a result, our aircraft provide excellent performance with **day-in and day-out** reliability, while being economical to acquire and cost-effective to operate and maintain. Equally important, we provide a superior product package, with comprehensive aircraft and after-sales support for parts, services, and technical assistance.

Embraer was Brazil's largest exporter from 1999 to 2001 and the second largest in 2002, 2003 and 2004. It currently employs more than 16, 853 people, 94.7% based in Brazil.

Embraer Material Support Division provides assistance on spares support and logistics as well as a range of special support programs to help operators reduce costs.

Embraer

Spares Support

Embraer maintains parts inventories, which are available to our customers 7 days a week, 24 hours a day. Service is provided through our Sales and Distribution Centers in São José dos Campos, SP, Brazil, Fort Lauderdale, FL, USA and Villepinte, France or through Embraer's Distribution Centers in Weybridge, UK.

Provisioning Services

Prior to delivery of aircraft, Embraer Material Support can provide customers with initial spares provisioning recommendation (the Initial Provisioning List or IPL) based on projected utilization, available maintenance capability and special requirements. Embraer's experience along with the utilization of advanced statistics techniques assures the best return over the investment in inventories.

In addition, Embraer Material Support can assess tools, equipment and facilities available at Customer sites and recommend additional items or modifications.

Special Programs

In addition to the sale of new parts and materials, Embraer provides options to reduce customers'investments in stocks through the following Customized Programs:
- Spare Parts Pool (Fleet Hour Agreement program)
- **Consignment** Stock
- Exchange Program
- Insurance Items Rental Program (high price and low-utilization items)
- Consumables Consignment
- Repair Management

Honeywell and Material Management

Honeywell is a leading global provider of integrated avionics, engines, wheels and brakes systems and service solutions for aircraft manufacturers, airlines, business and general aviation, military, space and airport operations.

Honeywell

Honeywell

Get the right parts, exactly when and where you need them.

By simplifying your maintenance, logistics and spare equipment availability, we provide needed aircraft equipment when and where it is needed to best support your operations.

Tailored to your specific needs and business requirements, you'll keep your aircraft operational and greatly reduce AOG delays by ensuring a rapid response from our comprehensive offering of asset availability solutions. From exchange and rental services to a full range of maintenance, logistics and materials management programs, our solutions are designed to reduce administrative costs and help you to better manage **up-front** capital investments, while lowering inventory carrying costs and facility space requirements. Each of our solutions additionally features a full range of 24/7 customer service and program support capabilities from Honeywell's global network of service and customer support centers. Our range of asset availability solutions is proven to deliver improved availability, shorter turnaround times, and the highest quality aerospace parts for lower total costs of aircraft ownership.

With the comprehensive Integrated Service Solution (ISS) support offering, Honeywell can manage the logistics, repair and spare equipment inventory required to support your aircraft fleet, so that spares are always available for your critical equipment.

You benefit from a single integrated program with one agreement and predictable periodic payments to guarantee global asset availability. Our Regional Asset Pools use negotiated rates for quick access to a regional pool of spare equipment inventory.

Here you'll find dispatch-critical **LRU**s on hand，and conditional equipment spares ready at a Honeywell facility for rapid exchange within a 24- to 72-hour turnaround time.

New Words & Phrases

quote　报价

inventory　库存

part interchangeability　可互换件

Proprietary Parts　专有件

substitution　可替代性

jeopardizing　危害；危及

AOG＝Aircraft On Ground　飞机在地面,意指飞机出现了紧急故障

7-series　波音公司"7"系列的飞机，如 B737、B767 等

repair the aircraft to as-new condition　飞机修复如新

streamline　使……高效率

Embraer　巴西航空工业公司

day-in and day-out　日复一日

IPL＝Initial Provisioning List　初始航材供应清单

consignment　寄售

tailored to　为……量身定做

up-front　提前的；预先

LRU＝Line Replaceable Unit　航线可更换件

Choose the Best Answer

1. AOG in this passage is short for ____.

A. arrival of goods　　　　　　　B. aviation overseas group

C. aircraft on ground　　　　　　D. augmented operator grammar

2. LRU is an acronym for ____.

A. line replaceable unit　　　　　B. lowest replaceable unit

C. least recently used　　　　　　D. las cruces

3. To quote is to ____.

A. order　　　B. bargain　　　C. purchase　　　D. name the price of

4. Embraer has been one of the largest ____ in Brazil.

A. importer

B. exporter

5. In 1999，Boeing granted ____ Aero services exclusive rights to market and sell Boeing commercial aircraft surplus inventory.

A. Volvo   B. SAAB   C. Embraer   D. Bae

6. An inventory is ____.

A. a supply or stock of something

B. a creation of something doesn't exist before

C. a list of sold products

D. a browser for internet surfing

7. IPL in this passage is short for ____.

A. illustrated parts list

B. initial program load

C. initial provisioning list

D. implemented program list

8. Day-in and day-out reliability means ____.

A. two day reliability

B. 24 hours reliability

C. half a day's reliability

D. constant reliability

9. You can order parts and view part information through the award winning ____ website (part analysis & requirement tracking).

A. Boeing component page

B. Boeing inventory page

C. Boeing unit page

D. Boeing PART page

10. Jeopardize means ____.

A. endanger   B. paralyze   C. minimize   D. secure

Translations of Long and Difficult Sentences

1. To provide more value and better service to our customers, we have developed a website on the World Wide Web to give customers direct access to our extensive part information and ordering system.

T：为了给我们的客户提供更多的价值和更好的服务，我们已经在万维网上开发了一个网站给客户直接进入，并能查询到我们大量的部件信息和进入订货系统。

2. These parts, available for both in and out of production aircraft, are built in accordance with Boeing's quality system and come with full traceability documentation.

T：这些部件，对国内外生产的飞机都有用，是按照波音质量系统制造的并且都有跟踪文件可以查询。

3. We offer technical expertise on a broad range of spares issues, such as part interchangeability and substitutions, providing ways for you to use your inventory and budget more effectively.

T：我们提供技术专家来解决有关备件的大量问题，例如部件的可互换性和可替代性，给您提供方法来更有效地利用你的产品和预算。

4. When your Boeing 7-series or MD-series airplane is disabled, we stand ready to help you return it to revenue service, wherever in the world it happens to be, with 24-hours-aday, seven-days-a-week dispatch availability.

T：无论在全世界的什么地方发生，当你们的波音7系列或MD系列飞机出故障时，我们时刻准备好帮助你们修理好它们并使它们返回运营服役，我们将保证飞机一周7天、一天24小时的放行可用性。

5. Our goal is to get you back in the air with as little disruption to your schedules as possible and to streamline your communication with all departments of Boeing, as well as with applicable regulatory agencies.

T：我们的目标是使你的飞机安全返回，给你的航班计划尽可能少的干扰，并且使你与波音所有部门的沟通都顺畅，也包括与管理局的沟通。

Questions

1. What information can you acquire from the Boeing part page?
2. What's the meaning of Proprietary Part?
3. What services can the Boeing and Volvo Aero Services supply?
4. How do you grasp the right meaning of the Right Parts at the Right Time?
5. What services can the 24-hour AOG Parts Support supply?
6. What's the feature of Embraer Provisioning Services?
7. How does the Embraer reduce the customers'investments in stocks?
8. What's Honeywell?

Extensive Reading

Composites and Advanced Materials in Aircraft

For many years, aircraft designers could propose theoretical designs that they could not build because the materials needed to construct them did not exist. (The term "unobtainium" is sometimes used to identify materials that are desired but not yet available.) For instance, large space planes like the Space Shuttle would have proven extremely difficult, if not impossible, to build without heat-resistant ceramic tiles to protect them during re-entry. And high-speed forward-swept-wing airplanes like Grumman's experimental X-29 or the Russian Sukhoi S-27 Berkut would not have been possible without the development of composite materials to keep their wings from bending out of shape.

The Lockheed F-22 uses composites for at least a third of its structure

Composites are the most important materials to be adapted for aviation since the use of aluminum in the 1920s. Composites are materials that are combinations of two or more organic or inorganic components. One material serves as a "matrix," which is the material that holds everything together, while the other material serves as a reinforcement, in the form of fibres embedded in the matrix. Until recently, the most common matrix materials were "thermosetting" materials such as epoxy, bismaleimide, or polyimide. The reinforcing materials can be glass fibre, boron fibre, carbon fibre, or other more exotic mixtures.

Fiberglass is the most common composite material, and consists of glass fibres embedded in a resin matrix. Fiberglass was first used widely in the 1950s for boats and automobiles, and today most cars have fiberglass bumpers covering a steel frame. Fiberglass was first used in the Boeing 707 passenger jet in the 1950s, where it comprised about two percent of the structure. By the 1960s, other composite materials became available, in particular boron fibre and graphite, embedded in epoxy resins. The U. S. Air Force and U. S. Navy began research into using these materials for aircraft control surfaces like ailerons and rudders. The first major military production use of boron fiber was for the horizontal stabilizers on the Navy's F-14 Tomcat interceptor. By 1981, the British Aerospace-McDonnell Douglas AV-8B Harrier flew with over 25 percent of its structure made of composite materials.

Making composite structures is more complex than manufacturing most metal structures. To make a composite structure, the composite material, in tape or fabric form, is laid out and put in a mould under heat and pressure. The resin matrix material flows and when the heat is removed, it solidifies. It can be formed into various shapes. In some cases, the fibres are wound tightly to increase strength. One useful feature of composites is that they can be layered, with the fibres in each layer running in a different direction. This allows materials engineers to design structures that behave in certain ways. For instance, they can design a structure that will bend in one direction, but not another. The designers of the Grumman X-29 experimental plane used this attribute of composite materials to design forward-swept wings that did not bend up at the tips like metal wings of the same shape would have bent in flight.

The greatest value of composite materials is that they can be both lightweight and strong. The heavier an aircraft weighs, the more fuel it burns, so reducing weight is important to aeronautical engineers.

Despite their strength and low weight, composites have not been a miracle solution for aircraft structures. Composites are hard to inspect for flaws. Some of them absorb moisture. Most importantly, they can be expensive, primarily because they are labour intensive and often require complex and expensive fabrication machines. Aluminum, by contrast, is easy to manufacture and repair. Anyone who has ever gotten into a minor car accident has learned that dented metal can be hammered back into shape, but a crunched fiberglass bumper has to be completely replaced. The same is true for many composite materials used in aviation.

Modern airliners use significant amounts of composites to achieve lighter weight. About ten percent of the structural weight of the Boeing 777, for instance, is composite material. Modern military aircraft, such as the F-22, use composites for at least a third of their structures, and some experts have predicted that future military aircraft will be more than two-thirds composite materials. But for now, military aircraft use substantially greater percentages of composite materials than commercial passenger aircraft primarily because of the different ways that commercial and military aircraft are maintained.

Aluminum is a very tolerant material and can take a great deal of punishment before it fails. It can be dented or punctured and still hold together. Composites are not like this. If they are damaged, they require immediate repair, which is difficult and expensive. An airplane made entirely from aluminum can be repaired almost anywhere. This is not the case for composite materials, particularly as they use different and more exotic materials. Because of this, composites will probably always be used more in military aircraft, which are constantly being maintained, than in commercial aircraft, which have to require less maintenance.

Thermoplastics are a relatively new material that is replacing thermosets as the matrix material for composites. They hold much promise for aviation applications. One of their big advantages is that they are easy to produce. They are also more durable and tougher than thermosets, particularly for light impacts, such as when a wrench dropped on a wing accidentally. The wrench could easily crack a thermoset material but would bounce off a thermoplastic composite material.

In addition to composites, other advanced materials are under development for aviation. During the 1980s, many aircraft designers became enthusiastic about ceramics, which seemed particularly promising for lightweight jet engines, because they could tolerate hotter temperatures than conventional metals. But their brittleness and difficulty to manufacture were major drawbacks, and research on ceramics for many aviation applications decreased by the 1990s.

Many modern light aircraft are constructed in composite material such as this Glasair

Aluminum still remains a remarkably useful material for aircraft structures and metallurgists have worked hard to develop better aluminum alloys (a mixture of aluminum and other materials). In particular, aluminum-lithium is the most successful of these alloys. It is approximately ten percent lighter than standard aluminum. Beginning in the later 1990s it was used for the Space Shuttle's large External Tank in order to reduce weight and enable the shuttle to carry more payload. Its adoption by commercial aircraft manufacturers has been slower, however, due to the expense of lithium and the greater difficulty of using aluminum-lithium (in particular, it requires much care during welding). But it is likely that aluminum-lithium will eventually become a widely used material for both commercial and military aircraft.

Questions for extensive reading
1. What's the definition of composite material?
2. What is the value of the composite materials?

Lesson 11

Customer Support

Boeing's disgraceful
downfall explained

Customer support

Airplane on Ground (AOG)—Incident Recovery and Repair Services

Who We Are: Our technical experts will provide **on-site** comprehensive, integrated assistance to recover a disabled airplane. Our goal is to recover damaged airplanes using methods and procedures that will avoid costly secondary damage. Boeing recovery experts have accumulated experience from numerous airplane recoveries around the world. We will use these prior experiences and our technical expertise to assist you in carrying out a successful recovery operation.

What We Do: Our airplane recovery team offers:

• On-site technical support to recover your airplane

• Consultation on appropriate airplane recovery equipment and methods for your operations

• Airplane recovery documents which provide critical information such as lifting, **tethering**, transporting and other data you will need to recover Boeing manufactured airplanes

• Training on aircraft recovery and establishing an airplane recovery team for your airline

Minimize Repair and Inventory Cost

A better way to manage repairs and inventory—With our Component Exchange Programs, you minimize component repair and inventory costs, and no longer need to worry about repair **turntime**. Boeing holds hundreds of replacement components, which are tested and overhauled to standards set by the **original equipment manufacturer** and are ready to ship within 24 hours of your order. This means you can **trim** inventory, which reduces holding costs and lets you put the capital to better use. Our programs also provide a single point of contact for components and handle inventory maintenance and warranties thereby simplifying administration.

Reduce repair costs of line replaceable units—Component Exchange Programs offer a ready supply of **dispatch-critical units** manufactured by Boeing and Boeing suppliers, including the high-value components that typically account for a large part of spares expense. At no additional charge to you, Boeing manages the repair, testing, and **recertification** of these units—reducing your costs.

Minimize service time—By taking advantage of our next-day shipping, you don't need to worry about how long it takes to repair a unit. With Component Exchange Programs, a replacement can be **en route** to your site before the damaged unit is even removed from the airplane, and you are no longer forced to cover lengthy repair turntimes with **in-stock** inventory.

Simplify supplier administration—Component Exchange Programs serve as a single point of contact for dozens of original equipment manufacturers, reducing your administrative burden for warranties, service, and deliveries. Your parts will be automatically shipped from the service center that provides the quickest response. As the programs expand, we will add new centers to serve you.

Additional benefits—

• **Fleet modification**. Our programs bear the cost of incorporating selected configuration changes, which minimizes the chance that you will stock outdated parts. Program parts will be upgraded as necessary with the latest modifications.

• Absolute **airworthiness**. Boeing guarantees that every part meets the specifications and performance standards of the original manufacturer and is certified by **regulatory agencies**.

Field Service Representatives

Aviation is a global, **round-the-clock** business. Boeing has developed a worldwide infrastructure to support airline schedules, resolve technical difficulties, provide quick access to technical information and deliver vital products and services when and where they're needed.

At the forefront of the Boeing global support team are more than 200 field service representatives in 65 countries. Highly qualified and experienced, they help customers keep their Boeing fleets in safe and profitable service, provide timely on-site technical advice and help assure a smooth introduction of new Boeing jetliners.

The field **reps** can **marshal** the full resources of the Boeing Company, including the **in-depth** expertise of service engineering specialists. Service engineers focus on preventing and resolving in-service technical problems. They have access to all commercial engineering data, and they share **fleetwide** information with customers via our **MyBoeingFleet. com** Web portal.

FLEET TEAM Issues

Boeing developed the FLEET TEAM **initiative** in late 1999 to streamline the delivery of engineering support to Boeing operators. At the heart of this effort is the FLEET TEAM Resolution Process to handle service-related problems. By accessing a FLEET TEAM Bulletin Board on the Boeing web site, customers can participate in deciding which fleet issues receive priority attention.

Industry Database Development and Hosting

The International Airlines Technical Pool (IATP) is a convention of airlines sharing technical resources to generate economic savings and to achieve on-time dispatch reliability and safe operation at line stations. Under the auspices of the IATP, members share aircraft parts, aircraft tooling, ground handling equipment, and **manpower**.

Supported by the **Air Transport Association**, the ATA Aviation Marketplace (SPEC 2000) provides a single"one-stop"commerce and information portal site for the aviation industry, bringing buyers and sellers of aviation parts and services together in a single interactive community.

Air Transport Association

ATA

CDG(Continental DataGraphics) is proud of its role as a comprehensive solutions provider to support parts and services transactions across the worldwide aviation community.

Boeing Commercial Airplanes Operations Center

Leading the industry with around-the-clock customer service

Boeing Commercial Airplanes is always looking for ways to better serve its airline customers. In December 2005, leaders of the Boeing Commercial Aviation Services organization opened the Boeing Commercial Airplanes Operations Center in Seattle, Washington, to provide around-the-clock support to airline customers with technical issues requiring resolution within 24 hours.

Resolution within 24 hours

Building upon the success of the **Boeing Rapid Response Center**, which was formed in 1999, the operations center assists airline customers with urgent technical problems, engineering issues and maintenance requirements 24 hours a day, seven days a week, 365 days a year. It is dedicated to around-the-clock customer support of the current fleet of some 12,000 Boeing and Douglas airplanes.

Direct response to airline demand

The Boeing Commercial Airplanes Operations Center is a direct response to increasing airline demand for around-the-clock support.

Continued cost and performance pressures have changed many airlines'operating models. Some have greatly reduced the size of their engineering departments or moved to a virtual model where such support is provided by a third party.

At the same time, a stricter regulatory environment has emerged, producing an increasing reliance on airplane manufacturers to provide greater customer support and technical expertise.

The Boeing Commercial Airplanes Operations Center provides comprehensive airplane support services, including structures, systems and maintenance issues. With Boeing experts in flight operations, spare parts and maintenance engineering, the center supports customers with speed, ease and a positive attitude.

Similar to airline operations or control centers, Boeing **staffs** its center with a mix of engineering and technical experts to address any question, issue or problem whenever an airline calls for help.

Foundation of Commercial Airplanes business

The Operations Center is another demonstration of how superior customer support is the foundation of Boeing Commercial Airplanes business. Boeing has a proud 70-year history of leading the industry with innovative customer support. Today, Commercial Aviation Services sets the standard for delivering the fundamentals of aviation support—spares, training, maintenance documents and technical advice—and offers the broadest range of support products and services in the industry.

Operations center of customer support

The origins of the Operations Center began on July 16, 1999, when Boeing formed the Rapid Response Center, or **RRC**, to provide commercial airplane operators with an unprecedented level of support during nights, weekends and holidays. The RRC's off-hours capability supplemented the ongoing daytime support by the highly trained Boeing technical experts in Service Engineering, the organization responsible for working closely with operators around the globe to prevent in-service problems and resolve technical issues.

Boeing established the RRC as a comprehensive, **one-stop** source of information to assist airline customers with "airplane-on-ground", or AOG situations. These are instances when an airplane is unexpectedly removed from service due to a problem with its systems or structure. Most often, AOG situations involve a minor technical problem with a back-up system or minor structural damage. Boeing conservatively estimates that a one-to-two-hour AOG delay costs an airline $10,000 in **downtime**. Actual costs of such delays can run as high as $150,000, depending on airplane model and the airline.

While the company had always offered around-the-clock assistance to customers, the RRC reflected the first time it had assembled a broad team of technical experts, equipped with sophisticated databases, in one room. Boeing was the first commercial airplane manufacturer to offer customers this type of service.

The RRC ultimately grew to three locations—Seattle and Everett, Wash., and Long Beach, Calif.—linked by high-speed telecommunications and staffed by a dedicated group of technical specialists, including structures engineers, systems engineers, field service representatives, spares personnel and maintenance engineers.

During the RRC's first year of operation, it saved airlines an estimated $50 million by reducing the time it took to solve technical problems that caused AOG situations. Some 400 operators with nearly 5,000 AOGs were assisted by RRC staff during that first year of operation, with an average response time of an hour and a half to resolve the technical issue.

Comprehensive and integrated response

The Operations Center builds upon the success and experience of the RRC and Service Engineering, and delivers an even more comprehensive and integrated response to the world's airlines, specifically to provide around-the-clock support for technical difficulties needed in 24 hours or less. RRC services were transitioned into the Operations Center and the partnership with Service Engineering continues. Service Engineering maintains its primary responsibility for addressing complex airplane issues that require longer resolution times while partnering with the Operations Center in dealing with urgent requirements.

Comprehensive and integrated response

Center staff represents a diverse array of Boeing expertise to address both AOG situations as well as other urgent airline requirements.

The center, located in the Duwamish area of Seattle, accommodates:

- Up to six controllers, who are responsible for all incoming center work
- Up to six functional leads, representing structures, systems, spares and other disciplines
- Up to 18 positions for functional engineering representatives from throughout the Commercial Aviation Services organization.

In addition, the center features four multimedia-equipped work rooms for teams to gather regarding a specific airline issue and a multimedia-equipped executive conference room for customer briefings and other large-scale meeting requirements.

How the center works

When a customer contacts the Operations Center, a controller discusses and defines the problem. The controller then works with leads from structures, systems and material management to develop options to resolve the problem. Following this collaboration, the customer and controller reach a joint decision on the optimum solution.

In addition to the 20 to 22 Operations Center staff per shift, structures and systems engineering support also is available from throughout Boeing Commercial Airplanes as needed.

Operations Center staff members are located at the Duwamish (south Seattle) as well as at extensions in Everett, Wash., and Long Beach, Calif. Having this extended operation allows Boeing to tap into more broad-based expertise at key Boeing locations. The Long Beach and Everett extensions opened May 24 and June 23, 2006, respectively. Functional leads and controllers will remain collocated at the Duwamish-based Operations Center for the long term.

The new Operations Center provides one more example of the Boeing commitment to be No. 1 in customer support.

Lufthansa Technik Group Capabilities

Lufthansa Technik has an international network and offers a vast portfolio of technology, training and logistics services, as well as supplementary services for all aspects of aircraft operations. As a competent partner for fleets of any size, we offer one-stop customized solutions.

The following summary(see Tab. 11-1, Tab. 11-2, Tab. 11-3)illustrates the complete **MRO** service portfolio of the Lufthansa Technik Group.

Tab. 11-1　Aircraft services（maintenance and overhaul）

Aircraft services (maintenance and overhaul)		
Airbus	**Boeing**	**Further types**
A300－600	737 (CL and NG)	Avro RJ/BAe 146
A310	747	Embraer Legacy
A318	757	Embraer 135/145
A319	767	Bombardier:
A320	777	(Challenger, Learjet, Global Express)
A321	MD-11	Gulfstream
A330	MD-80	Dassault Falcon Jet
A340	Boeing Business Jet (BBJ)	Cessna Citation
A380		Lockheed Jetstar
Airbus Corporate Jetliner (ACJ)		Raytheon Hawker
		IAI Westwind
		Sabreliner
		Saab 2000

Tab. 11-2　Engine services（maintenance and overhaul）

Engine services (maintenance and overhaul)		
General Electric	**Pratt & Whitney**	**Rolls-Royce**
CF6-50, －80C2, －80E1 CF34-3, －8, －10	JT9D-7, －7A, －7F, －7J, －7Q, －7R JT9D-59A, JT9D-70A JT15D PW4000-94, PW100, PW150	RB211-535 Trent 500 Trent 700 Trent 900 Spey, Tay
CFMI	**IAE**	**Honeywell**
CFM56-2C, －3, －5, －7B	V2500-A5, －D5	ALF502 TFE731 LF507
	APUs	
APS2000/3200 PWC901A	GTCP36-300 GTCP85-98, －129H GTCP131-9A, －9B GTCP331-200, －250, －350, －500, －600 GTCP660-4	TCSP700-4E

Tab. 11-3　Component services（maintenance and overhaul）

Component services（maintenance and overhaul）including Landing Gear services	
Airbus	**Boeing**
A300，-600	737
A310	747
A318，A319，A320，A321	757
A330	767
A340	777
A380	787
	MD-11
	MD-80（only Landing Gear）

Bombardier	**Embraer**	**Other regional aircraft**
CRJ 100，200，700，705，900 Q400	ERJ 135，140，145 Embraer 170，175，190，195	Only Landing Gear： Avro Raytheon Hawker Gulfstream

New Words & Phrases

Incident Recovery　故障修复

on-site　现场

tethering　系；拴

turntime　停场时间

original equipment manufacturer(OEM)　设备原厂家

trim　配平

dispatch-critical unit　与飞机放行相关的重要部件

recertification　再认证

en route　在途中

in-stock　有现货

fleet modification　机队改装

airworthiness　适航

regulatory agency　管理局

round-the-clock　全天候

reps＝representatives　代表

marshal　整合

in-depth　深入的；详细的

fleetwide　全球机队的

MyBoeingFleet.com　波音公司全球客户服务网站

initiative　项目

manpower　人工

Air Transport Association　航空运输协会(美国)

CDG＝Continental Data Graphics　大陆数字图文公司

Boeing Rapid Response Center　波音公司客户服务快速反应中心

staff　为……配备

RRC＝Rapid Response Center　快速反应中心

one-stop　一站式

downtime　停场时间，停工期

MRO＝maintenance，repair and overhaul　维护、修理和大修

Choose the Best Answer

1. MRO in this passage refers to ＿＿＿.

A. maintenance repair order

B. material release order

C. maintenance，repair and overhaul

D. movement report office

2. Original equipment manufacturer can be shortened to ＿＿＿.

A. OEMR　　　　B. OREM　　　　C. OEM　　　　D. OEMA

3. ATA in this passage is short for ＿＿＿.

A. actual time of arrival

B. air transport association

C. advance tactical aircraft

D. African technical association

4. Which one is not a regulatory agency?

A. FAA　　　　B. CAAC　　　　C. JAA　　　　D. Boeing

Translations of Long and Difficult Sentences

1. A Better Way To Manage Repairs and Inventory — With our Component Exchange Programs，you minimize component repair and inventory costs，and no longer need to worry about repair turntime.

T：我们的部件交换计划是一个管理维修和库存的更好办法,你可以最小化部件维修和库存成本,并且不再需要担心维修的停场时间。

2. Simplify supplier administration — Component Exchange Programs serve as a single point of contact for dozens of original equipment manufacturers，reducing your administrative burden for warranties，service，and deliveries.

T：简化供应商的管理——部件交换计划作为一个与很多原始设备制造商接触的独立通道,可以减少你用于担保、勤务和交付的行政负担。

3. Boeing has developed a worldwide infrastructure to support airline schedules, resolve technical difficulties, provide quick access to technical information and deliver vital products and services when and where they're needed.

T：波音公司已经开发了一个全世界的基础设施,无论什么时候、什么地点客户需要,它将支持客户的航线计划、解决技术困难、提供快速的技术信息通道,并且交付重要的产品和服务。

4. Highly qualified and experienced, they help customers keep their Boeing fleets in safe and profitable service, provide timely on-site technical advice and help assure a smooth introduction of new Boeing jetliners.

T：他们富有经验地、高质量地帮助客户保持他们的波音机队处于安全的状态和赚取利润,提供及时的在线技术建议并帮助提供波音新机队的机型知识培训。

5. The International Airlines Technical Protocol (IATP) is a convention of airlines sharing technical resources to generate economic savings and to achieve on-time dispatch reliability and safe operation at line stations.

T：国际航空技术协议是一个航空公司分享技术资源的公约,它使得航空公司节省经济成本并获得准时的放行可靠度和在航线站点的安全操作。

Questions

1. What's the meaning of AOG? And what will the Boeing do if AOG occurs?
2. What is the better way to manage repairs and inventory?
3. How can the customers minimize repair and inventory cost?
4. How do you explain Component Exchange Program?
5. What's the duty of field service representatives of Boeing company?
6. How does the Boeing Commercial Aircraft Operation Center work?
7. Which capability does the Lufthansa Technik Group have?

Extensive Reading

Customer Service Representative

Duties and Responsibilities

A customer service representative handles all sorts of correspondence, including inquiries and complaints, for the airlines. A representative using his or her own judgement, has the capabilities to refund fares and tickets, if they deem it necessary and justifiable. Often considered part of the management staff of an airline, a customer service representative has access to information and frequent flier accounts, personnel files and flight information.

Training Required

A customer service and/or management background, although not necessarily required, is a definite job. Most airline companies will hold training classes within the corporation.

A representative must know something about everything in airport operations to be able to field all types questions from clients. Therefore, most customer service reps will receive training in reservations, aircraft, personnel, company programs and policy, airline operations, ticketing and fares. Most airlines will also perform a background check before hiring.

Working Conditions

Generally in a professional office setting, the customer service representative will work a full 8.5 hours a day, weekends off. Paperwork, a telephone and a computer will fill the space in the office cubicle.

Personality Needed

A customer service rep must naturally be patient and professional. He or she must be able to listen to the client and communicate clearly and competently with them. A customer service rep must have the ability to break down a problem and to organize thoughts while someone else is talking.

Average Salary

As with most jobs, the salary of a customer service representative may vary depending on whether or not the candidate is outside the industry or has a college degree, among other things. Generally, a customer service representative may start at $25,000.

Employment Possibilities

Once established with an airline, the customer service representative may move up in the company, gain more responsibility, and/or obtain more privileged access to certain information.

The Best and the Worst

The best aspect of being a customer service representative is the chance to be presented with a problem and resolve the situation. A representative has the opportunity to educate a passenger that air travel is not always as simple as just buying a ticket. Irate passengers and irresolvable complaints can cloud up an otherwise sunny opportunity to help someone.

Questions for extensive reading

1. What's the responsibility of customer service representative?
2. Would you like to become a customer service representative?

Lesson 12

Next Generation Air Transportation System

Top 10 the fastest
airplane

Control tower in Beijing capital airport

The Next Generation Air Transportation System, or NextGen, is the transformation of the **radar-based** air traffic control system of today to a satellite-based system of the future. This transformation is essential in order to safely accommodate the number of people who fly in the United States. The already astronomical cost of delays will only increase if nothing is done. This will enhance runway safety on runways, taxiways and ramp areas and reduce delays, while also lowering emissions and fuel use.

New, **satellite-based** technologies will significantly improve safety, capacity and efficiency on runways and in the nation's skies while providing environmentally friendly procedures and technologies that reduce fuel burn, carbon emissions and noise.

Controllers and pilots communicate today largely by talking back and forth over radio. **Data Communications** (Data Comm) will improve safety and efficiency by replacing voice

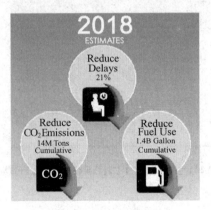

NextGen virtues

communications, which are labor intensive and susceptible to error. NextGen communications between controllers and flight crews will be handled by Data Comm transmissions, relieving radio frequency for more complex maneuvers and allowing complicated instructions to be provided electronically.

All of the FAA systems in NextGen will need to speak to one another—as well as to the systems used by other parts of the aviation community, including the airlines, the military and the Department of Homeland Security. **System Wide Information Management (SWIM)** is an information platform that will allow this to take place. SWIM is an essential part of NextGen, since the safe and efficient use of airspace depends on how well the different parts of the airspace system communicate with one another.

Weather accounts for 70 percent of all delays. **NextGen Network Enabled Weather (NNEW)** will improve aircraft operations over the nation's skies by reducing the impact of weather. NNEW will provide better weather forecasts, particularly for severe conditions such as thunder storms and icing. This will allow FAA air traffic managers and those who use the system to better manage traffic flow in bad weather.

The **Federal Aviation Administration (FAA)** is leveraging existing technologies and expanding their capabilities to bring the benefits of NextGen to the flying public today. In order to make the NextGen concept more easily understood, a fact sheet explains NextGen through the different phases of flight, describing some of the technologies being used as the foundation for NextGen. A list at the end shows the most recent of the many aviation community partners joining forces with the FAA to help transform the airspace system. These partners include airlines, manufacturers, state, local and foreign governments, universities and associations.

The FAA has also entered into agreements with international partners across the Atlantic and Pacific to accelerate the deployment of NextGen technologies and procedures to improve aviation safety, efficiency and capacity while reducing the environmental footprint during all phases of flight. The Atlantic Agreement, reached between the FAA and the European Union, is called the **Atlantic Interoperability Initiative to Reduce Emissions**

(**AIRE**). The Pacific Agreement, first reached with Australia and New Zealand and more recently joined by Japan and Singapore, is called the Asia and Pacific Initiative to Reduce Emissions.

The FAA's safety management systems approach, which is more proactive and data-driven, will help the agency achieve the next level of safety for the flying public. Ongoing investments in airport infrastructure—**runways**, terminals and technology—will ensure that maximum benefits will be gained from transforming the air traffic system and renovating aircraft fleets. The investment in advanced engines, **airframes** and sustainable fuels, along with new procedures, will help aviation's environmental footprint lessen over time.

Before Takeoff

The safe transportation of any air traveler begins on the ground. The FAA has different systems that allow air traffic controllers to see the location of aircraft and vehicles on airport runways and **taxiways** and keep them safely separated. One of these systems, called **Airport Surface Detection Equipment—Model X (ASDE-X)**, gets its information from a variety of surface surveillance sources, including radar, automatically transmitting the most accurate targets to monitors in the **tower**. The biggest improvement over systems that derive information solely by radar, which might show false targets during bad weather, will be the introduction of **Global Positioning System (GPS)** locations of both aircraft and surface vehicles. ASDE-X is fully operational at 27 airports.

GPS

A software tool called Surface Management uses ASDE-X to extend airport surface monitoring beyond runways and taxiways to the **ramp** areas. This extended coverage will improve common situational awareness, making pilots, controllers and airport operators better aware of the precise location of every aircraft, vehicle and obstacle on the airport surface.

After Takeoff

Aircraft flying in the U. S. today are tracked, for the most part, by radar. A new system called **Automatic Dependent Surveillance-Broadcast (ADS-B)** uses GPS satellite signals to more accurately identify the aircraft's location throughout the flight. In the near future, controllers will be able to safely reduce the separation standards between aircraft, which will provide increased capacity in the nation's skies. The FAA first rolled out ADS-B in **Alaska**, a site chosen because the rugged terrain severely limits radar coverage. Aircraft were equipped with ADS-B avionics, including a cockpit display. This display provided the pilot with the aircraft's location, the location of other aircraft, and graphical and textual weather information on a moving map. The accident rate for aircraft equipped with ADS-B avionics, which gives pilots a cockpit display showing where they are in relation to bad weather and terrain—dropped by 47 percent.

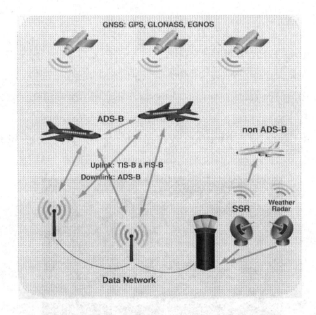

ADS-B

ADS-B now covers the Gulf of Mexico, where the FAA, in partnership with the **Helicopter Association International**, has installed a network of ADS-B ground stations on oil and natural gas platforms and the surrounding shoreline. This brings air traffic surveillance services, more precise aircraft locations and weather data to both low-altitude helicopters servicing the platforms and high-altitude commercial flights operating beyond radar coverage in the Gulf.

The FAA also has rolled out ADS-B in **Louisville**, where United Parcel Service (UPS) voluntarily equipped 107 of its aircraft with ADS-B avionics in order to save time, fuel and carbon emissions on flights to and from its Louisville hub. The system will soon be deployed for surveillance in **Philadelphia** and **Juneau.**

Pilots flying in aircraft equipped with ADS-B avionics in South Florida now receive free traffic and weather information on their cockpit displays. This marks the first time that pilots are able to see the same traffic information that's seen by air traffic controllers. The display of traffic information (called **Traffic Information Service-Broadcast, or TIS-B**) and weather information (**Flight Information Service-Broadcast, or FIS-B**) was made possible by the installation of 11 ground stations in South Florida by **ITT Corp.** The ground stations transmit satellite signals showing aircraft locations to pilots and controllers. Flight information now being broadcast free to pilots includes graphical displays of bad weather tracked by the National Weather Service and essential flight information, including special-use airspace and temporary flight restrictions.

ADS-B coverage has been nationwide in 2013.

A new software tool called **Traffic Management Advisor** (**TMA**) helps controllers sequence aircraft through high altitude airspace and into the airspace around major airports by calculating their precise routes as well as the minimum safe distances between aircraft. TMA is deployed at all 20 of the nation's en-route centers in the continental United States and 33 of the top 35 airports.

Over the Ocean

On flights over the Atlantic, the FAA and its partners (Single European Sky Air Traffic Management Research program, or SESAR; European air navigation service providers, aircraft manufacturers including Boeing and Airbus, and commercial airlines) are testing **Oceanic Trajectory Based Operations** (**TBOs**), which allow aircraft to operate the most efficient routes and altitudes. Seven test flights in May 2009 saved 330 gallons of fuel and 6,730 pounds of carbon dioxide. Tests in 2010 will also include Air France.

On Approach

The FAA has developed a toolbox of procedures to safely bring aircraft to their destination airport as quickly and efficiently as possible.

Beginning about 200 miles out, **Tailored Arrivals** allow controllers to look over an aircraft's flight path and tailor it to avoid certain conditions that might otherwise slow it down, such as bad weather and restricted airspace. More than 250 Tailored Arrivals have been flown into San Francisco by 747 and 777 aircraft, saving an estimated 27, 350 gallons of fuel.

As aircraft approach their destination airport, an **Optimized Profile Descent** keeps them at their most efficient altitude for as long as possible before they begin a continuous approach to the airport. The smooth descent—rather than the stepped-down approach required by current procedures—saves time and money while reducing carbon emissions and noise. **Delta** reduced carbon emissions by an estimated 200 to 1，250 pounds and saved 10 to 60 gallons of fuel per arrival into Atlanta during flight trials.

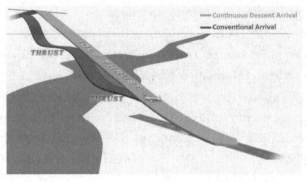

Optimized Profile Descent

Optimized Profile Descents maximize satellite-based approaches called **Area Navigation** （RNAV） and **Required Navigation Performance** （RNP），which provide precise approaches to runways. The FAA has published 341 RNAV and 205 RNP procedures. Both RNAV and RNP，like the other tools in the toolbox，allow aircraft to safely land as quickly and efficiently as possible.

New Words & Phrases

radar-based　基于雷达

satellite-based　基于卫星

Data Communications（Data Comm）　数据通信

System Wide Information Management（SWIM）　庞大信息管理系统

NextGen Network Enabled Weather（NNEW）　下一代主动网络气象

Federal Aviation Administration（FAA）　美国联邦航空局

Atlantic Interoperability Initiative to Reduce Emissions（AIRE）　大西洋积极协同减少
排放

runway　跑道

airframe　机身

taxiways　滑行道

Airport Surface Detection Equipment－Model Ⅹ（ASDE-Ⅹ）　机场地面探测设备——
型号 X

tower　塔台

Global Positioning System（GPS）　全球定位系统

ramp　机坪

Automatic Dependent Surveillance－Broadcast（ADS-B）　自动独立监控——广播

Alaska　阿拉斯加州（美国州名）

Helicopter Association International　国际直升机协会

Louisville　路易（斯）维尔（美国肯塔基州北部城市）

Philadelphia　费城(美国宾夕法尼亚州东南部港口城市)

Juneau　朱诺(美国阿拉斯加州首府)

Traffic Information Service-Broadcast，or TIS-B　交通信息服务广播

Flight Information Service-Broadcast，or FIS-B　飞行信息服务广播

ITT Corp(International Telephone and Telegraph Corp.)　美国国际电话电报公司

（=IT&T）

Traffic Management Advisor（TMA）　交通管理咨询

Oceanic Trajectory Based Operations（TBOs）　实用海洋航线

Tailored Arrivals　精心设计的到达

Optimized Profile Descent　以最佳剖面下降

Delta　美国达美航空公司

Area Navigation（RNAV）　区域导航

Required Navigation Performance（RNP）　所需导航性能

Choose the Best Answer

1. Controllers and pilots communicate today largely by talking back and forth over ____.

A. cell phone　　　　B. GPWS　　　　C. radio　　　　D. ACARS

2. Nextgen will use ____ to replace voice communications.

A. data communications　　　　　　B. words communications

C. code communications　　　　　　D. message communicaitons

3. FAA is short for ____.

A. final approach area

B. federal aviation administration

C. federal aviation authority

D. federal aviation agency

4. GPS is short for ____.

A. gallons per second

B. global positioning system

C. ground playback station

D. ground processing system

5. The FAA first rolled out ADS-B in ____, a site chosen because the rugged terrain severely limits radar coverage.

A. Nevada　　　　B. California　　　　C. Alaska　　　　D. New York

6. Optimized profile descents maximize satellite-based approaches called area navigation (____) and required navigation performance (____).

A. RNAV，RNP　　　　　　　　　B. AN，RNP

C. RNAV，RNAP　　　　　　　　　D. AN，RNAP

Translations of Long and Difficult Sentences

1. New, satellite-based technologies will significantly improve safety, capacity and efficiency on runways and in the nation's skies while providing environmentally friendly procedures and technologies that reduce fuel burn, carbon emissions and noise.

T：当提供环境友好型的程序和技术的时候（它们将减少燃油消耗、碳排放和噪声），新的、基于卫星的技术将极大地提高飞机在跑道和领空飞行的安全性、容量及效率。

2. Data Communications (Data Comm) will improve safety and efficiency by replacing voice communications, which are labor intensive and susceptible to error.

T：数据通信替代语音进行通信的方式将提高安全性和效率，因为语音通信属于高强度的劳动且容易出错。

3. In order to make the NextGen concept more easily understood, a fact sheet explains NextGen through the different phases of flight, describing some of the technologies being used as the foundation for NextGen.

T：为了使下一代的概念更容易理解，一张详情表格解释了下一代空管系统，它描述了一些用于下一代空管系统建设的技术。

4. Ongoing investments in airport infrastructure — runways, terminals and technology — will ensure that maximum benefits will be gained from transforming the air traffic system and renovating aircraft fleets.

T：机场基础设施的持续投资，包括跑道、航站和技术，将确保源于空管系统更换和飞机机队的更新所带来的最大收益。

Questions

1. What's the feature of Next Generation Air Transportation System? And how about its virtue?

2. How do the controllers and pilots communicate with the NextGen technology?

3. What's the function of System Wide Information Management (SWIM)?

4. To accelerate the application of NextGen technology, what role does the FAA play?

5. What can be used to keep the surface safety before takeoff?

6. What's the meaning of Optimized Profile Descent? Please explain it.

Extensive Reading

Next Generation Data Communications

Next Generation (NextGen) Data Communications, an element of the Next Generation Air Transportation System, will significantly reduce controller-to-pilot communications and controller workload, whilst improving safety.

Description

In the current United States National Airspace System, all communications with airborne aircraft is by voice communications. Aircraft route of flight revisions must be communicated through multiple change-of-course instructions or lengthy verbal reroute instructions, which must be repeated; are prone to verbal communications errors; and entry errors into an aircraft's flight management system. The use of voice communication is labor and time intensive and will limit the ability of the Federal Aviation Administration (FAA) to effectively meet future traffic demand in the United States.

Adding air-to-ground and ground-to-ground data communications will significantly reduce controller-to-pilot communications and controller workload. The data communications will enable ground automated message generation and receipt, message routing and transmission, and direct communications with aircraft avionics.

Initially, data communications will be an additional means for two-way exchange between controllers and flight crews for air traffic control clearances, instructions, advisories, flight crew requests and reports. Eventually, the majority of communications will be handled by data communications for appropriately equipped ground and airborne stations. Data communications will enable air traffic control to issue an entire route of a flight with a single data transmission directly to the aircraft's flight management system.

Benefits

Voice communications contribute to operational errors due to miscommunication, stolen clearances (an air traffic control clearance for one aircraft is heard and erroneously accepted by another aircraft) and delayed message transfers due to radio frequency congestion. Data communications will enable air traffic controller productivity improvements and will permit capacity growth without requisite growth in costs associated with infrastructure equipment, maintenance, labor and training. As a result, the resources required to provide air traffic management service per aircraft operation will decrease. The use of real-time aircraft data by ground systems to plot 4-dimensional trajectories (lateral and vertical navigation, ground speed and longitudinal navigation), and perform conformance management, will shift air traffic operations from minute-by-minute tactical control, to more predictable and planned strategic traffic management.

Questions for extensive reading

1. What benefits do next generation data communications have?
2. What is the distinction between voice communications and data communications?

Lesson 13

Composite Material Usage in Aircraft Structure

■ Carbon laminate
■ Carbon sandwich
■ Fiberglass
■ Aluminum
□ Aluminum steel titanium

Boeing Sonic
Cruiser

Composite Material Usage in Aircraft Structure

<Overview>

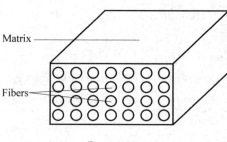

Matrix

Fibers

Composites

Composites are materials made of two or more **constituents** with different physical or chemical properties. When these materials are combined, the new material has different characteristic from the **individual** components. But the two or more materials which combine the composite materials must not **melt** in each other e. g. Glass Fiber Reinforced Plastic (**GPRP**), Continuous Fiber Ceramic Composites (**CFCC**), Carbon Fiber Reinforced Plastic (**CFRP**) and Aramid Fiber Reinforced Plastic (**AFRP**). These materials have been used in the aerospace industry as a new material according to the following features (Tab. 13-1).

Tab. 13-1 Composite materials' features and benefits

Features	Benefits
Light weight	It's lighter than steel by 5 times, which means less power consumption and reduce corrosion and cost.
High stiffness	It's more stiff than steel by two and half times.
High strength	It's stronger than steel by two and half times.
Few parts	It reduces the cost and stress because the number of cables are few between parts and that means less stress.

The best materials for the aircraft are those with high specific properties (mechanical property/density).

The light metalssuch as aluminum and titanium are popular aircraft materials, as composite materials like Glass or Carbon Fiber Reinforced Plastic. For example, if we make a comparison between the density of Aluminum alloy and Glass Fiber Reinforced Plastic, we find that the **densities** are 2,700 and 1,700 kg/m^3 respectively.

An advanced composite material is made of a **fibrous** material **embedded** in a **resin matrix**, generally laminated with fibers oriented in alternating directions to give the material **strength** and **stiffness**. Fibrous materials are not new; wood is the most common fibrous structural material known to man.

Applications of composites on aircraft include:
- Fairings
- Flight control surfaces
- Landing gear doors
- Leading and trailing edge panels on the wing and stabilizer
- Interior components
- Floor beams and floor boards
- Primary structure of vertical and horizontal stabilizer on large aircrafts
- Primary wing and fuselage structure on new generation large aircrafts
- Turbine engine fan blades
- Propellers

Weight saving through increased specific strength or stiffness is a major **driver** for the development of materials for airframes. There are many other **incentives** for the application of a new material.

A crucial issue in changing to a new material, even when there are clear performance benefits such as weight saving to be gained, is **affordability**. This includes **procurement** cost (currently the main criterion) and support cost through life (i. e. , cost of **ownership**, including maintenance and repair). Thus, the benefits of weight saving must be balanced against the cost. Approximate values may be placed on saving 1 kilogram of weight on a range of aircraft types.

In choosing new materials for airframe applications, it is essential to ensure that there are no **compromises** in the levels of safety achievable with conventional alloys. **Retention** of high levels of residual strength in the presence of typical damage for the particular material (damage tolerance) is a critical issue.

Durability, the resistance to cyclic stress or environmental degradation and damage, through the service life is also a major factor in determining through-life support costs. The rate of damage growth and tolerance to damage determine the frequency and cost of inspections and the need for repairs throughout the life of the structure.

History of Composites

Throughout history, humans have used composite type materials. One of the earliest uses of composite materials was that the ancient **Mesopotamians** around 3400 B. C. when they glued wood strips at different angles to create **plywood**.

Egyptians used cartonnage, layers of linen or **papyrus** soaked in plaster for death masks during the 2,181—2,055 B. C. Archeologists have found that natural composite building materials were in used in Egypt and Mesopotamia, since ancient builders and **artisans** used straw to reinforce mud bricks, pottery, and boats around 1,500 B. C.

Around 25 B. C. , The **Ten Books on Architecture** described concrete and distinguished various types of lime and **mortars**. Researchers have demonstrated that the cement described in the books is similar, and in some ways superior to the **Portland cement** used today.

In about 1,200 A. D. , the Mongols invented the first composite bows made from a combination of wood, bamboo, bone, cattle tendons, horns and silk bonded with natural pine resin. The bows were small, very powerful, and extremely accurate. Composite Mongolian bows were the most feared weapons on earth until the invention of effective **firearms** in the 14th century.

From the 1870's through the 1890's, a revolution was occurring in chemistry. **Polymerization** allowed new synthetic resins to be transformed from a liquid to solid state in a crosslinked **molecular** structure. Early **synthetic resins** included **celluloid**, **melamine** and **bakelite**.

In the early 1900's, plastics such as **vinyl**, **polystyrene**, **phenolic** and **polyester** were developed. As important as these innovations were, reinforcement was needed to provide the strength and rigidity.

Bakelite is an early innovative plastic. It is a thermosetting **phenol formaldehyde** resin, formed from an elimination reaction of phenol with formaldehyde. It was developed by Belgian-born chemist Leo Baekeland in New York in 1907.

One of the first plastics made from synthetic components, Bakelite was used for its electrical non-conductivity and heat-resistant properties in electrical insulators, radio and telephone casings, and such diverse products as kitchenware, jewelry, pipe stems, and children's toys. Bakelite was designated a National Historic Chemical Landmark in 1993 by the American Chemical Society in recognition of its significance as the world's first synthetic plastic. The "retro" appeal of old Bakelite products has made them collectible.

In 1935, Owens Corning launched the fiber reinforce polymer (FRP) industry by introducing the first glass fiber. In 1936, unsaturated polyester resins were patented. Because of their curing properties, they would become the dominant choice for resins in manufacturing today. In 1938, other higher performance resin systems like epoxies also became available.

World War Ⅱ brought the FRP industry from research into actual production. In addition to high strength to weight properties, fiberglass composites were found to be transparent to radio frequencies and were adopted for radar domes and used with other electronic equipment. In addition, the war effort developed first commercial grade boat hulls. While they were not deployed in the war effort, the technology was rapidly commercialized after the war.

By 1947 a fully composite body automobile had been made and tested. This car was reasonably successful and led to the development of the 1953 **Corvette**, which was made using fiberglass preforms impregnated with resin and molded in matched metal dies. During this period, several methods for molding were developed. Eventually two methods, compression molding of sheet molding compound (SMC) and bulk molding compound (BMC), would emerge as the dominant forms of molding for the automotive and other industries.

In early 1950's, manufacturing methods such included pultrusion, vacuum bag molding, and large-scale **filament winding** were developed. Filament winding became the basis for the large-scale rocket motors that propelled exploration of space in the 1960's and beyond. Pultrusion is used today in the manufacture of linear components such as ladders and moldings.

In 1961, first carbon fiber was patented, but it was several years before carbon fiber composites were commercially available. Carbon fibers improved thermoset part stiffness to weight ratios, thereby opening even more applications in aerospace, automotive, sporting goods, and consumer goods. The marine market was the largest consumer of composite materials in the 1960's.

Fiber development in the late 1960's led to fibers made from ultra-high molecular weight polyethylene in the early 1970's. Progress in advanced fibers led to breakthroughs in aerospace components, structural and personal armor, sporting equipment, medical devices, and many other applications. New and improved resins continued to expand composites market, especially into higher temperature ranges and corrosive applications. In the 1970's, the automotive market surpassed marine as the number one market—a position it retains today.

Mar-Bal Inc. was formed in 1970 and began their journey of becoming the most integrated thermoset composites solution provider of today. Mar-Bal began small and custom molded components for the electrical (e. g. breakers), motor assembly (e. g. housings) and small appliance (e. g. waffle makers) industries.

By the mid 1990's, composites hit mainstream manufacturing and construction. As a cost-effective replacement to traditional materials like metal and engineered thermoplastics, industrial designers and engineers began specifying thermoset composites for various components within the appliance, construction, electrical and transportation industries.

Composites began to impact the electrical transmission market with products such as pole line hardware, cross-arms and insulators.

Materials used in B787 body

Composite materials are not a stranger to the aerospace industry and as early as 1940's, Glass Fiber Reinforced Polymers (GFRP) began to find their way into the maritime industry. In 1944 the first aircraft with composites in its fuselage was flown in the USA, an experimentally modified **Vultee BT-15**.

In the early 1960's, composites were used in the form of "pre-pegs" which consist of a series of fiber reinforced plastics (FRP) pre-impregnated with an epoxy resin. Examples can be seen in the wings and forward fuselage of the AV-8B Harrier and the tail of the A320, as well as other military aircrafts such as the Eurofighters 2000.

Recently, Airbus increased its use of composites from 25% in the **iconic** A380 to 53% in the new A350 XWB. Boeing did the same: 12% of the structure of the B777 is made of composites and now their newest aircraft the B787 is comprised in 50% of composites. This produced a reduction in weight of 20% in the B787 and reduced scheduled and non-routine maintenance due to a reduced risk of corrosion and fatigue.

Although these composites have many features such as light weight, hight stiffness, etc. , but it also has many disadvantages, for example, it can be old under the effect of high temperature and humidity, medium resistance to shocks, difficulties in repairing and difficulties in series production.

They are using composite materials instead of aluminum in a wide range of the aircraft industry because of high specific solidity, light weight and high specific stiffness.

Composites have also been used in the designing of the UAVs industry. In 2009, a survey of 200 models by the composite world found that all of the models have composite components and number of cases.

However, the increasing demand for payload capacity and drone performance made the industry switch to another composite for the construction of the drone construction: carbon fiber reinforced polymers (CFRP) which is now the primary material used in the construction of the **UAV** airframes.

According to composite world, in 2007 and 2008, 231 and 247 **metric tons** of composites were produced to support UAVs and the market is expected to produce 738 metric tons of airframe structure by the year 2018.

As the market share of drones increases in civil and military applications, the demand for more maneuverable, payload effective UAVs is going to increase with composite materials playing a vital role in the development of these new aircrafts.

The use of additive manufacturing techniques such as Fused Deposition Modeling (FDM) and **Laser Sintering** (LS) in conjunction with composite materials is going to permit the development of more effective drones for security and military purposes.

Composite Manufacturing

The primary manufacturing methods used to produce composites include:
- Manual Lay-Up
- Automated Lay-Up
- Spray-Up
- Filament Winding
- Pultrusion
- Resin Transfer Molding

Manual **lay-up** involves cutting the reinforcement material to sizeby using a variety of hand and power-operated devices. These cut pieces are then impregnated with wet matrix material, and laid over a mold surface that has been coated with a release agent and then typically a resin gel-coat. The impregnated reinforcement material is then hand-rolled to ensure uniform distribution and to remove trapped air. More reinforcement material is added until the required part thickness has been built-up. Manual lay-up can also be performed using pre-impregnated reinforcement material, called "prepreg". The use of prepreg material eliminates separate handling of the reinforcement and resin, and can im-

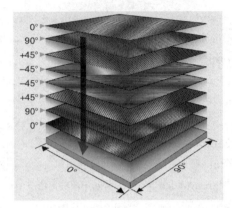

Composites lay-up

prove part quality by providing more consistent control of reinforcement and resin contents. Prepreg must be kept refrigerated prior to use, however, to prevent premature curing.

The productivity of the manual lay-up can be automated using **CNC** machines. These machines are used for both prepreg tape-laying and prepreg fiber-placement primarily in the aerospace industry.

In spray-up, resin is sprayed onto a prepared mold surface using a specially designed spray gun. This gun simultaneously chops continuous reinforcement into suitable lengths as it sprays the resin.

After lay-up, the composite parts must be cured. Curing can take place at room temperature, often with heated air assist. Ovens, heated-platen presses, and **autoclaves** may also be used. Curing times may range from a single hour to one-half day or longer. Curing is also accomplished with vacuum bag molding. Here, a non-adhering plastic film, usually polyester, is sealed around the lay-up material and mold plate. A vacuum is slowly created under the bag forcing it against the lay-up. This draws out entrapped air and excess resin. Vacuum bag molding is effective in producing large, complex shaped parts.

Filament winding refers to wrapping a narrow fiber tow or band of tows of resin impregnated fiber around a **mandrel** of the shape to be produced. When the mandrel is removed, a hollow shape is the result. Uses for filament winding include pipe, tubing, pressure vessels, tanks and items of similar shape. Filament winding is typically applied using either hoop or helical winding. In hoop winding, the tow is almost perpendicular to the axis of the rotating mandrel. Filament winding mandrels may be metallic or non-metallic and designed to either collapse to facilitate part removal or may be dissolvable after curing.

Pultrusion is a continuous process used primarily to produce long, straight shapes of constant cross-section.

Pultrusion is similar to extrusion except that the composite material is pulled, rather than pushed, through a die. Pultrusionis produced using continuous reinforcing fibers called "roving" that provide longitudinal reinforcement and transverse reinforcement in the form of mat or cloth materials. These reinforcements are resin impregnated by drawing through a resin wet-out station; and generally shaped within a guiding, or preforming system. They are then subsequently shaped and cured through a preheated die or set of dies.

Once cured, the pultrusion is saw-cut to length. Pultrusion can be hollow or solid, and applications include bar , rod, pipe, tubing, ladder rails and rungs, and supports of many kinds.

Resin transfer molding or "RTM" produces large, complex items such as bath and shower enclosures, cabinets, aircraft parts, and automotive components. In this process, a set of mold halves are loaded with reinforcement materials, then clamped together. Resin is then pumped or gravity fed into the mold infusing the reinforcement material. Once the mold is filled with resin, it is plugged and allowed to cure. After curing, the mold halves are separated and the part is removed for final trimming and finishing.

Composites Repair

Damage to radome honeycomb sandwich structure

Composites are used in a wide range of applications in aerospace, marine, automotive, surface transport and sports equipment markets. Damage to composite components is not always visible to the naked eye and the extent of damage is best determined for structural components by suitable Non-Destructive Test (**NDT**) methods.

Alternatively the damaged areas can be located by simply tapping the composite surface and alternatively listening to the sound. The damaged areas give a dull response to the tapping, and the boundary between the good and damaged composite can easily be mapped to identify the area for repair.

Awarenessof inspection for composite damage should be included in the regular maintenance schedules for composite structures. Particular attention would be made to areas which are more prone to damage.

Repairs to aircraft structures are controlled and should be carried out according to the Aircraft Structural Repair Manual (SRM). For other applications the repaired components would normally be expected to meet the original specification and mechanical performance requirements.

（1）Cosmetic repair

Cosmetic repair is designed to repair localized surface defects to the original profile and to prevent **UV** damage and moisture ingress. Cosmetic repair related to minor defects which have no significant effects on structural strength of the structure.

（2）Minor repair

Cirrus defines minor and major repair the same as the FARs do. So，minor repair would be repaired that is not major repair.

（3）Major repair

The repair might appreciably effect weight balance，structural strength，performance，powerplant operation，flight characteristic or other qualities，which effect airworthiness.

（4）Restricted repair

Any repairs occurring in no repair zones as listed in the maintenance manual are restricted.

New Words & Phrases

constituent　组成；组分

individual　单个的

melt　熔化；溶解

GPRP　玻璃纤维增强塑料

CFCC　连续纤维增强陶瓷基复合材料

CFRP　碳纤维增强塑料

AFRP　芳纶纤维增强塑料

densities　密度，density 的复数

fibrous　纤维的

embed　嵌入

resin　树脂

matrix　基体

strength　强度

stiffness　刚度

weight saving　减重

driver　动机

incentive　诱因；动机

affordability　可购性

procurement　采购

ownership　所有权

compromise　妥协

retention　保留

durability　耐久性

Mesopotamians 美索不达米亚人

plywood 胶合板

cartonnage 制造木乃伊盒的材料；埃及的木乃伊盒

papyrus 纸莎草纸

artisan 工匠

Ten Books on Architecture 书名：《建筑十书》

mortars 砂浆

Portland cement 硅酸盐水泥

firearms 枪支

polymerization 聚合

molecular 分子的

synthetic resin 合成树脂

celluloid 赛璐珞（明胶）

melamine 三聚氰胺

bakelite 酚醛树脂

vinyl 乙烯基

polystyrene 聚苯乙烯

phenolic 酚醛

polyester 聚酯

phenol 苯酚

formaldehyde 甲醛

Corvette 克尔维特牌汽车

filament winding 纤维缠绕

Vultee BT-15 美国 Vultee 公司的 BT-15 教练机

iconic 偶像的；标志性的

UAV＝Unmanned Aerial Vehicle 无人驾驶飞机

metric ton 公吨

Laser Sintering 激光烧结

lay-up 铺层

CNC＝Computerized Numerical Control 计算机数字控制

autoclave 热压器

mandrel 芯棒

NDT＝Non-Destructive Test 无损检测

UV＝ultraviolet 紫外线

Choose the Best Answer

1. When several materials are combined，the new material has ＿＿ characteristic from the individual components.

A. same   B. different   C. similar   D. common

2. Which one is not the feature of composite materials?

A. Heavy weight　　B. High stiffness　　　C. High strength　　　D. High density

3. Which one is not the application of composites on aircraft?

A. Fairings　　　　　　　　　　B. Flight control surfaces

C. Battery　　　　　　　　　　D. Landing gear doors

4. How many percent does the use of composites account for on A350 aircraft?

A. 25%　　　　　　B. 35%　　　　　　C. 53%　　　　　　D. 40%

5. What kinds of repair is it if the damagehas no significant effects on structural strength of the aircraft structure?

A. Cosmetic repair　　　　　　B. Minor repair

C. Major repair　　　　　　　　D. Restricted repair

Translations of Long and Difficult Sentences

1. An advanced composite material is made of a fibrous material embedded in a resin matrix, generally laminated with fibers oriented in alternating directions to give the material strength and stiffness.

T：先进的复合材料由嵌入树脂基体的纤维材料制成,通常由交替方向的纤维层压而成,以赋予材料强度和刚度。

2. Approximate values may be placed on saving 1 kilogram of weight on a range of aircraft types.

T：一定范围内机型的一千克重量也值得减小。

3. Retention of high levels of residual strength in the presence of typical damage for the particular material (damage tolerance) is a critical issue.

T：在特定材料的典型损伤(损伤容限)的存在下保持高强度残余强度是一个关键问题。

4. Durability, the resistance to cyclic stress or environmental degradation and damage, through the service life is also a major factor in determining through-life support costs.

T：在全寿命周期中,耐久性(防止循环应力或环境衰退造成的损伤)也是决定全寿命维护成本的主要因素。

Questions

1. What is composites?

2. What types of composites are often used into aircraft structure?

3. What are the benefits of composite materials?

4. Give some examples for the composite materials applied into aircraft structure.

5. What are the primary manufacturing methods used to produce composites?

Extensive Reading

Nondestructive Inspection（NDI）of Composites

Visual Inspection

A visual inspection is the primary inspection method for in-service inspections. Most types of damage scorch, stain, dent, penetrate, abrade, or chip the composite surface, making the damage visible. Once damage is detected, the affected area needs to be inspected closer using flashlights, magnifying glasses, mirrors, and borescopes. These tools are used to magnify defects that otherwise might not be seen easily and to allow visual inspection of areas that are not readily accessible. Resin starvation, resin richness, wrinkles, ply bridging, discoloration（due to overheating, lightning strike, etc.）, impact damage by any cause, foreign matter, blisters, and disbonding are some of the discrepancies that can be detected with a visual inspection. Visual inspection cannot find internal flaws in the composite, such as delaminations, disbondings, and matrix crazing. More sophisticated NDI techniques are needed to detect these types of defects.

Audible Sonic Testing（Coin Tapping）

Sometimes referred to as audio, sonic, or coin tap, this technique makes use of frequencies in the audible range（10 to 20 Hz）. A surprisingly accurate method in the hands of experienced personnel, tap testing is perhaps the most common technique used for the detection of delamination and/or disbonding. The method is accomplished by tapping the inspection area with a solid round disk or lightweight hammer-like device and listening to the response of the structure to the hammer. A clear, sharp, ringing sound is indicative of a well-bonded solid structure, while a dull or thud-like sound indicates a discrepant area.

The tapping rate needs to be rapid enough to produce enough sound for any difference in sound tone to be discernable to the ear. Tap testing is effective on thin skin to stiffener bondlines, honeycomb sandwich with thin face sheets, or even near the surface of thick laminates, such as rotorcraft blade supports. Again, inherent in the method is the possibility that changes within the internal elements of the structure might produce pitch changes that are interpreted as defects, when in fact they are present by design. This inspection should be accomplished in as quiet an area as possible and by experienced personnel familiar with the part's internal configuration. This method is not reliable for structures with more than four plies. It is often used to map out the damage on thin honeycomb face sheets.

Automated Tap Test

This test is very similar to the manual tap test except that a solenoid is used instead of a hammer. The solenoid produces multiple impacts in a single area. The tip of the impactor has a transducer that records the force versus time signal of the impactor. The magnitude of the force depends on the impactor, the impact energy, and the mechanical properties of the structure. The impact duration (period) is not sensitive to the magnitude of the impact force; however, this duration changes as the stiffness of the structure is altered. Therefore, the signal from an unflawed region is used for calibration, and any deviation from this unflawed signal indicates the existence of damage.

Ultrasonic Inspection

Ultrasonic inspection has proven to be a very useful tool for the detection of internal delaminations, voids, or inconsistencies in composite components not otherwise discernable using visual or tap methodology. There are many ultrasonic techniques; however, each technique uses sound wave energy with a frequency above the audible range. A high-frequency (usually several MHz) sound wave is introduced into the part and may be directed to travel normal to the part surface, or along the surface of the part, or at some predefined angle to the part surface. You may need to try different directions to locate the flow. The introduced sound is then monitored as it travels its assigned route through the part for any significant change. Ultrasonic sound waves have properties similar to light waves. When an ultrasonic wave strikes an interrupting object, the wave or energy is either absorbed or reflected back to the surface. The disrupted or diminished sonic energy is then picked up by a receiving transducer and converted into a display on an oscilloscope or a chart recorder. The display allows the operator to evaluate the discrepant indications comparatively with those areas known to be good. To facilitate the comparison, reference standards are established and utilized to calibrate the ultrasonic equipment.

The repair technician must realize that the concepts outlined here work fine in the repetitious manufacturing environment, but are likely to be more difficult to implement in a repair environment given the vast number of different composite components installed on the aircraft and the relative complexity of their construction. The reference standards would also have to take into account the transmutations that take place when a composite component is exposed to an in-service environment over a prolonged period or has been the subject of repair activity or similar restorative action. The four most common ultrasonic techniques are discussed next.

Through Transmission Ultrasonic Inspection

Through transmission ultrasonic inspection uses two transducers, one on each side of the area to be inspected. The ultrasonic signal is transmitted from one transducer to the other transducer. The loss of signal strength is then measured by the instrument. The instrument shows the loss as a percent of the original signal strength or the loss in decibels. The signal loss is compared to a reference standard. Areas with a greater loss than the reference standard indicate a defective area.

Pulse Echo Ultrasonic Inspection

Single-side ultrasonic inspection may be accomplished using pulse echo techniques. In this method, a single search unit is working as a transmitting and a receiving transducer that is excited by high voltage pulses. Each electrical pulse activates the transducer element. This element converts the electrical energy into mechanical energy in the form of an ultrasonic sound wave. The sonic energy travels through a Teflon® or methacrylate contact tip into the test part. A waveform is generated in the test part and is picked up by the transducer element. Any change in amplitude of the received signal, or time required for the echo to return to the transducer, indicates the presence of a defect. Pulse echo inspections are used to find delaminations, cracks, porosity, water, and disbonds of bonded components. Pulse echo does not find disbonds or defects between laminated skins and honeycomb core.

Ultrasonic Bondtester Inspection

Low-frequency and high-frequency bondtesters are used for ultrasonic inspections of composite structures. These bondtesters use an inspection probe that has one or two transducers. The high-frequency bondtester is used to detect delaminations and voids. It cannot detect a skin-to-honeycomb core disbond or porosity. It can detect defects as small as 0.5-inch in diameter. The low-frequency bondtester uses two transducers and is used to detect delamination, voids, and skin to honeycomb core disbands. This inspection method does not detect which side of the part is damaged, and cannot detect defects smaller than 1.0-inch.

Phased Array Inspection

Phased array inspection is one of the latest ultrasonic instruments to detect flaws in composite structures. It operates under the same principle of operation as pulse echo, but it uses 64 sensors at the same time, which speeds up the process.

Radiography

Radiography, often referred to as X-ray, is a very useful NDI method because it essentially allows a view into the interior of the part. This inspection method is accomplished by passing X-rays through the part or assembly being tested while recording the absorption of the rays onto a film sensitive to X-rays. The exposed film, when developed, allows the inspector to analyze variations in the opacity of the exposure recorded onto the film, in effect creating a visualization of the relationship of the component's internal details. Since the method records changes in total density through its thickness, it is not a preferred method for detecting defects such as delaminations that are in a plane that is normal to the ray direction. It is a most effective method, however, for detecting flaws parallel to the X-ray beam's centerline. Internal anomalies, such as delaminations in the corners, crushed core, blown core, water in core cells, voids in foam adhesive joints, and relative position of internal details, can readily be seen via radiography. Most composites are nearly transparent to X-rays, so low energy rays must be used. Because of safety concerns, it is impractical to use around aircraft. Operators should always be protected by sufficient lead shields, as the possibility of exposure exists either from the X-ray tube or from scattered radiation. Maintaining a minimum safe distance from the X-ray source is always essential.

Thermography

Thermal inspection comprises all methods in which heat-sensing devices are used to measure temperature variations for parts under inspection. The basic principle of thermal inspection consists of measuring or mapping of surface temperatures when heat flows from, to, or through a test object. All thermographic techniques rely on differentials in thermal conductivity between normal, defect free areas, and those having a defect. Normally, a heat source is used to elevate the temperature of the part being examined while observing the surface heating effects. Because defect free areas conduct heat more efficiently than areas with defects, the amount of heat that is either absorbed or reflected indicates the quality of the bond. The type of defects that affect the thermal properties include debonds, cracks, impact damage, panel thinning, and water ingress into composite materials and honeycomb core. Thermal methods are most effective for thin laminates or for defects near the surface.

Neutron Radiography

Neutron radiography is a nondestructive imaging technique that is capable of visualizing the internal characteristics of a sample. The transmission of neutrons through a medium is dependent upon the neutron cross sections for the nuclei in the medium. Differential attenuation of neutrons through a medium may be measured, mapped, and then visualized.

The resulting image may then be utilized to analyze the internal characteristics of the sample. Neutron radiography is a complementary technique to X-ray radiography. Both techniques visualize the attenuation through a medium. The major advantage of neutron radiography is its ability to reveal light elements such as hydrogen found in corrosion products and water.

Moisture Detector

A moisture meter can be used to detect water in honeycomb sandwich structures. A moisture meter measures the RF power loss caused by the presence of water. The moisture meter is often used to detect moisture in nose radomes.

Questions for extensive reading

1. What is the NDT technology?
2. What are the NDT technologies for composites?

Lesson 14

Weight and Balance

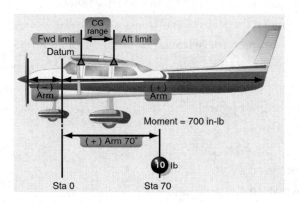

perfect commercial
aircraft

Weight and balance

Introduction

Compliance with the weight and balance limits of any aircraft is critical to flight safety. Operating above the maximum weight limitation compromises the structural integrity of an aircraft and adversely affects its performance. Operation with the center of gravity (**CG**) outside the approved limits results in control difficulty.

Weight Control

Aerodynamics of Flight, weight is the force with which gravity attracts a body toward the center of the Earth. It is a product of the mass of a body and the acceleration acting on the body. Weight is a major factor in aircraft construction and operation, and demands respect from all pilots.

The force of gravity continuously attempts to pull an aircraft down towardthe earth. The force of lift is the only force that **counteracts** weight and sustains an aircraft in flight.

The amount of lift produced by an airfoil is limited by the airfoil design, angle of attack (AOA), airspeed, and air density. To assure that the lift generated is sufficient to counteract weight, loading an aircraft beyond the manufacturer's recommended weight must be avoided. If the weight is greater than the lift generated, the aircraft may be incapable of flight.

Effects of Weight

Any item aboard the aircraft that increases the total weight is undesirable for performance. Manufacturers attempt to make an aircraft as light as possible without **sacrificing** strength or safety.

The pilot should always be aware of the consequences of overloading. An overloaded aircraft may not be able to leave the ground, or if it does become airborne, it may exhibit unexpected and unusually poor flight characteristics. If not properly loaded, the initial indication of poor performance usually takes place during takeoff.

Excessive weight reduces the flight performance in almost every respect. For example, the most important performance **deficiencies** of an overloaded aircraft are:

- Higher takeoff speed
- Longer takeoff run
- Reduced rate and angle of climb
- Lower maximum altitude
- Shorter range
- Reduced cruising speed
- Reduced **maneuverability**
- Higher stalling speed
- Higher approach and landing speed
- Longer landing roll
- Excessive weight on the nose wheel or tail wheel

The pilot must be knowledgeable about the effect of weight on the performance of the particular aircraft being flown. **Preflight** planning should include a check of performance charts to determine if the aircraft's weight may contribute to hazardous flight operations. Excessive weight in itself reduces the safety margins available to the pilot, and becomes even more hazardous when other performance-reducing factors are combined with excess weight. The pilot must also consider the consequences of an overweight aircraft if an emergency condition arises. If an engine fails on takeoff or airframe ice forms at low altitude, it is usually too late to reduce an aircraft's weight to keep it in the air.

Weight Changes

The operating weight of an aircraft can be changed by simply altering the fuel load. Gasoline has considerable weight—6 pounds per gallon. Thirty gallons of fuel may weigh more than one passenger. If a pilot lowers airplane weight by reducing fuel, the resulting decrease in the range of the airplane must be taken into consideration during flight planning.

During flight, fuel burn is normally the only weight change that takes place. As fuel is used, an aircraft becomes lighter and performance is improved.

Changes of fixed equipment have a major effect upon the weight of an aircraft. The installation of extra radios or instruments, as well as repairs or modifications may also affect the weight of an aircraft.

Balance, Stability, and Center of Gravity

Balance refers to the location of the **CG** of an aircraft, and is important to stability and safety in flight. The CG is a point at which the aircraft would balance if it were suspended at that point.

The primary concern in balancing an aircraft is the fore and aft location of the CG along the longitudinal axis. The CG is not necessarily a fixed point; its location depends on the distribution of weight in the aircraft. As variable load items are shifted or expended, there is a resultant shift in CG location. The distance between the forward and back limits for the position of the center for gravity or CG range is certified for an aircraft by the manufacturer. The pilot should realize if the CG is displaced too far forward on the longitudinal axis, a nose-heavy condition will result. Conversely, if the CG is displaced too far aft on the longitudinal axis, a tail-heavy condition results. It is possible that the pilot could not control the aircraft if the CG location produced an unstable condition.

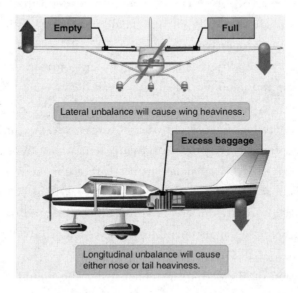

Lateral and longitudinal unbalance

Location of the CG with reference to the lateral axis is also important. For each item of weight existing to the left of the fuselage centerline, there is an equal weight existing at a corresponding location on the right. This may be upset by unbalanced lateral loading. The position of the lateral CG is not computed in all aircraft, but the pilot must be aware that adverse effects arise as a result of a laterally unbalanced condition. In an airplane, lateral unbalance occurs if the fuel load is mismanaged by supplying the engine(s) **unevenly** from tanks on one side of the airplane. The pilot can compensate for the resulting wing-heavy condition by adjusting the trim or by holding a constant control pressure. This action places the aircraft controls in an **out-of-streamline** condition, increases drag, and results in decreased operating efficiency. Since lateral balance is addressed when needed in the aircraft flight manual (**AFM**) and longitudinal balance is more critical, further reference to balance in this handbook means longitudinal location of the CG. A single pilot operating a small rotorcraft, may require additional weight to keep the aircraft laterally balanced.

Flying an aircraft that is out of balance can produce increased pilot fatigue with obvious effects on the safety and efficiency of flight. The pilot's natural correction for longitudinal unbalance is a change of trim to remove the excessive control pressure. Excessive trim, however, has the effect of reducing not only aerodynamic efficiency but also primary control travel distance in the direction the trim is applied.

Effects of Adverse Balance

Adverse balance conditions affect flight characteristics in the same manner as those mentioned for an excess weight condition. It is vital to comply with weight and balance limits established for all aircraft, especially **rotorcraft**. Operating above the maximum weight limitation compromises the structural integrity of the rotorcraft and adversely affects performance. Balance is also critical because on some fully loaded rotorcraft, CG deviations as small as three inches can dramatically change handling characteristics. Stability and control are also affected by improper balance.

Loading in a nose-heavy condition causes problems in controlling and raising the nose, especially during takeoff and landing. Loading in a tail-heavy condition has a serious effect upon longitudinal stability, and reduces the capability to recover from stalls and spins. Tail-heavy loading also produces very light control forces, another undesirable characteristic. This makes it easy for the pilot to **inadvertently** overstress an aircraft.

It is important to reevaluate the balance in a rotorcraft whenever loading changes. In most aircrafts, off-loading a passenger is unlikely to adversely affect the CG, but off-loading a passenger from a rotorcraft can create an unsafe flight condition. An out-of-balance loading condition also decreases maneuverability since cyclic control is less effective in the direction opposite to the CG location.

Limits for the location of the CG are established by the manufacturer. These are the fore and aft limits beyond which the CG should not be located for flight. These limits are published for each aircraft in the Type Certificate Data Sheet (**TCDS**), or aircraft specification and the AFM or Pilot's Operating Handbook (**POH**). If the CG is not within the allowable limits after loading, it will be necessary to relocate some items before flight is attempted.

The forward CG limit is often established at a location that is determined by the landing characteristics of an aircraft. During landing, one of the most critical phases of flight, exceeding the forward CG limit may result in excessive loads on the nose wheel, a **tendency** to nose over on tailwheel type airplanes, decreased performance, higher stalling speeds, and higher control forces.

In extreme cases, a CG location that is beyond the forward limit may result in nose heaviness, making it difficult or impossible to flare for landing. Manufacturers purposely place the forward CG limit as far rearward as possible to aid pilots in avoiding damage when landing. In addition to decreased static and dynamic longitudinal stability, other undesirable effects caused by a CG location aft of the allowable range may include extreme control difficulty, violent stall characteristics, and very light control forces which make it easy to overstress an aircraft inadvertently.

A restricted forward CG limit is also specified to assure that sufficient elevator/control deflection is available at minimum airspeed. When structural limitations do not limit the forward CG position, it is located at the position where full-up elevator/control deflection is required to obtain a high **AOA** for landing.

The aft CG limit is the most rearward position at which the CG can be located for the most critical maneuver or operation. As the CG moves aft, a less stable condition occurs, which decreases the ability of the aircraft to right itself after maneuvering or turbulence.

For some aircrafts, both fore and aft CG limits may be specified to vary as gross weight changes. They may also be changed for certain operations, such as **acrobatic** flight, retraction of the landing gear, or the installation of special loads and devices that change the flight characteristics.

The actual location of the CG can be altered by many variable factors and is usually controlled by the pilot. Placement of baggage and cargo items determines the CG location. The assignment of seats to passengers can also be used as a means of obtaining a favorable balance. If an aircraft is tail-heavy, it is only logical to place heavy passengers in forward seats.

Fuel burn can also affect the CG based on the location of the fuel tanks. For example, most small aircrafts carry fuel in the wings very near the CG and burning off fuel has a little effect on the loaded CG. On rotorcrafts, the fuel tanks are often located behind the CG and fuel consumption from a tank aft of the rotor mast causes the loaded CG to move forward. A rotorcraft in this condition has a nose-low attitude when coming to a hover following a vertical takeoff. Excessive rearward displacement of the cyclic control is needed to maintain a hover in a no-wind condition. Flight should not be continued since rearward cyclic control fades as fuel is consumed. Deceleration to a stop may also be impossible. In the event of engine failure and autorotation, there may not be enough cyclic control to flare properly for a landing.

Management of Weight and Balance Control

Title 14 of the Code of Federal Regulations (14 **CFR**) section 23. 23 requires establishment of the ranges of weights and CGs within which an aircraft may be operated safely. The manufacturer provides this information, which is included in the approved AFM, TCDS, or aircraft specifications.

While there are no specified requirements for a pilot operating under 14 CFR part 91 to conduct weight and balance calculations prior to each flight, 14 CFR section 91. 9 requires the pilot in command (**PIC**) to comply with the operating limits in the approved AFM. These limits include the weight and balance of the aircraft. To enable pilots to make weight and balance computations, charts and graphs are provided in the approved AFM.

Weight and balance control should be a matter of concern to all pilots. The pilot controls loading and fuel management (the two variable factors that can change both total weight and CG location) of a particular aircraft. The aircraft owner or operator should make certain that up-to-date information is available for pilot use, and should ensure that appropriate entries are made in the records when repairs or modifications have been accomplished. The removal or addition of equipment results in changes to the CG.

Weight changes must be accounted for and the proper **notations** made in weight and balance records. The equipment list must be updated, if appropriate. Without such information, the pilot has no foundation upon which to base the necessary calculations and decisions.

Standard parts with negligible weight or the addition of minor items of equipment such as nuts, bolts, washers, rivets, and similar standard parts of negligible weight on fixed-wing aircraft do not require a weight and balance check. Rotorcrafts are, in general, more critical with respect to control with changes in the CG position. The following criteria for negligible weight change is outlined in Advisory Circular (AC) 43. 13-1 (as revised), Methods Techniques and Practices—Aircraft Inspection and Repair:

• One pound or less for an aircraft whose weight empty is less than 5,000 pounds;

• Two pounds or less for aircraft with an empty weight of more than 5,000 pounds to 50,000 pounds;

• Five pounds or less for aircraft with an empty weight of more than 50,000 pounds.

Negligible CG change is any change of less than 0. 05 percent Mean Aerodynamic Chord (**MAC**) for fixed-wing aircrafts, 0. 2 percent of the maximum allowable CG range for rotorcrafts. Exceeding these limits would require a weight and balance check.

Before any flight, the pilot should determine the weight and balance condition of the aircraft. Simple and orderly procedures based on sound principles have been devised by the manufacturer for the determination of loading conditions. The pilot uses these procedures and exercises good judgments when determining weight and balance. In many modern aircrafts, it is not possible to fill all seats, baggage compartments, and fuel tanks, and still remain within the approved weight and balance limits. If the maximum passenger load is carried, the pilot must often reduce the fuel load or reduce the amount of baggage.

14 CFR part 125 requires aircrafts with 20 or more seats or weighing 6,000 pounds or more to be weighed every 36 calendar months. Multi-engine aircrafts operated under a 14 CFR part 135 are also required to be weighed every 36 months. Aircrafts operated under 14 CFR part 135 are **exempt** from the 36-month requirements if operated under a weight and balance system approved in the operations specifications of the certificate holder AC 43.13-1, Acceptable Methods, Techniques and Practices. Aircraft Inspection and Repair also requires that the aircraft mechanic must ensure the weight and balance data in the aircraft records is current and accurate after a 100-hour or annual inspection.

Weight and Balance Restrictions

An aircraft's weight and balance restrictions should be closely followed. The loading conditions and empty weight of a particular aircraft may differ from that found in the AFM/POH because modifications or equipment changes may have been made. Sample loading problems in the AFM/POH are intended for guidance only; therefore, each aircraft must be treated separately. Although an aircraft is certified for a specified maximum gross takeoff weight, it will not safely take off with this load under all conditions. Conditions that affect takeoff and climb performance, such as high elevations, high temperatures, and high humidity (high density altitudes) may require a reduction in weight before flight is attempted. Other factors to consider prior to takeoff are runway length, runway surface, runway slope, surface wind, and the presence of obstacles. These factors may require a reduction in weight prior to flight.

Some aircrafts are designed so that it is difficult to load them in a manner that will place the CG out of limits. These are usually small aircrafts with the seats, fuel, and baggage areas located near the CG limit. Pilots must be aware that within CG limits these aircrafts can be overloaded in weight. Other aircraft can be loaded in such a manner that they will be out of CG limits even though the useful load has not been exceeded. Because of the effects of an out-of-balance or overweight condition, a pilot should always be sure that an aircraft is properly loaded.

New Words & Phrases

counteract　抵消

sacrificing　牺牲

deficiencies　缺点（复数）

maneuverability　操纵性

preflight　航前

CG＝Center of Gravity　重心

unevenly　不均匀地

out-of-streamline　非流线型

AFM＝Aircraft Flight Manual　飞机飞行手册

rotorcraft 旋翼机

inadvertently 疏忽地

TCDS＝Type Certificate Data Sheet 机型认证数据表

POH＝Pilot's Operating Handbook 飞行员操作手册

tendency 趋势

AOA＝Angle of Attack 迎角

acrobatic 杂技般的(指高难度的飞行动作)

CFR＝Code of Federal Regulations 联邦航空规章代码

PIC＝Pilot in Command 机长

notation 记号

MAC＝Mean Aerodynamic Chord 平均空气动力弦

exempt 豁免

Choose the Best Answer

1. What's the importance to flight safety of compliance with the weight and balance limits of any aircraft?

A. Common.　　　　　　　　　B. It doesn't matter.

C. Key.　　　　　　　　　　　D. A little bit.

2. Manufacturers attempt to make an aircraft as ＿＿ as possible without sacrificing strength or safety.

A. heavy　　　B. light　　　C. big　　　D. small

3. Which one of the flight performances is not reduced by excessive weight?

A. Takeoff speed　　　　　　　B. Landing speed

C. Takeoff run　　　　　　　　D. Range

4. ＿＿ planning should include a check of performance charts to determine if the aircraft's weight may contribute to hazardous flight operations.

A. Postflight　　　B. Preflight　　　C. In flight　　　D. On ground

5. ＿＿ gallons of fuel may weigh more than one passenger.

A. Forty　　　B. Fifty　　　C. Sixty　　　D. Thirty

Translations of Long and Difficult Sentences

1. Operating above the maximum weight limitation compromises the structural integrity of an aircraft and adversely affects its performance.

T：超过最大重量限制的操作会损害飞机的结构完整性并对其性能产生不利影响。

2. To assure that the lift generated is sufficient to counteract weight，loading an aircraft beyond the manufacturer's recommended weight must be avoided.

T：为确保所产生的升力足够抵消重力，必须避免超出制造商所推荐重量的飞机负载。

3. An overloaded aircraft may not be able to leave the ground，or if it does become airborne，it may exhibit unexpected and unusually poor flight characteristics.

T：过载的飞机不能离开地面，否则如果飞起来，飞机可能出现未预料的和出乎意料差的飞行性能。

4. The CG is a point at which the aircraft would balance if it were suspended at that point.

T：重心指的是如果飞机悬挂在该点位置，它将处于平衡状态。

5. Excessive trim，however，has the effect of reducing not only aerodynamic efficiency but also primary control travel distance in the direction the trim is applied.

T：然而，额外的配平不仅减小了飞机的空气动力效能，而且减小了配平应用方向上的主控制舵面的偏转行程。

6. During landing，one of the most critical phases of flight，exceeding the forward CG limit may result in excessive loads on the nose wheel，a tendency to nose over on tailwheel type airplanes，decreased performance，higher stalling speeds，and higher control forces.

T：着陆时，作为最重要的飞行阶段之一，超出前重心点的限制将在前轮上导致过载，给带尾轮类型的飞机重心靠前的趋势，降低飞行性能，导致更高的失速速度和更大的控制力。

7. In addition to decreased static and dynamic longitudinal stability，other undesirable effects caused by a CG location aft of the allowable range may include extreme control difficulty，violent stall characteristics，and very light control forces which make it easy to overstress an aircraft inadvertently

T：除了降低飞机静态和动态的纵向稳定性之外，重心位置处于重心许可范围靠后会引起一些出乎意料的影响，如极端控制困难，明显的失速特征和不经意的非常轻的控制力即容易导致飞机过载。

Questions

1. Why should aircraft obey weight and balance limits?

2. What factors will limit the amount of lift produced by an airfoil?

3. What are the most important performance deficiencies of an overloaded aircraft?

4. What will happen when the CG location produced an unstable condition?

5. Where can a pilot find the specified requirements for the weight and balance control of certain airplane?

Extensive Reading

Aircraft Weight Definitions

Manufacturer's Empty Weight (MEW)：The weight of the structure，power plant，furnishings，systems and other items of equipment that are considered an integral part of the aircraft. It is essentially a "dry" weight，including only those fluids contained in closed systems (e. g. hydraulic fluid).

Operational Empty Weight (OEW)：The manufacturer's empty weight plus the operator's items，i. e. the flight and cabin crew and their baggage，unusable fuel，engine oil，emergency equipment, toilet chemicals and fluids, galley structure, catering equipment, seats, documents, etc.

Dry Operating Weight (DOW): The total weight of an aircraft ready for a specific type of operation excluding all usable fuel and traffic load. Operational Empty Weight plus items specific to the type of flight, i. e. catering, newspapers, pantry equipment, etc.

Zero Fuel Weight (ZFW): The weight obtained by addition of the total traffic load (payload including cargo loads, passengers and passenger's bags) and the dry operating weight.

Landing Weight (LW): The weight at landing at the destination airport. It is equal to the Zero Fuel Weight plus the fuel reserves.

Takeoff Weight (TOW): The weight at takeoff at the departure airport. It is equal to the landing weight at destination plus the trip fuel (fuel needed for the trip), or to the zero fuel weight plus the takeoff fuel (fuel needed at the brake release point including reserves).

$$TOW = DOW + \text{traffic load} + \text{fuel reserves} + \text{trip fuel}$$
$$LW = DOW + \text{traffic load} + \text{fuel reserves}$$
$$ZFW = DOW + \text{traffic load}$$

Maximum Structural Takeoff Weight (MTOW): The takeoff weight (TOW) must never exceed a Maximum Structural TOW (MTOW) which is determined in accordance with in flight structure resistance criteria, resistance of landing gear and structure criteria during a landing impact with a vertical speed equal to -1.83 m/s (-360 feet/min).

Maximum Structural Landing Weight (MLW): The landing weight (LW) is limited, assuming a landing impact with a vertical speed equal to -3.05 m/s (-600 feet/min). The limit is the maximum structural landing weight (MLW). The landing weight must comply with the relation:

$$\text{actual } LW = TOW - \text{Trip Fuel} \leqslant MLW$$
$$\text{actual } TOW \leqslant MLW + \text{Trip Fuel}$$

Maximum Structural Zero Fuel Weight (MZFW): Bending moments, which apply at the wing root, are maximum when the quantity of fuel in the wings is minimum. During flight, the quantity of fuel located in the wings decreases. As a consequence, it is necessary to limit the weight when there is no fuel in the tanks. This limit value is called Maximum Zero Fuel Weight (MZFW).

Maximum Structural Taxi Weight (MTW): The Maximum Taxi Weight (MTW) is limited by the stresses on shock absorbers and potential bending of landing gear during turns on the ground.

Nevertheless, the MTW is generally not a limiting factor and it is defined from the MTOW, so that:

$$MTW - \text{Taxi Fuel} > MTOW$$

Minimum Structural Weight: The minimum weight is the lowest weight selected by the applicant at which compliance with each structural loading condition and each applicable flight requirement of JAR/FAR Part 25 is shown.

Usually, the gusts and turbulence loads are among the criteria considered to determine that minimum structural weight.

Questions for extensive reading

1. What is the relation between LW and MLW?
2. What is the definition of MTW?

Lesson 15

Airworthiness of Aircraft

ETOPS

Fly for airworthiness certificate

Historical Background

Standards and recommended practices for the airworthiness of aircraft were adopted by the council on 1 March 1949 **pursuant** to the provisions of Article 37 of the Convention on International Civil Aviation (Chicago 1944) and designated as **Annex** 8 to the Convention.

The annex contained, in Part Ⅱ, general airworthiness procedures applicable to all aircrafts and in Part Ⅲ, minimum airworthiness characteristics for airplanes provided, or to be provided, with certificates of airworthiness classifying them in an established ICAO Category. Part Ⅰ contained definitions.

At its fourth session, the Airworthiness Division collaborating with the Operations Division made recommendations concerning the use of a performance code as an alternative to the one contained in theannex, in which the climb values had the status of Recommended Practices. Further, the Airworthiness Division made recommendations concerning certain aspects of the certification in ICAO categories. As a result of those recommendations, the council approved the incorporation of the alternative performance code as attachment.

The assembly at its seventh session (June 1953) **endorsed** the action already taken by the council and the Air Navigation Commission to initiate a fundamental study of ICAO policy on international airworthiness and directed the council to complete the study as rapidly as practicable.

In pursuing such study, the Air Navigation Commission was helped by an international body of experts designated as the "Airworthiness Panel", which contributed to the preparation of the work of the Third Air Navigation Conference.

As a result of these studies, a revised policy on international airworthiness was developed and it was approved by the council in 1956. According to this policy, the principle of certification in an ICAO Category was abandoned. Instead, Annex 8 included broad standards which defined, for application by the competent national authorities, the complete minimum international basis for the recognition by states of certificates of airworthiness. It was considered that this met the obligation of the organization under Article 37 of the convention to adopt international standards of airworthiness.

It was recognized that the ICAOstandards of airworthiness would not replace national regulations. Each state would establish its own comprehensive and detailed code of airworthiness or would select a comprehensive and detailed code established by another contracting state. The level of airworthiness defined by this code would be indicated by the standards, supplemented, if necessary, by acceptable means of compliance.

In application of those principles, the Annex was declared as constituting the minimum standards for the purpose of Article 33. It was also recognized that the Annex might, at the time of adoption, not include technical standards for all classes of aircrafts or even for all classes of airplanes, if the council felt that no technical standards were required at that time to render Article 33 operative. Furthermore, adoption or amendment of the Annex declared to be complete for the purpose of Article 33 did not constitute the end of ICAO's work in the airworthiness field, as there was a need to continue international collaboration in airworthiness matters.

A revised text for Annex 8 consistent with the above principles was prepared on the basis of the recommendations made by the Third Air Navigation Conference (Montreal, September-October 1956). Part III of the Annex was limited to broad standards stating the objectives rather than the methods of realizing those objectives. However, to indicate the level of airworthiness intended by some of the broad standards, specifications of a more detailed and quantitative nature were included under the title "Acceptable Means of Compliance". These specifications were intended to assist the contracting states in the establishment and application of comprehensive and detailed national airworthiness codes.

To adopt a code giving an appreciably lower level of airworthiness than that given in an Acceptable Means of Compliance was considered to be a violation of the standard supplemented by that Acceptable Means of Compliance.

The revised text for Annex 8 was included in thefourth edition of the Annex, which **superseded** the first, second and third editions.

Another recommendation of the Third Air Navigation Conference led to the establishment by the council in 1957 of the Airworthiness Committee, consisting of airworthiness experts with broad experience and selected from those contracting states and international organizations willing to contribute.

Present policy on international airworthiness

There had been some concerns about the slow progress that had been made over the years with respect to developing supplementary airworthiness specifications in the form of Acceptable Means of Compliance. It was noted that the majority of the Acceptable Means of Compliance in Annex 6 and 8 had been developed in 1957 and were therefore applicable to only those airplane types operating at that time. No effort had been made to update the specifications in these Acceptable Means of Compliance nor had there been any recommendations from the Airworthiness Committee for upgrading of any of the Provisional Acceptable Means of Compliance, which had been developed as potential material for full-**fledged** Acceptable Means of Compliance. The Air Navigation Commission therefore requested the Airworthiness Committee to review the progress made by it since its **inception** with a view to determining whether or not desired results had been achieved and to recommend any changes to improve the development of detailed airworthiness specifications.

The Airworthiness Committee at its ninth meeting (Montreal, November/December 1970) made a detailed study of the problems and recommended that the concept of developing airworthiness specifications in the form of Acceptable Means of Compliance and Provisional Acceptable Means of Compliance be abandoned. A provision should be made for an airworthiness technical manual to be prepared and published by ICAO, which include guidance material intended to facilitate the development and uniformity of national airworthiness codes by contracting states.

The Air Navigation Commission reviewed the recommendations of the Airworthiness Committee **in the light of** the history of the development of the airworthiness policy approved by the council in 1956. It came to the conclusion that the basic objectives and principles on which the ICAO airworthiness policy had been based were sound and did not require any significant change. It was also concluded that the main reason for the slow progress in the development of airworthiness specifications in the form of Acceptable Means of Compliance and Provisional Acceptable Means of Compliance was the degree of mandatory status to the former implied by the following statement included in the forewords of the fourth and fifth editions of Annex 8.

On 6 June 2000, the Air Navigation Commission reviewed the recommendation of the Continuing Airworthiness Panel and the Airworthiness Study Group, in light of the introduction of the type certification process, to introduce the Type Certificate concept. It came to the conclusion that this internationally used and known certificate was already introduced in the Airworthiness Technical Manual (Doc 9051) and that its introduction complements the type certification process, making the text of Annex 8 consistent with its international airworthiness use.

It was further noted that the state of registry, which is in charge of the issuance or validation of Certificates of Airworthiness **by virtue of** Article 31 of the Convention, and the state of design may be different states, with separate functions and duties, and two independent responsibilities. Accordingly, the requirements governing the issuance of Type Certificates in accordance with applicable provisions of Annex 8 are not part of "the minimum standards" which govern the issuance or validation of Certificates of Airworthiness, and lead to the recognition of their validity pursuant to Article 33 of the convention.

The Evolution of Airworthiness Certification Standards

Airworthiness standards and the processes utilized to implement these standards are mandated by the federal government; these standards have evolved over the years through legislative and regulatory changes. These changes have been driven mainly by four areas: (a) public and congressional concern about air transportation safety; (b) introductions of new technologies; (c) lessons learned from accidents or incidents; (d) harmonization with international air transportation policies and regulations.

Airworthiness standards state that no person may lawfully operate a civil aircraft in the U.S. unless the aircraft has an airworthiness certificate. The requirements for the certification of civil aircraft date back to the Air Commerce Act of 1926 (Komons, 1978). These regulations were codified in the U.S. Department of Commerce Bureau of Air Commerce Aeronautics Bulletin No. 7 titled: Airworthiness Requirements for Aircraft by the Department of Commerce Bureau of Air Commerce (1926). On March 29, 1927, the Department of Commerce Aeronautics Branch issued the first aircraft type certificate to the Buhl Airster CA-3. In the late 1930's, the Civil Aeronautics Authority (CAA) was established and a replacement for Bulletin No. 7 was issued. The new regulation was the Civil Air Regulation (CAR) Part4. This regulation recognized the need for separate regulations for small aircrafts and larger transport aircrafts. CAR Part 4 covered small aircrafts, while CAR Part 4T covered transport aircrafts. Helicopters were later added to the certification regulations (Kimberlin, 2003).

The Civil Aeronautics Act of 1938 resulted in the issuance of new regulations: CAR 4A for small aircrafts and CAR 4B for transport aircrafts. These designations were later changed to CAR Part 3 for small aircrafts, defined as aircraft with a maximum certificated takeoff weight of 12,500 pounds or less, and CAR Part 4B for transport aircrafts, defined as those aircrafts with maximum certificated takeoff weight in excess of 12,500 pounds (Kimberlin, 2003).

The FAA believes that the creators of CAR 3 selected 13,000 pounds as the weight division between what they considered the largest small airplane and the smallest large airplane (FAA, 2009). Since 13,000 pounds was considered a number of bad luck, the creators of CAR 3 chose 12,500 instead. The DC-3 was one of the large airplanes at the time, with a seating capacity of up to 13 passengers and a maximum certificated takeoff weight of 25,000 pounds. Around the same time, the largest light twin-engine airplane was the Beech 18, which had a maximum certificated takeoff weight of about 8,000 pounds. Historically, smaller, lighter airplanes were typically simpler and slower, while larger and heavier airplanes were more complex and faster. While splitting aircraft categories based on weight had a logical foundation, one of the problems of aircraft certification is the wide spectrum of complexity of Part 23 airplanes: (a) ranging from slow single-engine airplanes to very fast jets, and (b) all with maximum certificated gross weights of 12,500 pounds or less (Bowles, 2010).

Many of today's light aircrafts and some transport aircrafts are still certified using the CARs as their type certification regulatory basis if the manufacturer applied for the original type of certificate when these regulations were in effect (Kimberlin, 2003). In 1965, after the Civil Aeronautics Authority became the Federal Aviation Agency, new aircraft certification regulations were issued. Aircraft with maximum certificated takeoff weights of 12,500 pounds and below were governed by 14 CFR Part 23, while aircraft with maximum certificated takeoff weights in excess of 12,500 pounds were governed by 14 CFR Part 25 (Part 25). Initially, these rules were very similar to the CAR 3 rules; however, changes in technology and accidents have caused the rules to be revised and changed considerably.

In the 1960's, the development of the jet engine allowed civilian jets to be produced. The early civilian jets had a maximum certificated takeoff weight of over 12,500 pounds, so they naturally fell within the CAR 4 or Part 25 transport category. Bill Lear created the Learjet 23 and intentionally set the maximum certificated takeoff weight at exactly 12,500 pounds so as to remain in the Part 23 category. Lear's intent was to simplify certification and save time. Lear wanted the Learjet to be one of the first business jet in history and also wanted to complete the aircraft certification process before that of one of its competitors, the Jet Commander (Slocum, 1978). The Learjet 23 was allowed to be certified under Part 23 with the exception that it was required to have a crew of two pilots, a requirement that previously applied only to Part 25 airplanes. The next Learjet model built was the Learjet 24, which was almost identical to the Learjet 23, but it was certified under Part 25 (Slocum, 1978). In more modern times the Cessna Citation, which weighed much less than 12,500 pounds, because it was a jet, was certified under Part 25 and was required to have two pilots. A few years later, Cessna built the Model 501 Citation I-SP that was certified for single-pilot operations under Part 23; this airplane was almost identical to the Citation 500 (Slocum, 1978).

In the 1970's, the 19 passenger turboprops, such as the Beech 1900 and the Merlin Metro, emerged on the market and started being used for airline feeder routes. The FAA decided to use Part 23 certification standards for this new **commuter** class, supplementing many sections with Part 25 Special Federal Airworthiness Regulation (SFAR) requirements (FAA, 2009).

Initially, the commuter class within Part 23 was reserved for airplanes already certified and in production; however, new business jets, like the Beech Premier and Citation CJ2 emerged. These jets were built with maximum certificated takeoff weights of less than 12,500 pounds in order to remain under Part 23. To certify other high performance jets such as the Citation CJ4 or the Embraer Phenom 300 under Part 23, the FAA created a new set of SFAR documents with the special conditions the airplanes had to meet. These jets were required to meet the same engine failure minimum climb take-off profile of the large jets, which is imposed as a special condition on those airplanes and did not extend to all airplanes in Part 23. In 2006, the FAA certified the Eclipse 500 very light jet. Since the Eclipse 500 weighed less than 6,000 pounds, it was exempt from meeting the engine fail-ure minimum climb performance. The FAA allowed this exception since propeller air-planes that weigh less than 6,000 pounds do not have engine-out climb requirements (Eclipse Aviation Corporation [EAC], 2008).

The special conditions necessary to fit high performance jets into certification standards originally designed for piston single-engine and twin-engine airplanes resulted in rule chan-ges catered to the certification of higher performance and more complex aircraft. Between 1994 and 1996, approximately 800 rule changes to Part 23 were enacted. The rule changes ranged from corrections, to harmonization with European rules, to rules that addressed new technologies. While these changes addressed the needs of more sophisticated Part 23 airplanes, the overall certification complexity increased, making it more costly to certify less complex aircraft (FAA, 2009).

The Aircraft Certification Process

The Federal Aviation Regulations (FARs) contain the airworthiness standards and are contained separately in Chapter I of Title 14 of the CFR. The FARs provide the type cer-tification requirements or airworthiness standards. These airworthiness standards include requirements for aircraft design, manufacturers' production quality control systems, oper-ations standards, and maintenance standards for air carriers and repair facilities.

The main goals of aircraft certification and continued airworthiness standards are: (a) to increase the reliability of safety-critical systems, and (b) to ensure that the probability of the failure for a particular safety-critical system is less than one in one billion for each flight hour. The FAA has sought to achieve these goals through regulations that contains standards for design, analysis, tests, inspection, maintenance, and operations.

The Aircraft Certification Service (AIR) is the department within the FAA that devel-ops and administers safety standards for aircraft and related products manufactured in the U. S., or utilized by operators of U. S. registered aircraft. The FARs administered by the AIR can be seen in Tab. 15-1.

Tab. 15-1　FARs Administered by the AIR

FAR	Descriptions
FAR Part 21	Certification procedures for products and parts
FAR Part 23	Airworthiness standards for normal, utility, aerobatic, and commuter category aircraft
FAR Part 25	Airworthiness standards for transport category airplanes

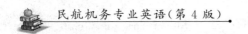
(Continued)

FAR	Descriptions
FAR Part 27	Airworthiness standards for normal category rotorcraft
FAR Part 29	Airworthiness standards for transport category rotorcraft
FAR Part 33	Airworthiness standards for aircraft engines
FAR Part 35	Airworthiness standards for propellers
FAR Part 39	Airworthiness directives

Aircraft certification regulations, Parts 21-39, are intended to ensure the airworthiness of aircraft by requiring the manufacturers of aircraft, engines, propellers, and any other component to comply with approved type designs. Aircraft certification regulations also require the development of operations limitations and maintenance requirements. The AIR consists of six policy centers located at the FAA headquarters in Washington, DC and four **directorates**: (a) the Transport Airplane Directorate in Seattle, Washington; (b) the Small Airplane Directorate in Kansas City, Missouri; (c) the Rotorcraft Directorate in Forth Worth, Texas; and (d) the Engine and Propeller Directorate in Burlington, Massachusetts.

Each directorate is also assigned a geographic area that covers about one-fourth of the U. S. and designated areas overseas. Within its assigned areas, each directorate is responsible for all the administrative aspects of aircraft certifications and continued airworthiness. An infrastructure of Aircraft Certification Offices (ACOs) and Manufacturing Inspection District Offices (MIDOs) are assigned to each directorate's geographic area. The ACOs approve the design for all types of new aircraft, engines, and propellers; aircraft and system modifications; new materials; and spare parts. The MIDOs approve production certificates for manufacturers of all types of regulated products and **oversee** the production quality control systems. Both the ACOs and the MIDOs have continued operational safety functions that involve participation in aircraft accidents and incidents, reviewing service difficulty reports, developing ADs, and enforcing regulations.

Airworthiness certificates

Airworthiness certificates are the cornerstones of AIR's overall certification process. In order to receive an airworthiness certificate, the aircraft must conform to its FAA approved type design and be in safe operating condition. The FAA issues standard and special airworthiness certificates. Special airworthiness certificates do not meet these international certification standards set by the International Civil Aviation Organization (ICAO). Special airworthiness certificates include the following categories: primary, restricted, limited, provisional, **light-sport**, experimental, and special flight permits (FAA, 2010a).

Type certificates

The FAA grants approval of every new and modified design of aircraft, aircraft engines, and propellers through a type certificate. The type certification process includes design approvals for materials, spare parts, and any other parts or equipment installed on a type-certificated aircrafts, engines, and propellers.

The FAA grants approval of initial type designs of new products such as aircraft, engines, and propellers after the type of certification basis under 14 CFR 21. 17 has been established. The type certification basis includes applicable airworthiness standards in effect and may include special conditions. These special conditions will have been developed to address novel and unusual design features of the product that are not specifically covered in the basic airworthiness standards.

The type certification basis may be amended throughout the certification process; however, once the type certificate is issued, the type certificate basis becomes part of the type certificate and cannot be changed. However, manufacturers may make design changes throughout the life of a particular product. These changes are classified as either major or minor changes. The FAA issues a Supplemental Type Certificates (STC) when an entity other than the manufacturer or holder of the type certificate has been approved to make a major change to a product in order to improve reliability, performance, or safety. Other approval documents used for type certification include Technical Standard Order Authorizations (TSOAs) for the design of equipment, parts, materials, and Parts Manufacturing Approvals (PMAs) for the design of spare and replacement parts not included in the type certificate.

Production certificates

The FAA issues four different types of production approvals: production certificates, production inspection system letters, PMAs, and TSOAs. Production certificates are issued for products that have already received a type certificate. Production inspection system letters are similar to production certificates with the exception that they are issued to small manufacturers of aircraft, engines, and propellers. Each holder of a production approval is responsible for incorporating quality control systems and ensuring that all of the suppliers operate in accordance with the FAA approved production quality control system.

Continued airworthiness

The FAA continuously monitors the safety performance of aircraft in service. Airworthiness Directives (ADs) are issued by the FAA to prevent unsafe conditions that could arise while an aircraft is in service. Feedback from manufacturers, operators, pilots, mechanics, and from aircraft investigators, as well as recommendations from the NTSB are taken into account to determine when corrective actions are necessary. In some cases, public confidence, often manifested by political pressures, can become a factor in the decision making process. As a result, ADs have been issued to restore public confidence even before a technical investigation has been concluded.

New Words & Phrases

pursuant 依据

annex 附录

endorse 批准

render 给予

supersede 取代

fledge 使……完善

inception 开始；开端

in the light of 根据

by virtue of 由于

commuter 上班族

directorate 董事会；理事会

oversee 监督

light-sport 轻型运动

Choose the Best Answer

1. Standards and recommended practices for the airworthiness of aircraft were designated as Annex ____ to the Convention.

A. 9　　　　　　B. 10　　　　　　C. 11　　　　　　D. 8

2. There had been some concerns about the ____ progress that had been made over the years with respect to developing supplementary airworthiness specifications in the form of Acceptable Means of Compliance.

A. rapid　　　　B. fast　　　　　C. slow　　　　　D. quick

3. Which one is not the reason to drive the changes of airworthiness standards?

A. public and congressional concern about air transportation safety

B. introductions of new materials

C. lessons learned from accidents or incidents

D. harmonization with international air transportation policies and regulations

4. In ____, the Civil Aeronautics Authority became the Federal Aviation Agency.

A. 1965　　　　B. 1966　　　　　C. 1975　　　　　D. 1979

5. These airworthiness standards include requirements for aircraft design, manufacturers'production quality control systems, operations standards, and ____ for air carriers and repair facilities.

A. repair standards　　　　　　　B. maintenance standards

C. check standards　　　　　　　D. modification standards

Translations of Long and Difficult Sentences

1. The Annex contained, in Part Ⅱ, general airworthiness procedures applicable to all aircrafts and in Part Ⅲ, minimum airworthiness characteristics for airplanes provided, or to be provided, with certificates of airworthiness classifying them in an established ICAO category. Part Ⅰ contained definitions.

T：附件包括第二部分——适用于所有飞机的一般适航程序和第三部分——已交付或即

将交付飞机的最小适航特征,附带按国际民航组织目录分类的适航认证。第一部分包括定义。

2. To adopt a code giving an appreciably lower level of airworthiness than that given in an Acceptable Means of Compliance was considered to be a violation of the standard supplemented by that Acceptable Means of Compliance.

T:采取低水平的适航代码,而不是适航性验证方法,被认为是违反了适航性验证方法的标准。

3. No effort had been made to update the specifications in these Acceptable Means of Compliance nor had there been any recommendations from the Airworthiness Committee for upgrading of any of the Provisional Acceptable Means of Compliance, which had been developed as potential material for full-fledged Acceptable Means of Compliance.

T:至今,没有努力去更新适航性验证方法,也没有来自适航委员会的任何临时适航性验证方法更新的推荐或建议,这些临时方法是潜在的材料,可以用来完善适航性验证方法。

Questions

1. When were the airworthiness standards issued?

2. What are the main contents of Annex 8?

3. Why would not the ICAO standards of airworthiness replace national regulations?

4. What areas have changes of airworthiness standards been driven mainly by?

Extensive Reading

PART II. PROCEDURES FOR CERTIFICATION AND CONTINUING AIRWORTHINESS

(Extracted from Annex 8)

Note—Although the Convention on International Civil Aviation allocates to the State of Registry certain functions which that State is entitled to discharge, or obligated to discharge, as the case may be, the Assembly recognized, in Resolution A23-13, that the State of Registry may be unable to fulfill its responsibilities adequately in instances where aircraft are leased, chartered or interchanged—in particular without crew—by an operator of another State and that the Convention may not adequately specify the rights and obligations of the State of an Operator in such instances until such time as Article 83 bis of the Convention enters into force. Accordingly, the Council urged that if, in the abovementioned instances, the State of Registry finds itself unable to discharge adequately the functions allocated to it by the Convention, it delegate to the State of the Operator, subject to acceptance by the latter State, those functions of the State of Registry that can more adequately be discharged by the State of the Operator. It was understood that pending entry into force of Article 83 bis of the Convention, the foregoing action would only be a matter of practical convenience and would not affect either the provisions of the Chicago Convention prescribing the duties of the State of Registry or any third State. However, as Article 83 bis entered into force on 20 June 1997, such transfer agreements will have effect in respect of those Contracting States which have ratified the related Protocol (Doc 9318) upon fulfillment of the conditions established in Article 83 bis.

CHAPTER 1. TYPE CERTIFICATION

1. 1　Applicability

The Standards of this chapter shall be applicable to all aircraft of types for which the application for certification was sub-mitted to a Contracting State on or after 13 June 1960, except that the provisions of 1. 4 of this part shall only be applicable to an aircraft type for which an application for a Type Certificate is submitted to the State of Design on or after 2 March 2004.

Note— Normally, a request for a type certificate is submitted by the aircraft manufacturer when the aircraft is intended for serial production.

1. 2　Design aspects of the appropriate

airworthiness requirements

1. 2. 1　The design aspects of the appropriate airworthiness requirements, used by a Contracting State for type certification in respect of a class of aircraft or for any change to such type certification, shall be such that compliance with them will ensure compliance with the Standards of Part Ⅱ of this Annex and, where applicable, with the Standards of Parts ⅢA, ⅢB and Ⅳ of this Annex.

1. 2. 2　The design shall not have any features or characteristics that render it unsafe under the anticipated operating conditions.

1. 2. 3　Where the design features of a particular aircraft render any of the design aspects of the appropriate airworthiness requirements or the Standards in Parts ⅢA, ⅢB or Ⅳ inappropriate, the Contracting State shall apply appropriate requirements that will give at least an equivalent level of safety.

1. 2. 4　Where the design features of a particular aircraft render any of the design aspects of the appropriate airworthiness requirements or the Standards in Parts ⅢA, ⅢB or Ⅳ inadequate, additional technical requirements that are considered by the Contracting State to give at least an equivalent level of safety shall be applied.

Note— An Airworthiness Manual (Doc 9760) containing guidance material has been published by ICAO.

1. 3　Proof of compliance

with the design aspects of the appropriate airworthiness requirements

1. 3. 1　There shall be an approved design consisting of such drawings, specifications, reports and documentary evidence as are necessary to define the design of the aircraft and to show compliance with the design aspects of the appropriate airworthiness requirements.

Note— The approval of the design is facilitated, in some States, by approving the design organization.

1.3.2   The aircraft shall be subjected to such inspections and ground and flight tests as are deemed necessary by the State to show compliance with the design aspects of the appropriate airworthiness requirements.

1.3.3   In addition to determining compliance with the design aspects of the appropriate airworthiness requirements for an aircraft, Contracting States shall take whatever other steps they deem necessary to ensure that the design approval is withheld if the aircraft is known or suspected to have dangerous features not specifically guarded against by those requirements.

1.3.4   A Contracting State issuing an approval for the design of a modification, of a repair or of a replacement part shall do so on the basis of satisfactory evidence that the aircraft continues to comply with the design aspects of the appropriate airworthiness requirements used for the type certification of that aircraft type or amended Type Certificate.

Note— The approval of the design of a modification to an aircraft is signified, in some States, by the issuance of a supplemental Type Certificate or amended Type Certificate.

1.4   Type Certificate

1.4.1   The State of Design, upon receipt of satisfactory evidence that the aircraft type is in compliance with the design aspects of the appropriate airworthiness requirements, shall issue a Type Certificate to define the design and to signify approval of the design of the aircraft type.

1.4.2   When a Contracting State, other than the State of Design, issues a Type Certificate for an aircraft type, it shall do so on the basis of satisfactory evidence that the aircraft type is in compliance with the design aspects of the appropriate airworthiness requirements.

Questions for extensive reading

1. What is the definition of continuing airworthiness?
2. Who will supply a request for a type certificate?

Vocabulary

A

A/P＝autopilot　自动驾驶

A/T＝autothrottle　自动油门

AC＝Alternating Current　交流电

accessory　附件

ACMP＝AC Motor Pump　交流电动泵

acquisition price　购买价格

acrobatic　杂技般的(指高难度的飞行动作)

ADC＝Air Data Computer　大气数据计算机

ADP＝Air-driven Pump　空气驱动泵

AFDS＝Autopilot Flight Director System　自动飞行定位系统

affordability　可购性

AFM＝Aircraft flight Manual　飞机飞行手册

AFRP　芳纶纤维增强塑料

AI＝Aviation Industry　航空工业

aileron　副翼

Air Transport Association　航空运输学会(美国)

aircraft electrical power systems（EPS）　飞机电源系统

airflow　气流

airfoil　机翼

airframe　机身

airlifter　运输机

airlines　航空公司

Airplane Health Management（AHM）　飞机健康管理

Airplane on Ground（AOG）　飞机在地面(喻示：飞机因突发故障需要维修，而且情况紧急)

Airport Surface Detection Equipment—Model X（ASDE-X）　机场地面探测设备——型号X

airworthiness　适航

airworthiness inspector　适航检查员

aisle stand　中央控制台

Alaska　阿拉斯加州(美国州名)

Allied Signal　联信公司(APU 制造商)

alternate form　备用方式

amphibious　两栖的

ANA＝All Nippon Airways　全日空航空公司

angle of incidence　入射角

annex　附录

AOA ＝Angle of Attack　迎角

AOG＝Aircraft on Ground　飞机在地面,意指飞机出现了紧急故障

APB＝Auxiliary Power Breaker　辅助电源断路器

APU ＝Auxiliary Power Unit　辅助动力装置

Area Navigation(RNAV)　区域导航

ARINC＝Aeronautical Radio Incorporation　美国航空无线电公司,该缩写代表航空无线电的通信标准

arm　预位

around the clock　全天候

arrester hook　制动钩

artisan　工匠

ASA＝Autoland Status Annunciator　自动着陆状态报警器

Atlantic Interoperability Initiative to Reduce Emissions（AIRE）　大西洋积极协同减少排放

attitude　姿态

autoclave　热压器

Automatic Dependent Surveillance—Broadcast(ADS-B)　自动独立监控——广播

autopilot servo　自动驾驶伺服机构

autothrottle　自动油门

AVAIL＝available　有用的

Aviation Maintenance Technician（AMT）　航空维修技术员

aviator　飞行员

axial flow　轴流式的

B

bakelite　酚醛树脂

biofuel　生物燃料(指曾经为活质的燃料，如煤)

BITE＝Built-in Test Equipment　机内自检设备

bleed valve　引气活门

blow　撞击

Boeing Rapid Response Center　波音公司客户服务快速反应中心

BPCU＝Bus Power Control Unit　汇流条电源控制组件

BTB＝Bus Tie Breaker　汇流条连接断路器

bus　汇流条

by virtue of　由于

C

capped test port　封盖的测试端口

captain　机长

cartonnage　制造木乃伊盒的材料；埃及的木乃伊盒

CDG＝Continental Data Graphics　大陆数字图文公司

celluloid　赛璐珞(明胶)

centrifugal　离心的

CFCC　连续纤维增强陶瓷基复合材料

CFR ＝Code of Federal Regulations　联邦航空规章代码

CFRP　碳纤维增强塑料

CG ＝Center of Gravity　重心

chassis　底盘

check valve　单向活门

chronology　年表

climbout　改出

CNC ＝Computerized Numerical Control　计算机数字控制

cockpit　驾驶舱

combustion chamber　燃烧室

commercial-off-the shelf(COTS)　商业成品零件

commuter　上班族

composite material　复合材料

compromise　妥协

Condition Based Maintenance(CBM)　视情维修

consignment　寄售

constituent　组成；组分

control column　驾驶杆

control wheel　驾驶盘

Corvette　克尔维特牌汽车

cost-effective　有成本效益的；划算的

counteract　抵消

cowled pod　整流罩罩体

cradle　支架

crankshaft　曲轴

cross-sectional　代表性的

CT＝Connecticut　美国康涅狄格州

cutting-edge　最前沿的

D

Data Communications(DataComm)　数据通信

day-in and day-out　日复一日

DC＝Directive Current　直流电

deadline　截止日期

deficiencies　缺点(复数)

deflection　偏转

Delta　美国三角航空公司

densities　密度,density 的复数

deploy　调动

directorate　董事会；理事会

DISC＝discharged　未通电的

disconnect　脱开

dispatch-critical unit　与飞机放行相关的重要部件

distributed　分布式的

downtime　停场时间；停工期

drag　阻力

drain　排泄

dreamliner　梦想飞机(即 B787 飞机)

drill press　钻床

driver　动机

durability　耐久性

Dutch roll　荷兰滚

dynamic maneuver　空气动力试验

dynamic　空气动力的

E

EADI＝Electronic Attitude Director Indicator　电子姿态定位指示器

eco-friendly　对生态环境友好的；不妨害生态环境的

ECS＝Engine Control System　发动机控制系统

ECU＝Electronic Control Unit　电子控制组件

EDP＝engine-driven pump　发动机驱动泵

EFBs＝electronic flight bags　电子飞行包

EGT＝Exhaust Gas Temperature　发动机排气温度

EICAS＝Engine Indication and Crew Alert System　发动机指示与机组警告系统

electrodynamic　电力学的

elevator feel shift　升降舵感觉漂移

elevator feel system　升降舵感觉系统

elevator　升降舵

embed   嵌入

Embraer   巴西航空工业公司

empennage   尾翼

en route   在途中

endorse   批准

engage   预位(通电)

EPC＝External Power Contactor   外电源接触器

Europe's Joint Aviation Authorities(JAA)   欧洲联邦航空局

Everett facility   埃弗里特工厂

executive aviation   公务航空

exempt   豁免

exhaust   排气

F

fairing   整流

FAR part 147   （美国）联邦航空规章(Federal Aviation Rules)147 部

fastener   紧固件

FBO＝Fixed Base Operator   固定基地运营商

FCU＝Fuel Control Unit   燃油控制组件

Federal Aviation Administration(FAA)   美国联邦航空局

feedback   反馈

fibrous   纤维的

filament winding   纤维缠绕

firearms   枪支

first officer   副驾驶

fishpole   钓鱼竿

fix-or-fly   修理或是放飞

flagship   旗舰

flap   襟翼

fledge   使……完善

fleet modification   机队改装

fleetwide   全球机队的

flight crew   飞行机组人员（一般包括飞行员和空中乘务员）

flight deck   驾驶舱

flight envelope   飞行任务包

Flight Information Service-Broadcast(FIS-B)   飞行信息服务广播

flight line   航线

Flight Standards District Office(FSDO)   飞行标准区域办公室

FMA＝Flight Mode Annunciator   飞行模式报警器

FMC＝Flight Management Computer　飞行管理计算机

formaldehyde　甲醛

fuel-burn　油耗

fuse　液压保险

fuselage　机身

G

GCB＝Generator Circuit Breaker　发电机电路断路器

GCU＝Generator Control Unit　发电机控制组件

gearbox　齿轮箱

General Electric　美国通用电气公司

generator　发电机

GHR＝Ground Handling Relay　地面处理继电器

glideslope　下滑道

Global Positioning System(GPS)　全球定位系统

go-around　复飞

GPM ＝Gallons Per Minute　每分钟加仑数

GPRP　玻璃纤维增强塑料

GRD＝ground　地面

ground jumper cable　搭铁线

gust-induced　由阵风所引起的(风切变)

H

hangar　机库(供飞机维修、储藏的库房)

health-monitoring systems　健康监控系统

heat exchanger　热交换器

Helicopter Association International　国际直升机协会

HMG＝Hydraulic Motor Generator　液压马达发电机

horizontal stabilizer　水平安定面

hydrogen　氢

I

iconic　偶像的;标志性的

IDG＝Integrated Drive Generator　整体驱动发电机

ignition　点火

ILS＝Instrument Landing System　仪表着陆系统

in the light of　根据

in the weeks ahead　在未来几个星期

inadvertently　疏忽地

incentive　诱因；动机

inception　开始；开端

Incident Recovery　突发事件恢复

in-depth　资深的

individual　单个的

initial airworthiness　初始适航

initiative　方案

inlet guide vane(IGV)　进口导向叶片

INOP＝inoperation　失效

in-stock　有现货

intake　吸入

interface　交互

intermediate stop　中转站

inventory　库存

IPL ＝Initial Provisioning List　初始航材供应清单

IRU＝Inertial Reference Unit　惯性参考组件

ITT Corp(International Telephone and Telegraph Corp.)　美国国际电话电报公司(＝IT&T)

J

jeopardizing　危害、危及

Juneau　朱诺[美国阿拉斯加州首府]

K

kVA　千伏安

L

landing gear　起落架

landing　着陆

Laser Sintering　激光烧结

lathe　车床

launch customer　启动客户

lay-up　铺层

LCCA＝Lateral Central Control Actuator　侧向中央控制作动筒

leading　前面的；前端的

lift　升力

light-sport　轻型运动

line replaceable unit　航线可更换件

load compressor　负载压气机

load shedding circuit　负载屏蔽电路

long-haul　长途运输的

Louisville　路易(斯)维尔[美国肯塔基州北部城市]

lower hold　腹舱(即一般客机的货舱)

LRU＝Line Replaceable Unit　航线可更换件

M

MAC＝Mean Aerodynamic Chord　平均空气动力弦

Mach trim　马赫配平

magnetic chip　磁屑

MAINT＝maintenance　维护；保养

make　构造

mandrel　芯棒

maneuverability　操纵性

manpower　人工

marshal　整合

matrix　基体

MCDP＝maintenance control and display panel　维修控制与显示面板

MCP＝mode control panel　模式控制面板

mechanic　机械工(指机务,即飞机维修人员)

melamine　三聚氰胺

melt　熔化；溶解

MES＝Main Engine Start　主发动机起动

Mesopotamians　美索不达米亚人

metric ton　公吨

modal suppression accelerometer　模式抑制加速计

mode selector　模式选择器

molecular　分子的

monopole　电极

mortars　砂浆

MRO＝maintenance，repair and overhaul　维护、修理和大修

MyBoeingFleet.com　波音公司全球客户服务网站

N

nautical mile　海里

NDT＝Non-Destructive Test　无损检测

NextGen Network Enabled Weather(NNEW)　下一代主动网络气象

next-generation　下一代

nm.＝nautical mile　海里

No-Fault-Found(NFF)　无故障被检查到(指送修的零部件没有检测到故障)

nose　机头

nose landing gear　前起落架

nose wheel steering　前轮转弯

notation　记号

O

Oceanic Trajectory Based Operations(TBOs)　实用海洋航线

one-stop　一站式

on-order　订购的

on-site　现场

on-the-job　在职

OPC＝Operational Configuration File　操纵配置文件

OPS＝Operational Program Software　操纵程序软件

Optimized Profile Descent　最佳下降剖面

original equipment manufacturer(OEM)　设备原厂家

oscillation　振荡

outmoded　过时的

out-of-streamline　非流线型

override　超控

oversee　监督

ownership　所有权

P

papyrus　纸莎草纸

part interchangeability　可互换件

payload　有效载荷

PCA＝Power Control Actuator　动力控制作动筒

pedal　脚蹬

phenol　苯酚

phenolic　酚醛

Philadelphia　费城(美国宾夕法尼亚州东南部港口城市)

PIC＝Pilot in Command　机长

piezoelectric　压电的

pilot　飞行员

pitch　俯仰

pitch enhancement system　动力增强系统

pivoted　转动的，回转的，装在枢轴上的

planform　俯视图

plenum　整流腔

plywood　胶合板

pneumatic　气源的

POH＝Pilot's Operating Handbook　飞行员操作手册

polyester　聚酯

polymerization　聚合

polystyrene　聚苯乙烯

Portland cement　硅酸盐水泥

power plant　动力装置(一般简称发动机或引擎)

predecessor　前辈；前任；(被取代的)原有事物

preflight　航前

pressure regulating valve　压力调节活门

procurement　采购

proprietary parts　专有件

PTU＝Power Transfer Unit　动力转换组件

pulse jet　脉冲喷气

pursuant　依据

Q

quote　报价

R

radar-based　基于雷达的

ram jet　冲压喷气

ramp　机坪

RAT＝Ram Air Turbine　冲压空气涡轮

recertification　再认证

regulatory agency　管理局

render　给予

repair the aircraft to as-new condition　飞机修复如新

reps＝representatives　代表

Required Navigation Performance(RNP)　所需导航性能

reserve brake　备用刹车

reservoir　油箱

resin　树脂

retention　保留

RH＝right　右

rocket　火箭

Rolls-Royce　英国罗尔斯-罗伊斯公司

rotorcraft　旋翼机

round-the-clock　全天候

route　航程

RPS＝Resident Operational Software　保留操纵软件

RRC＝Rapid Response Center　快速反应中心

rudder ratio changer　方向舵比例变换器

rudder　方向舵

runway　跑道

S

sacrificing　牺牲

satellite-based　基于卫星的

schedule interruption　航班中断

serviceability　有用性

shock-absorbing strut　减振支柱

shutdown　关断

skydrol　（防护及润滑用）特种液压工作油

slat　缝翼

SMI(Scientific Monitoring Inc.)　一家软件公司

solenoid　线圈

spoiler　扰流板

stabilator　平尾

stabilizer　安定面

staff　为……配备

stall test　失速测试

standby power　备用电源

standpipe　竖管；管体式水塔

static inverter　静变流机

stiffness　刚度

stowage bin　储物箱

streamline　使成……流线型

strength　强度

strut　吊架

substitution　可替代性

supersede　取代

surface　舵面

surge valve　喘振活门

switch　电门

synthetic resin　合成树脂

System Wide Information Management(SWIM)　庞大信息管理系统

T

tail assembly　尾翼组件

tail cone　尾锥

Tailored Arrivals　精心设计的到达

tailored to　为……量身定做

takeoff　起飞

taxiways　滑行道

TCDS ＝Type Certificate Data Sheet　机型认证数据表

Ten Books on Architecture　书名:《建筑十书》

tendency　趋势

tethering　保养

thermocouple　热电偶

thermoelectric　热电的

threshold　门槛值

throttle　油门

thrust force　推力

thrust reverser　反推装置

thrust　推力

tiller　舵柄

TMC　推力管理计算机

TMSP＝Thrust Mode Select Panel　推力模式选择面板

top-tier　顶级

tower　塔台

Traffic Information Service-Broadcast(TIS-B)　交通信息服务广播

Traffic Management Advisor(TMA)　交通管理咨询

trailing edge　后缘

trim tab　调整片

trim　配平

troubleshooting　故障排除(排故)

TRU＝Transformer Rectifier Unit　变压整流器

turbine　涡轮

turbojet　涡轮喷气

turboprop　涡轮螺旋桨

turn coordination　协调转弯

turn-back　返航

turntime　停场时间

twin-aisle　双通道

two-generation jump　跨越两代的

U

UAV ＝Unmanned Aerial Vehicle　无人驾驶飞机

UBR＝Utility Bus Relay　可用汇流条继电器

undercarriage　(飞机的)起落架;车盘;着陆装置

unevenly　不均匀地

UNSCHEDULED STAB TRIM　非计划(无指令)的安定面配平

up-front　提前的;预先

UV　紫外线

V

vent　排气

vertical stabilizer　垂直安定面

vinyl　乙烯基

VNAV＝Vertical Navigation　垂直导航

Vultee BT-15　美国 Vultee 公司的 BT-15 教练机

W

weight saving　减重

weldment　焊接件

wheel well　轮舱

wide bodies　宽体客机

widebody　宽体的

William Boeing　威廉·波音(波音公司创始人)

windshear　风切变

winglet　翼梢小翼

wire harness　导线保护管(套)

Wright brother　莱特兄弟

wye　Y 字;Y 字形物

Y

yaw damper　偏航阻尼器

yaw　偏航

YSM＝Yaw damper/Stabilizer trim Module　偏航阻尼器/安定面配平组件

others

737-a short-to-medium-range airplane　737 中短程飞机

7-series　波音公司"7"系列的飞机(如 B737、B767 等)

Appendix Ⅰ
B737NG After Flight Routine Jobcard

飞机注册号 A/C No.	地点 Station	日期 Date	预计工时 Planned Manhours	实际工时 Actual Manhours
			60 分钟 60 Minutes	

项序 Item	工作内容 Task Description	S	T
	Ⅰ 初始工作 Preliminary Tasks		
1	确认灭火瓶在位。确保停机坪飞机移动区域内无杂物。 Make sure fire extinguisher bottles in place, no abnormal object at aircraft move and parking area.		
2	确保放好轮挡，插好前轮转弯销(1 根)和起落架下位锁销(共 3 根，前起落架、左主起落架和右主起落架各 1 根)，并松开刹车。 Make sure the chocks have been set. Install nose gear steering pin (1) and landing gear downlock pins (3). Release the parking brake.		
	Ⅱ 按照程序法检查飞机外部 Aircraft External Area		
	机头区域 Nose Area		
1	目视检查机头蒙皮外表无损伤。 Visually check the nose fuselage skin for no damage.		
2	目视检查排放孔/排放口区域无异常渗漏。 Visually check fuselage areas of drain masts and drains for no abnormal leakage.		
3	目视检查雷达罩无损伤。 Visually check the radome for no damage.		
4	目视检查皮托管(3 个)、全温探头(1)、迎角传感器(2 个)无损伤，无堵塞和覆盖物。目视检查皮托管周围区域蒙皮无损伤、起皱。 Visually check the pitot probes (3), TAT (1), and AOA sensors (2) for no damage and blockage. Visually check the skin area adjacent to the pitot probes is not damaged and wrinkled.		
5	目视检查前电子设备舱门、外部口盖及勤务面板无丢失和损伤。 Visually check forward equipment compartment access door, external access doors and panels for no missing and damage.		
6	目视检查前起落架和舱门区域无损伤、无渗漏、无异物。 Visually check nose landing gear and gear door area for no damage, fluid leakage and obstruction.		

（Continued）

飞机注册号 A/C No.	地点 Station	日期 Date	预计工时 Planned Manhours	实际工时 Actual Manhours
			60 分钟 60 Minutes	

项序 Item	工作内容 Task Description	S	T
7	目视检查前轮刹车片磨损情况，确保固定螺杆顶部和刹车片表面的距离大于 1.5 mm。 Visually check nose wheel spin brake lining, make sure the distance from the head of each bolt to the wear brake lining surface is more than 1.5 mm.		
8	目视检查前起滑行灯外表无损伤，并清洁灯罩外表。 Visually check the taxi light lenses for clean and no damage.		
9	目视检查前起落架减振支柱无损伤，液压油渗漏不超标（渗漏标准参考 AMM 32-21-11）。 Visually check the nose landing gear shock strut for no damage and leakage (leakage limits refer to AMM 32-21-11).		
10	检查前轮轮胎损伤不超标，轮毂及轮缘无损伤、无螺栓剪切。 前轮磨损检查标准：外站磨二见三更换；基地见一线更换。 Check the nose tires for not too worn, no damage, and no damage to wheels and bolts. (Replace the tire if the first fabric ply be seen while the aircraft at base, replace the tire if the second fabric ply worn and the third fabric ply be seen while the aircraft not at base.)		
	右前机身和翼根区域 Right Forward Fuselage and Right Wing Root Area		
1	目视检查右前机身蒙皮外表无损伤，机翼至机身整流罩外表无损伤，客舱玻璃无损伤。 Visually check the right forward fuselage skin, the wing to body fairing, and the windows of passenger cabin for no damage.		
2	目视检查排放孔/排放口区域无异常渗漏。 Visually check fuselage areas of drain masts and drains for no abnormal leakage.		
3	目视检查右前勤务门和电子设备舱门、外部口盖及勤务面板无丢失和损伤。 Visually check the forward service door, electrical equipment compartment door, external access doors and panels for no missing and damage.		
4	目视检查通信/导航天线完整无损。 Visually check the communication and navigation antennas for integrity and no damage.		
5	目视检查静压孔(3)无堵塞和覆盖物。目视检查红白角标(RVSM 敏感区域)范围内蒙皮无损伤、起皱。 Visually check the static ports (3) for no blockage. Visually check skin area inside of red-white mark (RVSM sensitive area) is not damage and wrinkled.		
6	目视检查机组氧气系统绿色释放指示片完好。 Visually check the crew oxygen green discharge disc in place.		

（Continued）

飞机注册号 A/C No.	地点 Station	日期 Date	预计工时 Planned Manhours	实际工时 Actual Manhours
			60 分钟 60 Minutes	

项序 Item	工作内容 Task Description	S	T
7	目视检查前货舱门和门槛区域无损伤。 Visually check the forward cargo door and the doorsill area for no damage.		
8	目视检查右机翼照明灯、右可收放着陆灯、下机身防撞灯、右翼根着陆灯和转弯灯、应急灯外表无损伤。 Visually check the lights lenses of the following lights for no damage：the right wing illumination light，the right retractable landing light，the anti-collision light on the bottom fuselage，the right fixed landing light，the right runaway turnoff light，the emergency lights.		
9	目视检查右空调进/排气口无损伤、无堵塞。 Visually check the right air conditioner inlet and exhaust ports for no damage and blockage.		
10	目视检查右内侧前缘襟翼无损伤、无外来物、无液压油渗漏。 Visually check the right inboard leading edge flap for no damage，no obstruction，and no fluid leakage.		
	右发动机区域 Right Engine Area		
1	目视检查右发动机进气道、进气整流锥和风扇叶片无明显损伤。目视检查右发动机进气道处的 T12 探头无堵塞和损伤。 Visually check the right engine fan cowl，inlet spinner，and fan blades for no obvious damage. Visually check the right engine T12 sensor for no damage and blockage.		
2	目视检查右发动机整流罩、反推罩和吊挂无损伤，各口盖关闭，锁扣扣好。检查右发动机各余油管/排放管油液泄漏不超标。（漏油标准参考 AMM TASK 71-71-00-200-801-F00） Visually check the right engine fan cowl，thrust reverser and struts for no damage. Make sure all the panels and latches are latched. Check the right engine drain tubes for leakage. （Refer to AMM TASK 71-71-00-200-801-F00）		
3	目视检查右发动机外涵道、尾喷管、尾锥、反推折流门及其连杆，可见涡轮叶片无损伤，无外来物。 Visually check the right engine secondary air flow path，exhaust nozzle，exhaust plug，thrust reverser block door and the linkage，visible LPT blades for no damage and obstruction.		
	右机翼区域 Right Wing Area		
1	目视检查右机翼下表面及各口盖、翼尖、油箱通气口无损伤和燃油渗漏。 Visually check the right wing lower surface，all access panels，wing tip and fuel tank vent for no damage and no fuel leakage.		

（Continued）

飞机注册号 A/C No.	地点 Station	日期 Date	预计工时 Planned Manhours	实际工时 Actual Manhours
			60 分钟 60 Minutes	

项序 Item	工作内容 Task Description	S	T
2	目视检查右机翼各操纵舵面（缝翼、副翼、襟翼）无损伤、无外来物、无液压油渗漏。 Visually check the control surfaces (aileron, slat, flap) on the right wing for no damage, no obstructions, and no fluid leakage.		
3	目视检查燃油加油面板无损伤、锁好。 Visually check the fueling station door for no damage and make sure it is latched.		
4.	目视检查右机翼前/后位置灯、防撞灯外部无损伤。 Visually check lights lenses of the right wing position lights and the anti-collision light for no damage.		
5	目视检查右机翼上的放电刷无缺失、无损伤。 （无翼上小翼的飞机每侧机翼 4 个，有翼上小翼的飞机每侧机翼 2 个）。 Visually check the static dischargers on the right wing for no missing and damage. (4 for the aircraft without winglet, 2 for the aircraft with winglet).		
	右主起落架区域　Right Main Landing Gear Area		
1	目视检查右主起落架及其舱门区域无损伤、无渗漏、无异物。 Visually check right main landing gear and gear door area for no damage, fluid leakage, obstruction.		
2	目视检查右主起落架减振支柱无损伤，液压油渗漏不超标。（渗漏标准参考 AMM 32-11-21） Visually check the right main landing gear shock strut for no damage and too leakage (leakage limits refer to AMM 32-11-21).		
3	检查右主起落架上的刹车组件无损伤、无渗漏、无外来物，刹车磨损指示销未超标。 刹车磨损检查标准：设置停留刹车时，指示销伸出量基地时应≥1 mm；外站时≥0 mm。 Check the right main landing gear brake assembly for no damage, no fluid leakage and no obstruction. When parking brake is set, the brake wear indicating pin must be out of the bracket surface ≥1 mm while the aircraft at base, and it should be out of the bracket surface ≥0 mm while the aircraft not at base.		
4	检查右主起落架的轮胎损伤不超标，轮毂及轮缘无损伤、无螺栓剪切。 轮胎磨损检查标准：外站磨二见三更换；基地见一线更换。 Check right main landing gear tires for not too worn, no damage, and no damage to wheels and bolts. (Replace the tire if the first fabric ply seen while the aircraft at base, replace the tire if the second fabric ply worn and the third fabric ply be seen while the aircraft not at base.)		

（Continued）

飞机注册号 A/C No.	地点 Station	日期 Date	预计工时 Planned Manhours	实际工时 Actual Manhours
			60 分钟 60 Minutes	

项序 Item	工作内容 Task Description	S	T
	右后机身区域　Right After Fuselage Area		
1	目视检查右后机身蒙皮外表无损伤，客舱玻璃无损伤。 Visually check right after fuselage skin, and windows of passenger cabin for no damage.		
2	目视检查排放孔/排放口区域无异常渗漏。 Visually check fuselage areas of drain masts and drains for no abnormal leakage.		
3	目视检查应急灯外部无损伤。 Visually check emergency lights lenses for no damage.		
4	目视检查右翼上应急门(737-700 有 1 处,737-800 有 2 处)和右后勤务门、外部口盖及勤务面板无损伤。 Visually check right wing emergency exit door (1 for 737-700, 2 for 737-800), after service door, external access doors and panels for no missing and damage.		
5	目视检查通信导航天线完整无损。 Visually check the communication and navigation antennas for integrity and no damage.		
6	目视检查后货舱门和门槛区域无损伤。 Visually check the after cargo door and the doorsill area for no damage.		
7	目视检查客舱增压系统的正释压活门(2 个)应在关闭位,外流活门(1 个)应在打开位且无阻塞。 Visually check positive pressure relief valves (2) and out-flow valve (1) for no blockage. Make sure the positive pressure relief valves in closed position and the out-flow valve in open position.		
	机尾区域　Empennage Area		
1	目视检查机尾蒙皮外表无损伤。 Visually check the skin in empennage for no damage.		
2	目视检查机尾外部口盖及勤务面板无损伤。 Visually check external access doors and panels for no missing and damage.		
3	目视检查排放孔/排放口区域无异常渗漏。 Visually check fuselage areas of drain masts and drains for no abnormal leakage.		

（Continued）

飞机注册号 A/C No.	地点 Station	日期 Date	预计工时 Planned Manhours	实际工时 Actual Manhours
			60 分钟 60 Minutes	

项序 Item	工作内容 Task Description	S	T
4	目视检查升降舵感觉皮托管（2 个）无损伤，无堵塞和覆盖物。 Visually check the elevator feel pitot probes (2) for no damage and blockage.		
5	目视检查各操纵舵面（升降舵、安定面、方向舵）的可见部分无损伤、无外来物，无液压油渗漏。 Visually check the visible portion of control surfaces (elevator, stabilizers, rudder) for no damage, no obstructions, and no fluid leakage.		
6	**注意：该项只适用于 B737-800 飞机。当警告标牌的上端与整流罩对齐时表明尾橇缓冲器组件在正常位。** 目视检查尾橇可压缩缓冲器有无擦地的迹象。若有擦地的迹象，则检查尾橇缓冲器组件的警告标牌能否可见绿区部分，若看不见绿区，则更换缓冲器。 **NOTE：This task is only applicable to B737-800. The tailskid assembly is in normal position if the upper edge of the warning decal is in line with the fairing.** Visually check the tailskid crushable cartridge for evidence of tail Strike. If there has been a tail strike, and the green part of the warning decal can be seen, the crushable cartridge is still acceptable. If any of the green part of the warning decal can not be seen, then replace the crushable cartridge.		
7	目视检查机尾防撞灯外表无损伤。 Visually check anti-collision lights lenses for no damage.		
8	目视检查 APU 进气口、APU 冷却空气进口及排气口无损伤、无阻塞，APU 余油口无渗漏或漏油不超标。（漏油标准参考 AMM TASK 49-16-00-200-801） Visually check the APU air intake duct, APU cooling air inlet port and exhaust port for no damage and blockage. Check the APU drain port for leakage (Refer to AMM TASK 49-16-00-200-801).		
9	目视检查放电刷无缺失、无损伤（每侧平尾 3 个，垂尾 4 个）。 Visually check the static dischargers for no missing and damage. (3 on each horizontal stabilizer, 4 on vertical stabilizer)		
	左后机身区域　Left After Fuselage Area		
1	目视检查左后机身蒙皮外表无损伤，客舱玻璃无损伤。 Visually check the left after fuselage skin, and the windows of passenger cabin for no damage.		
2	目视检查排放孔/排放口区域无异常渗漏。 Visually check fuselage areas of drain masts and drains for no abnormal leakage.		

(Continued)

飞机注册号 A/C No.	地点 Station	日期 Date	预计工时 Planned Manhours	实际工时 Actual Manhours
			60 分钟 60 Minutes	

项序 Item	工作内容 Task Description	S	T
3	目视检查左翼上应急门（B737-700 有 1 处，B737-800 有 2 处）和左后登机门、外部口盖及勤务面板无损伤。 Visually check the left wing emergency exit door (1 for B737-700, 2 for B737-800), the after service door, external access doors and panels for no missing and damage.		
4	目视检查应急灯外部无损伤。 Visually check the emergency lights lenses for no damage.		
左主起落架区域　Left Main Landing Gear Area			
1	目视检查左主起落架及其舱门区域无损伤、无渗漏、无异物。 Visually check left main landing gear and gear door area for no damage, fluid leakage and obstruction.		
2	目视检查左主起落架减振支柱无损伤，液压油渗漏不超标（渗漏标准参考 AMM 32-11-21）。 Visually check the left main landing gear shock strut for no damage and no leakage (leakage limits refer to AMM 32-11-21).		
3	检查左主起落架上的刹车组件无损伤、无渗漏、无外来物，刹车磨损指示销未超标。 刹车磨损检查标准：设置停留刹车时，指示销伸出量基地时应≥1 mm；外站时≥0 mm。 Check the left main landing gear brake assembly for no damage, no fluid leakage and no obstruction. When parking brake is set, the brake wear indicating pin must be out of the bracket surface ≥1 mm while the aircraft at base, and it should be out of the bracket surface ≥0 mm while the aircraft not at base.		
4	检查左主起落架的轮胎损伤不超标，轮毂及轮缘无损伤、无螺栓剪切。 轮胎磨损检查标准：外站磨二见三更换；基地见一线更换。 Check left main landing gear tires for not too worn, no damage, and no damage to wheels and bolts. (Replace the tire if the first fabric ply be seen while the aircraft at base, replace the tire if the second fabric ply worn and the third fabric ply be seen while the aircraft not at base.)		
左机翼区域　Left Wing Area			
1	目视检查左机翼下表面及各口盖、翼尖、油箱通气口无损伤和燃油渗漏。 Visually check the left wing lower surface, all access panels, wing tip and fuel tank vent for no damage and no fuel leakage.		
2	目视检查左机翼各操纵舵面（缝翼、副翼、襟翼）无损伤、无外来物，无液压油渗漏。 Visually check the control surfaces (aileron, slat, flap) on the left wing for no damage, no obstructions, and no fluid leakage.		
3	目视检查左机翼前/后位置灯、防撞灯外部无损伤。 Visually check light lenses of the left wing position lights and the anti-collision light for no damage.		

（Continued）

飞机注册号 A/C No.	地点 Station	日期 Date	预计工时 Planned Manhours	实际工时 Actual Manhours
			60 分钟 60 Minutes	

项序 Item	工作内容 Task Description	S	T
4	目视检查左机翼上的放电刷无缺失、无损伤。 （无翼上小翼的飞机每侧机翼 4 个，有翼上小翼的飞机每侧机翼 2 个）。 Visually check the static dischargers on the left wing for no missing and damage. （4 for the aircraft without winglet，2 for the aircraft with winglet）		
	左发动机区域　Left Engine Area		
1	目视检查左发动机进气道、进气整流锥和风扇叶片无明显损伤；目视检查左发动机进气道处的 T12 探头无堵塞和损伤。 Visually check the left engine fan cowl, inlet spinner, and fan blades for no obvious damage. Visually check the right engine T12 sensor for no damage and blockage.		
2	目视检查左发动机整流罩、反推罩和吊挂无损伤，各口盖关闭，锁扣扣好；检查左发动机各余油管/排放管油液泄漏不超标。（漏油标准参考 AMM TASK 71-71-00-200-801-F00） Visually check the left engine fan cowl, thrust reverser and struts for no damage. Make sure all the panels and latches are latched. Check the left engine drain tubes for leakage.（Refer to AMM TASK 71-71-00-200-801-F00）		
3	目视检查左发动机外涵道、尾喷管、尾锥、反推折流门及其连杆、可见涡轮叶片无损伤，无外来物。 Visually check the left engine secondary air flow path, exhaust nozzle, exhaust plug, thrust reverser block door and the linkage, visible LPT blades for no damage and obstruction.		
	左前机身和翼根区域　Left Forward Fuselage and Left Wing Root Area		
1	目视检查左前机身蒙皮外表无损伤，机翼至机身整流罩外表无损伤，客舱玻璃无损伤。 Visually check the left areward fuselage skin, the wing to body fairing, and the windows of passenger cabin for no damage.		
2	目视检查排放孔/排放口区域无异常渗漏。 Visually check fuselage areas of drain masts and drains for no abnormal leakage.		
3	目视检查左内侧前缘襟翼无损伤、无外来物，无液压油渗漏。 Visually check the left inboard leading edge flap for no damage, no obstruction, and no fluid leakage.		
4	目视检查左空调进/排气口无损伤、无堵塞。 Visually check the left air conditioner inlet and exhaust ports for no damage and blockage.		
5	目视检查左可收放着陆灯、左机翼照明灯、下机身防撞灯、左翼根着陆灯和转弯灯、应急灯外表无损伤。 Visually check the light lenses of the following lights for no damage：the left wing illumination light，the left retractable landing light，the anti-collision light on the bottom fuselage，the left fixed landing light，the left runaway turnoff light，the emergency lights.		

(Continued)

飞机注册号 A/C No.	地点 Station	日期 Date	预计工时 Planned Manhours	实际工时 Actual Manhours
			60 分钟 60 Minutes	

项序 Item	工作内容 Task Description	S	T
6	目视检查静压孔(3)无堵塞和覆盖物。目视检查红白角标(RVSM 敏感区域)范围内蒙皮无损伤、起皱。 Visually check the static ports (3) for no blockage. Visually check skin area inside of red-white mark (RVSM sensitive area) is not damaged and wrinkled.		
7	目视检查左前登机门、外部口盖及勤务面板无丢失和损伤。 Visually check the forward entry door, external access doors and panels for no missing and damage.		
Ⅲ 检查机上区域 Cabin Area			
驾驶舱区域 Flight Cabin Area			
1	查阅飞行记录本的故障和缺陷,视情做相应处理,处理后应按规定填写记录。检查飞机外表结构损伤记录本在位,按需进行填写。 Review the flight log book, make sure the faults have been dealt with and the related information has been recorded in the book.		
2	将驾驶舱内门框上谐音模块上的驾驶舱门锁电源开关置于"OFF"位,并保持红色电门罩打开。 Put the flight deck access system switch on the chime module to "OFF" position. Hold the switch guard (red) in open position.		
3	确保驾驶舱内发动机滑油量指示不低于 17 夸脱,否则需添加滑油至油箱满刻度线。 **注意:添加发动机滑油应在发动机停车后 5 至 30 分钟内进行。** Make sure the engine oil quantity indication in flight cabin is not less than 17 quarts, if low need add oil to FULL scale of the oil tank. **NOTE:Engine oil should be added within 5 to 30 minutes after engine shutdown.** 记录 DU 上发动机滑油量的实际指示值（Record the engine oil indication displayed on DU）： 左(left)_____；右(right)_____。		
4	确保 DU 显示液压油量指示应大于 90%。若不符合以上要求,则补充液压油。 Make sure hydraulic fluid quantity indication on DU is more than 90%. If low add fluid as required. 记录在 DU 上指示的液压油量（Record the hydraulic fluid indication displayed on DU）： A 系统(A system)：_____%；B 系统(B system)：_____%。		
5	检查机组氧气瓶的压力: 有第二观察员座椅的飞机:要求压力值需大于等于 1050PSI; 无第二观察员座椅的飞机:要求压力值需大于等于 850PSI。 Check the pressure of crew oxygen bottle. For airplanes with second observer seat, the pressure should be at least 1050PSI; For airplanes without second observer seat, the pressure should be at least 850PSI. 记录氧气指示压力值(record the pressure of crew oxygen bottle)：(PSI)。		

（Continued）

飞机注册号 A/C No.	地点 Station	日期 Date	预计工时 Planned Manhours	实际工时 Actual Manhours
			60 分钟 60 Minutes	

项序 Item	工作内容 Task Description	S	T
6	在 CDU 做左/右发动机 EEC 自检，检查"当前故障"和"超差"页面上的故障代码/超差记录。 （注意：若飞机在外站过夜，此项可不执行。） Do EEC BITE test of both engines on CDU. Check the fault code at RECENT FAULTS page and exceedance data at EXCEEDANCE page. （NOTE：This task is not necessary to be performed while aircraft not at base. ）		
7	在 CDU 上做 APU 自检，检查"当前故障"页面上故障代码，并检查 APU 滑油量。 （注意：若飞机在外站过夜，此项可不执行。） Do the BITE test on CDU. Check the fault code at Current status page and check the APU oil quantity at Oil quantity page. （NOTE：This task is not necessary to be performed while aircraft not at base. ）		
8	将任一飞行控制电门 A 或 B 置于"STANDBY RUDDER"（备用方向舵）位，确认备用液压泵工作正常。分别接通 A、B 电动液压泵，确认泵工作压力稳定在 2850 至 3200PSI。 Set the FLT CONTROL A or B switch to the STBY RUD position. Make sure the STANDBY HYD STBY RUD ON light is on. Set A and B pump switch respectively to the ON position，Make sure the HYD P indicator for the applicable hydraulic system becomes stable between 2850 and 3200PSI.		
9	操作检查发动机/APU/货舱火警探测和灭火系统工作正常。操作检查轮舱、机翼和机身过热探测系统正常。在爆炸帽测试面板上操作检查各个爆炸帽正常。 Operationally test the fire detection system of engine，APU and cargo. Operationally test the overheat detection system of wheel well, wing and body. Operating check all the squibs on the squib test panel.		
10	检查驾驶舱内各电门位置在规定位，跳开关在闭合位（用套环固定在断开位除外）；按压灯光测试电门，确保指示灯指示正常；检查备用灯泡箱并配齐备用灯泡。 Make sure all switches in normal position，circuit breakers in close position（except those fixed in open position with clamp）. Push the light test switch, make sure all the lights go on. Check the spare bulbs in its position at spare bulb stowage box.		
11	检查驾驶舱风挡玻璃无裂纹、刮伤、分层和过热现象；滑动窗完好，操作灵活；检查雨刷无损伤. Check flight cabin windows for sign of crack, scratch, delamination，and overheat. Make sure slide windows can be operated freely and no damage. Check windshield wiper blades for no damage.		
12	按照应急设备分布图检查驾驶舱内应急设备齐全在位，无破损。 Check the emergency equipment in flight cabin in place and no damage according to the aircraft Emergency Equipment Distribution Figure.		
13	检查驾驶舱内手提式灭火瓶保险销完好，压力指示在绿区。 Check the portable extinguishing bottle pin are in place, the pressure indicator is in the green range.		

(Continued)

飞机注册号 A/C No.	地点 Station	日期 Date	预计工时 Planned Manhours	实际工时 Actual Manhours
			60 分钟 60 Minutes	

项序 Item	工作内容 Task Description	S	T
14	进行飞机防撞系统 TCAS 的自检,确保工作正常。 Do the BITE test of TCAS system.		
15	如安装,检查打印机打印纸余量。当打印纸量指示窗口显示空或缺纸 PAPER 灯亮时,更换打印纸。 If install,check the printer paper,replace it when paper level display shows empty or paper indicator comes on.		
16	检查国籍登记证、适航证、电台执照齐全在位。按随机资料清单确保随机资料齐全。 Check the Aircraft Nationality Registration Certification,Airworthiness Certification,Aircraft Station Licence in place. Check all the documents in place according to the Aircraft Documents List.		
17	清洁驾驶舱风挡玻璃。 Clean windshields windows.		
客舱区域　Passenger Cabin			
1	查阅客舱记录本上的故障和缺陷,视情做相应处理,处理后应按规定填写记录。 Review the cabin log book,make sure the faults have been dealt with and the related informetion has been recorded in the log book.		
2	检查磁带放音机、机内电话和旅客娱乐系统齐全在位。操作检查旅客放像系统工作正常。 Check the boarding music tape reproducer,interphone and passenger entertainment system in place. Operationally check passenger video system.		
3	检查客舱内部应急灯无缺损。 Check the emergency lights in passenger cabin for no missing damage.		
4	操作检查客舱顶灯,侧壁灯(窗灯),登机门灯,乘务员工作灯,厨房顶灯,厨房工作灯,厕所顶灯,厕所镜灯,客舱标志灯(FASTEN SEAT BELT, NO SMOKING,包括厨房中的),厕所"请回座位灯",厕所 OCCUPIED 灯工作正常。 Operationally check the general lights.		
5	按照应急设备分布图检查客舱内应急设备齐全在位(旅客救生衣除外),无损坏。检查客舱内应急设备标牌在位无缺损并与应急设备实际存放位置相符合。检查应急手电指示灯闪亮。 Check the emergency equipment in passenger cabin for no missing and damage according to the aircraft Emergency Equipment Distribution Figure. Check the emergency equipment placards for no missing and damage. Check the emergency flashlight indicator flashing.		

民航机务专业英语（第 4 版）

（Continued）

飞机注册号 A/C No.	地点 Station	日期 Date	预计工时 Planned Manhours	实际工时 Actual Manhours
			60 分钟 60 Minutes	

项序 Item	工作内容 Task Description	S	T
6	检查客舱内手提式灭火瓶手柄上的保险销完好，HALON 灭火瓶的压力指示在绿区；检查手提式氧气瓶的压力指示大于 1500PSI 且不得超过 1850PSI，检查氧气面罩的塑料包装未破损。 Check handle safety pin of the portable extinguisher in place, the indicator of the HALON pressure extinguisher is in the green range. Make sure the pressure indicator of the portable oxygen bottle is more than 1500PSI and less than 1850PSI. Check plastic packing of the oxygen mask for no damage.		
7	检查各登机门和勤务门上的应急滑梯气瓶压力指示在绿区。 Check the entry doors and service doors emergency exit slides pressure indications are at green band.		
8	通过客舱窗户检查机翼上表面可视扰流板、涡流发生器无损坏。 Check visible portions of the spoiler and vortex generator for no damage through the windows.		
9	检查厨房、储物箱和厨房插件（烤箱、咖啡壶、烧水杯等）固定在位，无缺损。检查厨房废物箱箱盖工作正常，关闭位时封严有效。 Check galley, box and compartment (oven, coffee maker, water boiler, hot cup) in its position, no lack and damage. Check galley waster cover in its position, and the seal work normally when closed.		
10	检查厕所部件（包括厕所门、装饰板、地板及相关附件）固定在位，无缺损。 Check lavatory module (include door, floor, furnishing, equipment) in position, no lack and damage.		
11	检查厕所废物箱内灭火瓶未释放，废物箱箱盖工作正常，在关闭位时封严有效。 Check the extinguishers in the waste container are not discharged. Check the waste container cover in its position, and the seal works normally when closed.		
12	检查厕所洗脸盆的冷热水龙头出水/排水正常，无泄漏。检查厕所马桶冲洗工作正常、出水量正常。不冲洗时马桶无漏气声音。 Check the lavatory faucet water flows normally, drain normally and no leakage. Check toilets work normally and flush water flows normally. The toilet is no air leaking when not flush.		
货舱区域　Cargo Area			
1	检查前货舱门可操纵、关严锁住且封严密封完好。目视检查前货舱内地板无严重压坑、破裂及腐蚀；侧壁板、天花板无损坏和脱落；货舱胶带无缺损，栏网无损坏；各通气口无异物堵塞。确保货舱内无积水（见备注）、无异物。检查前货舱门拉绳安装可靠，无缺损。 Check forward cargo door operating normally, the seal in its position. Check forward cargo floor for no large dent, damage, hole and corrosion. Check the sidewall and ceiling liners for no damage and loose. Check the cargo tape for no damage and loose. Check cargo nets for no damage and missing. Check the vent hole for no blockage. Make sure there is no water and waster in the cargo. Check forward cargo door bungee lanyard for no damage and security of installation.		
2	检查前货舱照明灯工作正常，灭火瓶的释放口无阻塞。 Operationally check the forward cargo compartment light. Check the extinguishing bottle discharge nozzle for no blockage.		

(Continued)

飞机注册号 A/C No.	地点 Station	日期 Date	预计工时 Planned Manhours	实际工时 Actual Manhours
			60 分钟 60 Minutes	

项序 Item	工作内容 Task Description	S	T
3	检查后货舱门可操纵、关严锁住且封严完好密封。目视检查后货舱内地板无严重压坑、破裂及腐蚀;侧壁板、天花板无损坏和脱落;货舱胶带无缺损;栏网无损坏;各通气口无异物堵塞。确保货舱内无积水(见备注)、无异物。检查后货舱门拉绳安装可靠,无缺损。 Check after cargo door operating normally, the seal in its position. Check after cargo floor for no large dent, damage, hole and corrosion. Check the sidewall and ceiling liners for no damage and loose. Check the cargo tape for no damage and loose. Check cargo nets for no damage and missing. Check the vent hole for no blockage. Make sure there is no water and waster in the cargo. Check after cargo door bungee lanyard for no damage and security of installation.		
4	检查后货舱照明灯工作正常,灭火瓶的释放口无阻塞。 Operationally check after cargo compartment light. Check the extinguishing bottle discharge nozzle for no blockage.		
	IV 检查和勤务工作 Service and Inspection Tasks		
1	检查前起减振支柱镜面伸出长度,如小于 6 cm 按 AMM 12-15-41 进行检查/勤务工作。 Check the extension of nose gear shock strut, if less than 6cm additional check/service should be done refer AMM 12-15-41. 记录伸出长度(Record shock strut extension Dimension):_____ cm。 用干净抹布蘸液压油 MIL-H-5606 清洁前起支柱,目视检查减振支柱镜面表面应无划伤。 Use cloth with MIL-H-5606 to clean extension of the nose gear shock strut, check the surface of nose gear shock strut for no damage.		
2	检查左主起减振支柱镜面伸出长度,如小于 8 cm 按 AMM 12-15-31 进行检查/勤务工作。 Check the extension of left main gear shock strut, if less than 8cm additional check/service should be done refer AMM 12-15-31. 记录伸出长度(Record shock strut extension Dimension):_____ cm。 用干净抹布蘸液压油 MIL-H-5606 清洁左主起支柱,目视检查减振支柱镜面表面无划伤。 Use cloth with MIL-H-5606 to clean the extension of left main gear shock strut, check the surface of left main gear shock strut for no damage.		
3	检查右主起减振支柱镜面伸出长度,如小于 8 cm 按 AMM 12-15-31 进行检查/勤务工作。 Check the extension of right main gear shock strut, if less than 8cm additional check/service should be done refer AMM 12-15-31. 记录伸出长度(Record shock strut extension Dimension):_____ cm。 用干净抹布蘸液压油 MIL-H-5606 清洁右主起支柱,目视检查减振支柱镜面表面无划伤。 Use cloth with MIL-H-5606 to clean the extension of right main gear shock strut, check the surface of right main gear shock strut for no damage.		

（Continued）

飞机注册号 A/C No.	地点 Station	日期 Date	预计工时 Planned Manhours	实际工时 Actual Manhours
			60 分钟 60 Minutes	

项序 Item	工作内容 Task Description	S	T
4	操作检查应急灯系统工作正常。 Operationally check the emergency lights system.		
5	操作检查外部灯光系统（前起滑行灯、左/右可收放着陆灯、左/右机翼照明灯、上/下机身防撞灯、左/右翼根着陆灯、左/右翼根转弯灯、左/右机翼前/后位置灯、左/右机翼防撞灯、机尾防撞灯）工作正常。 Operationally check the following external lights：Taxi light，Retractable landing lights，Wing illumination lights，Anti-collision lights，Landing lights，Runaway turnoff lights，Position lights.		
6	操作检查前轮舱照明灯和左/右轮舱照明灯工作正常。 Operationally check the landing gear wheel well illumination lights.		
7	拔出饮用水水箱增压压气机跳开关（P91 板 A18 或 D11），关闭厕所水加热器电门，放空饮用水。 Open the potable water tank air compressor circuit breaker（A18 OR D11on p91），close the lavatory water heater switch. Drain potable water off.		
8	套上皮托管管套（3 个）。 Put covers on the pitot probes（3）.		
9	若有需求，则更换 QAR 光盘，将取下的光盘交有关部门。 Replace QAR disk as required，and send it to related department. 注明是否更换（Record if the disk replaced or not）：□是（yes）；□否（no）。		
10	注明是否拆装机轮（record if remove/install tire or not）：□是（yes）；□否（no） 如拆装，记录拆装机轮和刹车的位置、所用定力以及实测的轮胎压力值（仅换轮需记录轮胎压力） If any tire or brake has been removed/installed，record the position，the torque value and the actual tire pressure as following：（It is required to record tire pressure only when tire replaced. ） 位置（position）_____，轮胎压力（tire pressure）：_____ PSI 首次定力（first torque）_____磅·英尺 pound·feet，二次定力（second torque） _____磅·英尺 pound·feet 位置（position）_____，轮胎压力（tire pressure）：_____ PSI 首次定力（first torque）_____磅·英尺 pound·feet，二次定力（second torque） _____磅·英尺 pound·feet 位置（position）_____，轮胎压力（tire pressure）：_____ PSI 首次定力（first torque）_____磅·英尺 pound·feet，二次定力（second torque） _____磅·英尺 pound·feet		

（Continued）

飞机注册号 A/C No.	地点 Station	日期 Date	预计工时 Planned Manhours	实际工时 Actual Manhours
			60 分钟 60 Minutes	

项序 Item	工作内容 Task Description	S	T
10	注意：1. 前轮定力：首次 80～100，回至 5～15 后，第二次 30（＜60）。单位：磅·英尺 　　　　主轮定力：首次 500～600，回至 10～30 后，第二次 150（＜300）。单位：磅·英尺 　　　2. 轮胎压力标准值为（205±5）PSI NOTE： 　　1. Nose wheel nut torque value：first tighten the nut to 80～100 pound-feet，then loose the nut to 5～15 pound-feet，And then tighten the nut to 30（＜60）pound-feet. 　　　Main wheel nut torque value：first tighten the nut to 500～600 pound-feet，then loose the nut to 10～30 pound-feet. And then tighten the nut to 150（＜300）pound-feet. 　　2. The tire pressure should be（205±5）PSI.		
	Ⅴ 航后周检工作（每星期一执行，如飞机在外站次日回基地执行） Weekly Check (performed on every Monday, or on the next day while aircraft not at base)		
1	按随机设备清单清点随机设备齐全。 Check the equipment in aircraft for no missing according to the Equipment List.		
2	操作检查航徽灯工作正常。 Operationally check the logo light.		
3	操作检查旅客阅读灯工作正常。 Operationally check passenger reading lights.		
4	操作检查备用电源系统：Operationally check standby power control unit.		

序号 No.	"STBY PWR"电门位置 "STBY PWR" switch position	AC、DC 表选择在备用电源位 的指示 indication	"STBY PWR OFF"灯 "STBY PWR OFF" light
1	在"AUTO"位 in "AUTO" position	AC VOLTS＝110～120 CPS FREQ＝395～405 DC VOLTS＝22～30	灯灭 light off
2	在"OFF"位 in "OFF" position	AC VOLTS＝0 CPS FREQ＝BLANK DC VOLTS＝0	灯亮 light on
3	在"BAT"位 in "BAT" position	AC VOLTS＝110～120 CPS FREQ＝395～405 DC VOLTS＝22～30	灯灭 light off
4	在"AUTO"位 in "AUTO" position	确认电瓶已完全充电 make sure the battery fully charged	灯灭 light off

(Continued)

飞机注册号 A/C No.	地点 Station	日期 Date	预计工时 Planned Manhours	实际工时 Actual Manhours
			60 分钟 60 Minutes	

项序 Item	工作内容 Task Description	S	T
5	记录 CDU 上显示的下列读数： Record the following data on CDU： APU 序号（APU serial number）：＿＿＿＿＿＿；APU 小时数（APU hours）：＿＿＿＿＿＿； APU 循环数（APU cycles）＿＿＿＿＿＿。		
6	记录 APU 性能数据： Record the APU data as following： 环境温度（environment temperature）：OAT：＿＿＿＿＿＿℃； 仅供电状态（only supplier condition）：APU EGT：＿＿＿＿＿＿℃； CT5ATP：＿＿＿＿＿＿。 **注意：仅供电状态指 APU 在供电且不引气状态下稳定运行一分钟后的状态；在 CDU 上进入 APU 自检页面→进入 IDENT/CONFIG 的第 2 页→进入 DATA MEMORY MODULE 的 第 5 页，即可看到 CT5ATP 参数。** NOTE：Electric power supply mode means APU runs 1 minute without bleed. At CDU enter in APU BITE TEST page → entry in IDENT/CONFIG page 2 → entry in DATA MEMO- RY MODULE page 5，then record CT5ATP.		
7	用干净的布蘸取液压油来清洁前轮转弯计量活门的活塞杆、曲柄表面的灰尘、油脂和污物。清洁后检查牵引销操纵连杆和计量活门活塞杆，确认松开牵引销操纵连杆后，连杆和计量活门活塞杆能返回原位。 Use a clean cloth, moistened in hydraulic oil to clean the crank and plunger to remove dirt, grease and grime. Check the operation of the towing lever and plunger, the towing lever and plunger must return to the normal position when released.		
	Ⅵ 结束工作 Final Tasks		
1	审核上述所有工作项目已完成，飞行记录本和客舱记录本上的故障（如有）已处理并完成签章。 Review all the above tasks have been accomplished, the faults（if any）written in the flight log book and the cabin log book have been dealt with.	★	
2	**注意：关闭 APU 时，将 P5 板 APU 电门扳至 OFF 位后，须至少等待 60 秒以完成 APU 的冷却循环，然后再关闭主电瓶电门。** NOTE：It is required to obey the following procedure for APU shut down：Put the APU switch on P5 panel to OFF position, and wait at least 60 seconds for APU cooling, then close the main battery switch. 确保飞机断电，关好门窗。 Remove the electrical power, close all the doors, windows and panels.		

注解

NOTE：

1. "工作者"一栏中的带"★"的项目表示须由放行人员签署。

   In the "Operator" column，the items with "★"should be signed by dispatcher.

2. 备注：如检查发现货舱有积水，须先清除货舱内积水，并须：

   NOTE：If found water accumulated in the cargo，need clean out the water，then：

   （1）如在基地：须填写非例行单并处理。

   If at base，should write the Non Routing Card.

   （2）如在外站：飞机放行后须将飞机号、机场、有水货舱位置等信息通告 MCC。

   In not at base，need notify MCC after dispatch，including Aircraft No，Airport，Cargo position.

Appendix Ⅱ
Aviation Abbreviations and Acronyms

（注：部分缩写与缩略语可能与课文的 Vocabulary 重复，此处仅供学习和参考）

A

A/C   air conditioning   空气调节

A/G   air/ground   空/地

A/L   autoland   自动着陆

A/P   autopilot   自动驾驶

A/S   airspeed   空速

A/T   autothrottle   自动油门

ABNORM   abnormal   不正常的

AC   alternating current   交流电

ACARS   ARINC Communications Addressing and Reporting System 航空无线通信寻址与报告系统

ACCEL   acceleration，accelerate   加速，使增速

ACM   air cycle machine   空气循环机

ADC   air data computer   大气数据计算机

ADF   automatic direction finder   自动定向仪

ADI   attitude director indicator 姿态指引仪

ADP   air driven pump   空气驱动泵

ADV   advance   推进

AFCS   automatic flight control system   自动飞行控制系统

AGL   above ground level 地平线之上

AI   anti-ice   防冰

AIDS   aircraft integrated data system   飞机集成数据系统

AIL   aileron   副翼

ALT   altitude   高度

ALTM   altimeter   高度计

ALTN(ALTNT)   alternate   交替的

AMB   ambient 周围的

AMM   Aircraft Maintenance Manual   飞机修护手册

ANN   announcement   通告

ANNUNC   annunciator   信号牌

ANT   antenna   天线

AOA　angle of attack　攻角(迎角)

APB　auxiliary power breaker　辅助动力断路器

APD　approach progress display　进近过程显示

APL　airplane　飞机

APPR　approach　进近

APPROX　approximately　近乎,大约

APU　auxiliary power unit　辅助动力装置

ARINC　Aeronautical Radio Incorporated　(美国)航空无线电公司,主要股东为美国定期
　　　　的航空公司、航空运输公司、飞机制造厂和外国领队航空公司的组织。其目的是
　　　　制订和出版电子设备和系统的规范、标准。

ASA　autoland status annunciator　自动着陆指示器

ASP　audio selector panel 音频选择面板

ASYM　asymmetrical　非对称的

ATC　air traffic control　空中交通管制

ATT　attitude　姿态

ATTND　attendant　服务员

AUTO　automatic　自动装置的

AUX　auxiliary　辅助的

AVM　airborne vibration monitor　空中振动监视器

B

BCRS　back course　反航道

BARO　barometric　大气压力的

BAT　battery　电池,蓄电池

BFO　beat frequency oscillator　差频振荡器

BITE　built-in test equipment　机内自检设备

BK　brake　刹车

BKGRD　background　背景

BPCU　bus power control unit　汇流条电源控制组件

BRKR　breaker　断路器

BRT　bright　明亮的

BTB　bus tie breaker　汇流条连接断路器

BTL　bottle　瓶子

C

C/B　circuit breaker　断路器,断路开关

C　center　中央

CADC　central air data computer　中央大气数据计算机

CAPT　captain　机长

CB circuit breaker 断路器，断路开关

CCA central control actuator 中央控制作动器

CCW counterclockwise 逆时针方向的

CDU control display unit 控制显示器

CH(CHAN) channel 频道

CHG change 改变

CHR chronograph 计时器

CHRGR charger 充电器

CK check 检查

CKT circuit 电路,回路

CL close 关闭,盖上,合上

CLB climb 爬升

CLR clear 清除

CLSD closed 关闭的,封闭的,闭合的

CMD command 命令

CMPTR computer 计算机

CNX cancelled 取消,废除,中止

COL column 杆、圆柱,(报纸的)栏、段

COMM communication 通信

COMP compressor 压缩机

COMPT compartment 舱、隔间

CON continuous 连续的, 不断的

COND condition 状态

CONFG configuration 结构,配置

CONN connection 连接

CONT control 控制

CP control panel 控制面板

CPCS cabin pressure control system 座舱压力控制系统

CPS cycles per second 循环/秒

CRS course 航路

CRT cathode ray tube 阴极射线管

CRZ cruise 巡航

CSEU control system electronics unit 控制系统电子组件

CT current transformer 整流器

CTN caution 注意

CTR center 中央

CU control unit 控制元件

CUST customer 客户,买主

CW clockwise 顺时针方向的

CWS　control wheel steering　驾驶盘转弯

D

DADC　digital air data computer　数字式大气数据计算机

DC　direct current　直流电

DECEL　decelerate　减速

DECR　decrease　减少

DEG　degree　度数

DEPR　depressurize　释压

DEPT　departure　离开,出发

DEST　destination　目标,目的地

DET　detector　探测器

DETNT　detent　(机械上的)止动装置,棘爪

DEV　deviation　误差、偏航

DFDR　digital flight data recorder　数字飞行数据记录器(黑匣子)

DG　directional gyro　陀螺方向仪

DH　decision height　决断高度

DISC　disconnect　使分离,分开,断开,脱开

DISCH　discharge　释放,排出(液体、气体等)

DISCONT　discontinued　停止,中断

DISENG　disengage　解开,解除,使脱离

DISP　dispatch　派遣

DIST　distance　距离,路程

DK　deck　舱面,甲板

DME　distance measuring equipment　测距仪

DMU　data management unit　资料管理单元

DN　down　向下

DPCT　differential protection current transformer　差动保护电流互感器

DR　door　门

DSPLY　display　显示

DSPY　display　显示

E

EADI　electronic attitude director indicator　电子姿态指引仪

ECON　economy　节约,经济

ECS　environmental control system　环境控制系统

EDP　engine driven pump　发动机驱动泵

EEC　electronic engine control　电子发动机控制

EFIS　electronic flight instrument system　电子飞行仪表系统

EGT   exhaust gas temperature   排气温度

EHSI   electronic horizontal situation indicator   电子水平状态指示器

EICAS   engine indicating and crew alerting system   发动机指示与机组警告系统

ELEC   electrical   电气的,电气科学的

ELEV   elevation   高度,海拔

EMER   emergency   紧急情况

ENG   engine   发动机

ENT   entrance   入口,门口

ENTMT   entertainment   娱乐

EPC   external power contactor   外电源接触器

EPR   engine pressure ratio   发动机压力比

EPRL   engine pressure ratio limit   发动机压力比限制

EQUIP   equipment   装备,设备

ERR   error   错误

ESS   essential   基本的,必需品

EVAC   evacuation   撤空,排泄物

EVBC   engine vane and bleed control   发动机放气控制

EXH   exhaust   排出,排气

EXT   external   外部的

EXTIN   extinguish   灭火

F

F/D   flight director   飞行指引仪

F/F   fuel flow   燃油流量

F/O   first officer   副驾驶

FAA   Federal Aviation Administration   (美国)联邦航空局

FCC   flight control computer   飞行控制计算机

FCEU   flight controls electronic unit   飞行控制电子组件

FCU   fuel control unit   燃油控制组件

FDR   flight data recorder   飞行数据记录器(黑匣子)

FIM   Fault Isolation Manual   故障隔离手册

FL   flow   流量

FLD   field   (飞机)场,(广阔的一大片)地

FLT   flight   航班,飞行

FLUOR   fluorescent   发亮的、荧光的

FMC   flight management computer   飞行管理计算机

FMS   flight management system   飞行管理系统

FREQ   frequency   频率

FRM   Fault Reporting Manual   故障报告手册

FSEU   flap slat electronic unit   襟缝翼电子组件

FT   feet   英尺

FWD   forward   前面的

G

G/S   glide slope   下滑道

GA   go-around   复飞

GB   generator breaker   发电机断路器

GCB   generator circuit breaker   发电机电路断路器

GCR   generator control relay   发电机控制继电器

GCU   generator control unit   发电机控制组件

GEN   generator   发电机

GHR   ground handling relay   地面操作继电器

GND   ground   地面

GP   group   团体

GPWS   ground proximity warning system   地面临近警告系统

GR   gear   齿轮、传动装置

GS   ground speed   地速

GSSR   ground service select relay   地面勤务选择继电器

GSTR   ground service transfer relay   地面勤务转换继电器

GW   gross weight   总重

H

H/L   high/low   高/低

HDG   heading   航向

HF   high frequency   高频

HORIZ   horizontal   水平

HP   high pressure   高压

HSI   horizontal situation indicator   水平状态指示器

HTR   heater   加热器

HYD   hydraulic   液压

I

IAS   indicated airspeed   指示空速

IDENT   identification   识别，鉴定

IDG   integrated drive generator   整体驱动发电机

IGN   ignition   点火

ILLUM   illuminate   照明的，发光的

ILS   instrument landing system   仪表着陆系统

IN　in　输入

INBD　inboard　内侧的

INCR　increase　增加

IND　indicator　指示器

INFC　interface　分界面

INFLT　inflight　飞行过程中的

INHIB　inhibit　抑制,禁止

INIT　initiation　入门,初始

INOP　inoperative　不活动的

INPH　interphone　对讲机

INST　instrument　仪器,仪表

INTLK　interlock　内锁

INTMT　intermittent　间歇的,时断时续的,周期性的

IP　intermediate pressure　中间压力

IRS　inertial reference system　惯性基准系统

IRU　inertial reference unit　惯性基准组件

ISLN　isolation　隔离

M

MCDP　maintenance control display panel　维修控制显示面板

MCP　mode control panel　模式控制面板

MDA　minimum descent altitude　最低下降高度

MIC　microphone　扩音器,麦克风

MIN　minimum　最小量,最小数

MM　Maintenance Manual　维护手册

MOD　module　组件、单元

MON　monitor　监视器,监控器

MOT　motion　（机械的）运转

MPU　magnetic pickup　检波器

MSG　message　信息

MSTR　master　主要的,总的

MSU　mode selector unit　模式选择组件

MU　management unit　管理组件

MUX　multiplexer　多路传输器

N

N/A　not applicable　不适用的

NAC　nacelle　引擎舱

NAV　navigation　导航

NCD　no computed data　无计算数据

NEG　negative　否定的,负的

NEUT　neutral　中立的

NLG　nose landing gear　前起落架

NO.　number　数,数字

NRM　normal　正常的

O

OBS　observer　观察员

OPR　operate　运转

OPT　option　选择

OPRN　operation　操作

OUTBD　outboard　外部的

OVHD　overhead　头顶,顶板

OVHT　overheat　过热

OVRD　override　超控,越过

OXY　oxygen　氧气

P

P/RST　press to reset　按下复位

PA　passenger address　旅客广播

PASS　passenger　旅客

PCA　power control actuator　动力控制作动筒

PCT　percentage　百分比

PDI　pictorial deviation indicator　偏航图表示

PES　passenger entertainment system　旅客娱乐系统

PLA　power level angle　油门杆角度

PLT　pilot　驾驶员,飞行员

PMG　permanent magnet generator　永磁发电机

PNEU　pneumatic　气动

PNL　panel　面板

POR　point of regulation　调节点

POS　position　位置

PRESS　pressure　压力

PRIM　primary　首要的,主要的

PROC　procedure　程序,步骤

PROT　protection　保护,防护

PSI　pounds per square inch　磅/平方英寸

PSS　passenger service system　旅客勤务系统

PSU   passenger service unit   旅客勤务组件
PTT   push to talk   按压开始讲话
PTU   power transfer unit   动力转换组件
PWR   power   动力

Q

QAD   quick attach detach   快速拆装
QTS   quarts   夸脱
QTY   quantity   数量

R

R   right   右边的
RA   radio altimeter   无线电高度表
RAT   ram air turbine   冲压空气涡轮
RCVR   reciever   接收器
RDMI   radio distance magnetic indicator   磁场距离指示
REC   recorder   记录器
RECIRC   recirculate   再循环
REF   reference   参考
REFRIG   refrigeration   冷冻
REG   regulator   调节器
REL   release   释放,解放
REP   representative   代表性的,典型的
REQ   required   必须的
REV   reverse   反相的,相反的
RF   right front   右前
RH   right hand   右手
RLSE   release   释放,解放
RLY   relay   继电器
RLY/SW   relay/switch   继电器/开关(电门)
RMI   radio magnetic indicator   磁场方位指示器
ROT   rotation   旋转
RPM   revolutions per minute 转/分
RPTG   reporting   报告
RST   reset   重新设定,复位
RTO   rejected takeoff   中断起飞
RUD   rudder   方向舵
RW   right wing   右翼
RWY   runway   跑道

S

SAT   static air temperature   静压空气温度

SEC   second   第二次

SEI   standby engine indicator   备用发动机指示器

SEL   select   选择

SELCAL   selective calling   选择呼叫

SERV   service   服务

SG   signal generator   信号发生器

SLCTD   selected   选择

SLCTR   selector   选择器

SOV   shut off valve   关断阀

SP   speed   速度

SPD   speed   速度

SPD BK   speed brake   速度刹车

STA   station   驻地,站

STAB   stabilizer   安定装置,安定面

STBY   standby   备用

STS   system status   系统状况

SURF   surface 表面,舵面

SW   switch   开关,电门

SYNC   synchronous   同步的

T

T/R   thrust reverser   反推(反向推力装置)

T.O.   takeoff   起飞

TACH   tachometer   转速计

TAI   thermal anti-ice   热敏防冰

TAS   true airspeed   真空速

TAT   total air temperature   总温

TCC   turbine case cooling   涡轮壳体冷却

TE   trailing edge   后缘

TEMP   temperature   温度,气温

TFR   transfer   转换

THR   thrust   推力

THROT   throttle   油门

THRSH   threshold   门槛

THRT   thrust 推力

TLA   thrust lever angle   推力杆角度

TMC   thrust management computer   推力管理计算机

TMS thrust management system 推力管理系统

TMSP thrust mode select panel 推力方式选择面板

TO takeoff 起飞

TOL tolerance 公差,容限

TR transformer rectifier 变压整流器

TURB turbine 涡轮(机)

TURBL turbulence 湍流,(气体等的)紊流

U

UBR utility bus relay 正使用中的汇流条继电器

UPR upper 上面

V

V/NAV vertical navigation 垂直导航

V/S vertical speed 垂直速度

VERT vertical 垂直的

VFY verify 验证

VG vertical gyro 垂直陀螺仪

VHF very high frequency 甚高频

VIB vibration 振动

VLD valid 有效的

VLV valve 阀,活门

VOL volume 量

VOLT voltage 电压,伏特数

VOR VHF omni-directional range 甚高频全向信标

VOX voice 声音

VSI vertical speed indicator 垂直速度指示器

VTR video tape reproducer 磁带放像机

W

W/D wiring diagram 线路图解

W/W wheel well 轮舱

WARN warning 警告,警报

WG wing 机翼

WHL wheel 轮子

WPT waypoint 航路点

WSHLD windshield 风挡

WX weather 天气

WXR weather radar 气象雷达

X

X-CH   cross channel   交叉通道

XDCR   transducer   传感器

XMIT   transmit   发射

XMTR   transmitter   发射机

XPNDR   transponder   发射机应答器,询问机

Y

Y/D   yaw damper   偏航阻尼器

Appendix Ⅲ
Answers for "Choose the Best Answer" of 15 Lessons

Lesson 1

1	2	3	4	5	6	7	8	9	10	11	12	13	14	15	16
C	C	B	D	D	B	C	D	B	B	C	A	C	C	D	B

Lesson 2

1	2	3	4	5	6	7	8	9	10
B	C	A	B	C	D	B	B	C	C

Lesson 3

1	2	3	4	5	6	7	8	9	10
B	A	A	B	C	D	A	A	B	D

Lesson 4

1	2	3	4	5	6	7	8	9	10
D	A	B	C	D	B	D	A	D	C

Lesson 5

1	2	3	4	5	6	7	8	9	10
B	B	A	C	A	B	A	A	A	C

Lesson 6

1	2	3	4	5	6	7	8	9	10
A	C	A	B	A	A	A	B	B	A

Lesson 7

1	2	3	4	5	6	7	8	9	10
B	A	B	A	B	C	A	B	C	C

Lesson 8

1	2	3	4	5	6	7
A	B	B	A	C	D	A

Lesson 9

1	2	3	4	5	6
A	B	A	D	A	C

Lesson 10

1	2	3	4	5	6	7	8	9	10
C	A	D	B	A	A	C	D	D	A

Lesson 11

1	2	3	4
C	C	B	D

Lesson 12

1	2	3	4	5	6
C	A	B	B	C	A

Lesson 13

1	2	3	4	5
B	D	C	C	A

Lesson 14

1	2	3	4	5
C	B	B	B	D

Lesson 15

1	2	3	4	5
D	C	B	A	B

Appendix IV
Reference Answers for Questions of 15 Lessons

Lesson 1

1. Q: What components in common do all modern airplanes have?

A: They have the fuselage, wing, tail assembly and control surfaces, landing gear, and power plants.

2. Q: How does the airplane produce lift?

A: The wings generate most of the lift to hold the plane in the air. Lift is obtained from the dynamic action of the wing with respect to the air.

3. Q: What's the function of fuselage?

A: The fuselage is the body of the airplane that holds all the pieces of the aircraft together and many of the other large components are attached to it.

4. Q: What do the shape and the placement of the wing depend upon?

A: It depends upon the airplane mission and the best compromise necessary in the overall airplane design.

5. Q: What control surfaces does an airplane have? Please explain their functions respectively.

A: It has horizontal piece (called the horizontal stabilizer) and a fixed vertical piece (called the vertical stabilizer). The stabilizers provide stability for the aircraft—they keep it flying straight. The vertical stabilizer keeps the nose of the plane from swinging from side to side (called yaw), while the horizontal stabilizer prevents an up-and-down motion of the nose (called pitch).

Aileron is used to roll the wings from side to side.

Flaps are used to increase lift at reduced airspeeds, primarily at landing and takeoff.

Spoilers are devices used to disrupt the airflow over the wing so as to reduce the lift on an airplane wing quickly.

Slats at the front part of the wing are used at takeoff and landing to produce additional lift.

At the rear of both the aileron surfaces and elevators and rudders are small moving sections called trim tabs that are attached by hinges. Their function is to balance the airplane if it is too nose heavy, tail heavy, or wing heavy to fly in a stable cruise condition; maintain the elevator, rudder, and ailerons at whatever setting the pilot wishes without the pilot maintaining pressure on the controls; and help move the elevators, rudder, and ailerons and thus relieve the pilot of the effort necessary to move the surfaces.

6. Q: What are the main engine types?

A: There are piston engine ram jet, pulse jet, turbojet, turboprop, and rocket engines.

7. Q: Please retell the history of Boeing Company.

A: Boeing traces its history to aviation pioneer William Boeing who, in 1916, built the company's first airplane, a seaplane for two with a range of 320 nautical miles (515 km). Since then, Boeing has defined the modern jetliner.

8. Q: What effort will Boeing Company make in the aspect of carbon emission?

A: Aircraft entering today's fleet are 70 percent more fuel efficient than early commercial jet airplanes, consuming about 3.5 liters per passenger per 100 km. Boeing is actively driving the development of sustainable biofuels for use by the aviation industry. Technology is advancing faster than expected. Many airlines could be flying on a percentage of biofuels within the next five to ten years. Advanced technologies for generating and harnessing energy are reducing the need to produce electricity from non-renewable resources. Boeing is developing applications within key energy harvesting technologies, including electrodynamic, thermoelectric, piezoelectric, hydrogen fuel cells and solar cells.

9. Q: Please give a brief introduction to Airbus Company.

A: Airbus is one of the world's leading aircraft manufacturers, and it consistently captures approximately half or more of all orders for airliners with more than 100 seats. Airbus' mission is to provide the aircraft best suited to the market's needs and to support these aircraft with the highest quality of service. The Airbus product line comprises 14 aircraft models, from the 100-seat single-aisle A318 jetliner to the 525-seat A380-which is the largest civil airliner in service. Airbus also has expanded into the military transport aircraft sector.

10. Q: What's the feature of the A380 aircraft?

A: The feature is magnificent handling qualities and eco-friendly operation and more than 380 patent applications filed for A380 technologies.

11. Q: Please give a brief introduction to Bombardier.

A: Bombardier is a global transportation company, present in more than 60 countries on five continents. It operate two industry-leading businesses: Aerospace and Rail transportation. Bombardier Aerospace ranks as the world's third largest civil aircraft manufacturer.

12. Q: Please give a brief introduction to embraer Company.

A: Embraer was Brazil's largest exporter from 1999 to 2001 and the second largest in 2002, 2003 and 2004. Embraer has become one of the largest aircraft manufacturers in the world by focusing on specific market segments with high growth potential in commercial, defense, and executive aviation.

Lesson 2

1. Q: What's the Boeing philosophy of delivering of B737 aircrafts?

A: The 737—a short-to-medium-range airplane is based on a key Boeing philosophy of delivering added value to airlines with reliability, simplicity and reduced operating and maintenance costs

2. Q: What's the function of winglet?

A: Advanced technology winglets allow airlines to save on fuel, extend its range, carry more payload and reduce engine maintenance costs. Blended winglets are wing tip extensions which provide several benefits to airplane operators. The winglet option increases the Next-Generation 737's lead as the newest and most technologically advanced airplane in its class. These new technology winglets are now available on 737-700s, 737-800s and 737-900ER as well as on the Boeing Business Jet (737-700 and 737-800).

3. Q: Give a brief introduction to B737 family.

A: There are 11 family members in the B737.

(1) 737-100: first delivery in 12/28/67 and first airline in service is Lufthansa. Last delivery to NASA in 7/26/73.

(2) 737-200: first delivery in 12/29/67 and first airline in service is United. Last delivery to Xiamen Airlines in 08/08/88.

(3) 737-300: first delivery in 11/28/84 and first airline in service is Southwest. Last delivery to Air New Zealand in 12/17/99.

(4) 737-400: first delivery in 09/15/88 and first airline in service is Piedmont . Last delivery to CSA Czech Air in 02/25/00.

(5) 737-500: first delivery in 02/28/90 and first airline in service is Southwest . Last delivery to Air Nippon in 07/26/99.

(6) 737-600: first delivery in 09/19/98 and first airline in service is SAS.

(7) 737-700: first delivery in 12/17/97 and first airline in service is Southwest.

(8) 737-800: first delivery in 04/22/98 and first airline in service is Hapag-Lloyd.

(9) 737-900: first delivery in 05/16/01 and first airline in service is Alaska.

4. Q: Please memorize the important B737 aircraft milestones.

A: Boeing surpasses 7,000 737 orders with an order placed by Next-Generation 737-900ER launch customer Lion Air. Boeing announced the order at the Paris Air Show. In August, 737 employees commemorate the milestone by filling a giant "7,000" spanning an area about the length of two Next-Generation 737-700s.

Lesson 3

1. Q: What materials are used to make as much as 50% of the primary structure of B787?

A: Composite material is primary applied in B787 aircraft manufacture. A total of 3 million additional square feet.

2. Q: What is the Boeing international technology development team looking at?

A: The Boeing international technology development team is looking at incorporating health-monitoring systems that will allow the airplane to self-monitor and report maintenance requirements to ground-based computer systems.

3. Q: How do the advances in engine technology benefit B787?

A: Advances in engine technology will contribute as much as 8 percent of the increased efficiency of the new airplane, representing a nearly two-generation jump in technology for the middle of the market.

4. Q: What features does the B787 aircraft interior have?

A: Sweeping arches, dynamic lighting, larger lavatories, more spacious luggage bins and electronic window shades whose transparency they can change during flight.

5. Q: What's the meaning of B787 Power On?

A: Power On is a complex series of tasks and tests that bring electrical power onto the airplane and begin to exercise the use of the electrical systems.

6. Q: How do you understand the unparalleled performance of B787 aircraft?

A: B787 will bring big-jet ranges to mid-size airplanes and provide airlines with unmatched fuel efficiency, resulting in exceptional environmental performance as well. Passengers will also see improvements with the new airplane, from an interior environment with higher humidity to increased comfort and convenience.

Lesson 4

1. Q: What's the function of thrust management system?

A: The thrust management system does two functions. It moves the throttles and calculates the thrust limit for the EICAS display.

2. Q: What's the function of YSM?

A: YSM combines these functions: yaw damper; stabilizer trim; rudder ratio changer; speed brake; elevator feel limit; elevator feel shift; BITE.

3. Q: What control systems does the autopilot flight director system provide automatic control to?

A: Aileron, elevator, stabilizer and rudder.

4. Q: Please retell the yaw damper's function.

A: YSM combines these functions: yaw damper; stabilizer trim; rudder ratio changer; speed brake; elevator feel limit; elevator feel shift; BITE.

5. Q: How do you understand UNSCHEDULED STAB TRIM?

A: An UNSCHEDULED STAB TRIM (amber) light shows when the stabilizer moves without a command to trim.

6. Q: What's the function of AFDS?

A: The autopilot flight director system (AFDS) supplies automatic control of these flight control systems: ailerons; elevators; rudder (autoland). The AFDS also does the calculations for the flight director commands.

7. Q: How do we use the MCDP to maint the aircraft?

A: After each flight, it collects and stores flight fault data found by the FCC, TMC, and FMC during the flight. It makes this data available for display during FLT FAULT mode operation. During the GRD TEST mode, it allows display of ground fault data and fault information from ground tests. It also provides operator instructions and test control necessary to do ground tests of AFDS related devices.

The MCDP also supplies information about FCC software. It can show the FCC software and hardware part numbers and software loading faults.

8. Q: Please explain the meaning of go-around.

A: The go-around mode is a combined autopilot (or F/D) and autothrottle mode provided for climbout after an aborted approach. Go-around may be entered from a single channel, multi-channel, or F/D only approach.

Go-around is armed when glideslope is captured or flaps are not up. Go-around is inhibited in the take-off mode. Push either of the go-around switches on the throttles to enter the mode.

Lesson 5

1. Q: What's the function of electrical power system?

A: The electrical power system makes, supplies, and controls electrical power to the airplane.

2. Q: Why can not the power sources be put in parallel?

A: Only one power sources can be used to flight at the same time. Other power sources can be seen as standby power.

3. Q: What power can the electrical power system supply?

A: The electrical power system supplies AC and DC power to airplane systems.

4. Q: Please enumerate the buses of electrical power system.

A: left and right AC buses; ground handling bus; ground service bus; flight instrument transfer buses; center AC bus; AC standby bus; utility buses. left and right DC buses; center DC bus; DC standby bus; APU battery bus; battery bus; main hot battery bus.

5. Q: What's the quality of the aircraft electrical power?

A: The AC power system makes 115 V AC, a frequency of 400 Hz and is rated at 90 kVA.

6. Q: When do we use the APU electrical power?

A: When the APU generator operates and means a failure of either IDG, the APU generator automatically powers the correct load. The APU generator can be used as a power source and the galley loads can be applied again. Generally we don't operate APU in flight.

7. Q: How does the GCU control the circuit?

A: The three GCUs provide automatic control and protection functions for each channel by monitor of IDG output, BPCU status information and control switch positions.

Lesson 6

1. Q: What's the function of hydraulic system?

A: Hydraulic systems give power to aircraft components.

2. Q: What kind of fluid can be used in the aircraft?

A: Acceptable BMS 3-11, Type Ⅳ fluids such as skydrol can be used.

3. Q: What subsystems does the hydraulic power system include?

A: They are the left, right, and center systems.

4. Q: What's the difference between EDP and ACMP?

A: There are two engine-driven pumps (EDPs), one on each engine. These are the primary pumps in the left and right systems. There are four ac motor pumps (ACMPs). Two are the primary pumps in the center system, and one each is the demand pump in the left and right systems.

5. Q: When can a ram air turbine be used?

A: When the hydraulic system fails, RAT can be used.

6. Q: What systems does the center system supply hydraulic power to?

A: The center system supplies hydraulic power for primary and secondary flight controls.

7. Q: How does the hydraulic fluid flow?

A: Fluid goes to the engine-driven pump (EDP) through a reservoir standpipe. A supply shutoff valve operated by the fire switch is in this supply line.

8. Q: What systems does the left hydraulic system supply hydraulic power to?

A: The left hydraulic system supply hydraulic power to primary and some secondary flight controls, thrust reversers, etc.

9. Q: What systems does the right hydraulic system supply hydraulic power to?

A: The right hydraulic system supply hydraulic power to primary and some secondary flight controls, thrust reversers, the normal brakes, etc.

10. Q: How does the EDP shutoff valve work?

A: When the engine driven pump (EDP) supply shutoff valve closed, it shuts off the supply of hydraulic fluid to the EDP.

Lesson 7

1. Q: What's the function of APU?

A: APU supplies the auxiliary power system with electric and pneumatic power. This lets the airplane operate independently of ground external power sources or the main engines.

2. Q: When does the APU operate at 101 percent?

A: The APU operates at 101 percent during these modes: in the air; ECS demand; main engine start (MES).

3. Q: What subsystem does the APU system contain?

A: The APU system contains these subsystems: control system; power plant; engine; APU and generator lubrication system; oil indicating system; fuel system; ignition/starting system; air system; indicating system; exhaust system.

4. Q: What systems does the APU have interfaces with?

A: The APU has interfaces with these systems that have information in other chapters/sections: electrical power; pneumatics; fire protection; EICAS.

5. Q: What's the function of FCU?

A: The fuel control unit (FCU) does these functions for the fuel supply: shuts off; filters; pressurizes; meters.

6. Q: How do you install or remove the APU?

A: The APU is removed with two fishpole hoists or a single hydraulic lift. Either method, the installation of an APU cradle, that supports the APU during installation and removal, is necessary. The cradle attaches to the left forward and both right side mounting brackets.

7. Q: How are the waste fuel, oil and water removed from the APU?

A: Waste fuel, oil, and water are removed from the APU by gravity-fed drains and vents.

8. Q: How does the APU exhaust?

A: The APU exhaust system sends the APU exhaust overboard through the exhaust duct.

Lesson 8

1. Q: In your opinion, what's a mechanic job like?

A: (as a reference) The job is difficult and would make persons feel very tired since the mechanics have to work through the colock, seven days a week.

2. Q: What is the differrence between the mechanic certificate and the repairman certificate?

A: The FAA issues mechanics and repairman certificates. Mechanics can get either an airframe certificate or a power plant certificate—most mechanics get both. Repairmen get certificates to perform only one or two specific tasks, and they must be supervised by FAA-approved Repair Stations, commercial operators, or air carriers where these specific tasks are done daily.

3. Q: What condition do you have to reach if you want to work on avionic equipment?

A: If you have an airframe certificate you don't need any other certificate, but you must be properly trained and qualified and have the proper tools and equipment. You can even work on avionics equipment without a certificate if you have avionics repair experience from the military or from working for avionics manufacturers and related industries.

4. Q: What requirements do you have to meet if you want to get a repairman's certificate?

A: We should achieve basic requirement, experience requirements, and pass oral, practical & written tests. To get a repairman's certificate, we must be recommended by a repair station, commercial operator, or air carrier.

5. Q: What tests do you have to take for a FAA certificate?

A: To become an aircraft mechanic, we must take oral and practical tests as well as written tests.

Lesson 9

1. Q: What's AHM?

A: AHM is a decision support capability provided via the MyBoeingFleet.com portal. Airplane Health Management uses real-time airplane data to provide enhanced fault forwarding, troubleshooting and historical fix information to reduce schedule interruptions and increase maintenance and operational efficiency. It delivers valuable information when and where it's needed.

2. Q: What's the function of AHM?

A: AHM integrates the remote collection, monitoring and analysis of airplane data to determine the status of an airplane's current and future serviceability or performance. It converts the data into information that you can use to make the operational or "fix-or-fly" decisions that can make the difference between profit and loss.

Airplane Health Management is part of the Boeing commitment to providing its customers with the solutions they need to improve profitability. AHM is a system for reducing delays, cancellations, air turn-backs, and diversions through the innovative use of existing aircraft data. AHM also supports long-term fleet-reliability programs by helping airlines identify and respond to faults before they occur.

3. Q: What can the British Airways do through the MyBoeingFleet.com portal?

A: British airline will feature Boeing's Airplane Health Management system to monitor the in-flight condition of more than 100 Boeing twin-aisle jetliners. AHM will be used on the airline's current 777 and 747-400 fleets and future deliveries, including 787 Dreamliners.

Through the MyBoeingFleet.com portal, British Airways will be able to track in-flight faults and make real-time operational decisions regarding maintenance, in order to deploy the necessary people, parts and equipment to address the issue before the airplane arrives at the gate.

4. Q: How many airplanes will the Boeing AHM be applied into for Air China and Air China cargo?

A: AHM is a component in Boeing's larger vision of Lifecycle Solutions-improving airline efficiency with digital productivity tools, product and industry expertise and the power of aviation's leading integrated supply chain, supporting Boeing airplanes from order placement through retirement.

Air China operates 10 Boeing 777-200s and 10 747-400s. Air China Cargo operates seven 747-400 freighters, including two Boeing Converted Freighters.

5. Q: Please explain the Lifecycle Solutions of Boeing's larger vision.

A: It enhances operational performance to the aerospace industry.

6. Q: Please introduce all kinds of aircraft monitoring system in detail.

A: The various on-wing health monitoring systems of today, which are a collection of separate, unrelated technologies, provide a basic level of monitoring. Their capabilities are relatively limited and the information they provide is used mostly to initiate maintenance actions, not for real-time decision-making.

Current engine vibration monitoring systems sample at a relatively low frequency—too low to capture much significant or useful information on the vibratory modes of the system. They check the vibration magnitude to determine that it is within a normal range. Magnitudes that are too high might indicate a bearing failure or engine imbalance, magnitudes that are too low might indicate a faulty sensor or seized engine.

Lesson 10

1. Q: What information can you acquire from the Boeing part page?

A: Through the Boeing PART Page, current data such as part inventories, prices, part interchangeability, quotes and purchase order status are at your fingertips.

2. Q: What's the meaning of Proprietary Part?

A: Genuine Boeing proprietary parts are those for which Boeing owns the engineering drawings. These parts, available for both in and out of production aircraft, are built in accordance with Boeing's quality system and come with full traceability documentation.

3. Q: What services can the Boeing and Volvo Aero Services supply?

A: Boeing and Volvo Aero Services can supply Parts Leasing and Redistribution Services.

4. Q: How do you grasp the right meaning of the Right Parts at the Right Time?

A: When your Boeing 7-series or MD-series airplane is disabled, we stand ready to help you return it to revenue service, wherever in the world it happens to be, with 24-hours-a-day, seven-days-a-week dispatch availability.

5. Q: What services can the 24-Hour AOG Parts Support supply?

A: We handle diagnosis, repairs, logistics, parts procurement, warranty and certification issues, and more.

6. Q: What's the feature of Embraer Provisioning Services?

A: Prior to delivery of aircraft, Embraer Material Support can provide customers with initial spares provisioning recommendation based on projected utilization, available maintenance capability and special requirements.

7. Q: How does the Embraer reduce the customers' investments in stocks?

A: Spare Parts Pool, Consignment Stock, Exchange Program, Insurance Items, Rental Program (high price and low-utilization items), Consumables Consignment, Repair Management can reduce the customers' investments in stocks.

8. Q: What's Honeywell?

A: Honeywell is a leading global provider of integrated avionics, engines, wheels and brakes systems and service solutions for aircraft manufacturers, airlines, business and general aviation, military, space and airport operations.

Lesson 11

1. Q: What's the meaning of AOG? And what will the Boeing do if AOG occurs?

A: AOG means Airplane On Ground. Their technical experts will provide on-site comprehensive, integrated assistance to recover a disabled airplane. Boeing established the RRC as a comprehensive, one-stop source of information to assist airline customers with "airplane-on-ground", or AOG situation.

2. Q: What is the better way to manage repairs and inventory?

A: With Component Exchange Programs, you minimize component repair and inventory costs, and no longer need to worry about repair turntime. Also programs provide a single point of contact for components and handle inventory maintenance and warranties thereby simplifying administration.

3. Q: How can the customers minimize repair and inventory cost?

A: Component Exchange Programs offer a ready supply of dispatch-critical units manufactured by Boeing and Boeing suppliers, including the high-value components that typically account for a large part of spares expense. With Component Exchange Programs, a replacement can be en route to your site before the damaged unit is even removed from the airplane, and you are no longer forced to cover lengthy repair turntimes with in-stock inventory.

4. Q: How do you explain Component Exchange Program?

A: Component Exchange Programs serve as a single point of contact for dozens of original equipment manufacturers, reducing your administrative burden for warranties, service, and deliveries.

5. Q: What's the duty of field service representatives of Boeing Company?

A: They help customers keep their Boeing fleets in safe and profitable service, provide timely on-site technical advice and help assure a smooth introduction of new Boeing jetliner.

6. Q: How does the Boeing Commercial Aircraft Operation Center work?

A: When a customer contacts the Operations Center, a controller discusses and defines the problem. The controller then works with leads from structures, systems and material management to develop options to resolve the problem. Following this collaboration, the customer and controller reach a joint decision on the optimum solution.

7. Q: What capability does the Lufthansa Technik Group have?

A: Lufthansa Technik has an international network and offers a vast portfolio of technology, training and logistics services, as well as supplementary services for all aspects of aircraft operations. As a competent partner for fleets of any size, they offer one-stop customized solution.

Lesson 12

1. Q: What's the feature of Next Generation Air Transportation System? And how about its virtue?

A: The Next Generation Air Transportation System is the transformation of the radar-based air traffic control system of today to a satellite-based system of the future.
Virtue: The Next Generation Air Transportation System will enhance runway safety on runways, taxiways and ramp areas and reduce delays, while also lowering emissions and fuel use.

2. Q: How do the controllers and pilots communicate with the NextGen technology?

A: NextGen communications between controllers and flight crews will be handled by Data Comm transmissions, relieving radio frequency for more complex maneuvers and allowing complicated instructions to be provided electronically.

3. Q: What's the function of System Wide Information Management (SWIM)?

A: All of the FAA systems in NextGen will need to speak to one another-as well as to the systems used by other parts of the aviation community, since the safe and efficient use of airspace depends on how well the different parts of the airspace system communicate with one another.

4. Q: To accelerate the application of NextGen technology, what role does the FAA play?

A: The Federal Aviation Administration (FAA) is leveraging existing technologies and expanding their capabilities to bring the benefits of NextGen to the flying public today The FAA has also entered into agreements with international partners across the Atlantic and Pacific to accelerate the deployment of NextGen technologies and procedures to improve aviation safety, efficiency and capacity while reducing the environmental footprint during all phases of flight.

5. Q: What can be used to keep the surface safety before takeoff?

A: One of these systems, called Airport Surface Detection Equipment-Model X (ASDE-X), gets its information from a variety of surface surveillance sources, including radar, automatically transmitting the most accurate targets to monitors in the tower. The biggest improvement over systems that derive information solely by radar, which might show false targets during bad weather, will be the introduction of Global Positioning System (GPS) locations of both aircraft and surface vehicles.

6. Q: What's the meaning of Optimized Profile Descent? Please explain it.

A: As aircraft approach their destination airport, an Optimized Profile Descent keeps them at their most efficient altitude for as long as possible before they begin a continuous approach to the airport. The smooth descent-rather than the stepped-down approach required by current procedures-saves time and money while reducing carbon emissions and noise.

Lesson 13

1. Q: What is composites?

A: Composites are materials made of two or more constituents with different physical or chemical properties. When these materials are combined, the new material has different characteristic from the individual components.

2. Q: What types of composites are often used into aircraft structure?

A: Glass fiber reinforced plastic,carbon fiber reinforced plastic and aluminum alloy.

3. Q: What are the benefits of composite materials?

A: They are with high specific properties, such as high specific strength, high specific stiffness.

4. Q: Give some examples for the composite materials applied into aircraft structure.

A: Applications of composites on aircraft include fairings, flight control surfaces, landing gear doors, leading and trailing edge panels on the wing and stabilizer, interior components, etc.

5. Q: What are the primary manufacturing methods used to produce composites?

A: The primary manufacturing methods used to produce composites include manual lay-up, automated lay-up, spray-up, filament winding, pultrusion and resin transfer molding.

Lesson 14

1. Q: Why should aircraft obey weight and balance limits?

A: Compliance with the weight and balance limits of any aircraft is critical to flight safety. Operating above the maximum weight limitation compromises the structural integrity of an aircraft and adversely affects its performance. Operation with the center of gravity outside the approved limits results in control difficulty.

2. Q: What factors will limit the amount of lift produced by an airfoil?

A: The amount of lift produced by an airfoil is limited by the airfoil design, angle of attack (AOA), airspeed, and air density.

Q: What are the benefits of composite materials?

3. Q: What are the most important performance deficiencies of an overloaded aircraft?

A:Higher takeoff speed, longer takeoff run, reduced rate and angle of climb, lower maximum altitude, shorter range, reduced cruising speed, reduced maneuverability, higher stalling speed, higher approach and landing speed, longer landing roll, and excessive weight on the nose wheel or tail wheel.

4. Q: What will happen when the CG location produced an unstable condition?

A: It is possible that the pilot could not control the aircraft if the CG location produced an unstable condition. The pilot should realize if the CG is displaced too far forward on the longitudinal axis, a nose-heavy condition will result. Conversely, if the CG is displaced too far aft on the longitudinal axis, a tail-heavy condition results.

5. Q: Where can a pilot find the specified requirements for the weight and balance control of certain airplane?

A: The manufacturer provides this information, which is included in the approved AFM, TCDS, or aircraft specifications.

Lesson 15

1. Q: When were the airworthiness standards issued?

A: Standards and recommended practices for the airworthiness of aircraft were adopted by the council on 1 March 1949 pursuant to the provisions of Article 37 of the Convention on International Civil Aviation (Chicago 1944) and designated as Annex 8 to the Convention.

2. Q: What are the main contents of Annex 8?

A: The annex contained, in Part II, general airworthiness procedures applicable to all aircrafts and in Part III, minimum airworthiness characteristics for airplanes provided, or to be provided, with certificates of airworthiness classifying them in an established ICAO category. Part I contained definitions.

3. Q: Why would not the ICAO standards of airworthiness replace national regulations?

A: Each state would establish its own comprehensive and detailed code of airworthiness or would select a comprehensive and detailed code established by another contracting state.

4. Q: What areas have changes of airworthiness standards been driven mainly by?

A: These changes have been driven mainly by four areas: (a) public and congressional concern about air transportation safety; (b) introductions of new technologies; (c) lessons learned from accidents or incidents; (d) harmonization with international air transportation policies and regulations.

References

［1］ http://www.eads.com.

［2］ http://www.airliners.net.

［3］ http://www.boeing.com/commercial.

［4］ http://www.bombardier.com.

［5］ http://www.embraer.com/english/content/home.

［6］ http://www.faa.gov.

［7］ http://aviationknowledge.wikidot.com/aviation.

［8］ 白杰,张帆.民航机务英语教程[M].北京:中国民航出版社,1997.

［9］ 常士基.现代民用航空维修工程管理[M].太原:山西科学技术出版社,2002.

［10］ 李永平,魏鹏程.民航机务专业英语[M].2版.北京:国防工业出版社,2014.

［11］ 李永平.民航机务专业英语[M].3版.北京:清华大学出版社,2018.